Luc Boudreaux
doguedebordeauxsurvival.com

Field Manual
No. 3-05.201

FM 3-05.201
HEADQUARTERS
DEPARTMENT OF THE ARMY
Washington, DC, 30 April 2003

Special Forces
Unconventional Warfare Operations

Contents

DISTRIBUTION RESTRICTION: Approved for public release; distribution is unlimited.

Preface

Field manual (FM) 3-05.201 provides the doctrinal basis for the conduct of unconventional warfare (UW) missions across the operational continuum. It continues the doctrinal education process that begins with Joint Publications (JPs) 3-05, Doctrine for Joint Special Operations; 3-05.1, Joint Tactics, Techniques, and Procedures for Joint Special Operations Task Force Operations; 3-05.5, Joint Special Operations Targeting and Mission Planning Procedures; and FMs 100-25, Doctrine for Army Special Operations Forces, and 3-05.20, Special Forces Operations. This manual informs and guides Special Forces (SF) commanders, staffs, and operational personnel primarily at battalion and lower echelons (Special Forces operational detachments [SFODs] A, B, and C) in their planning for and conduct of UW.

This manual provides historical examples to highlight key points throughout the text. It offers tactics, techniques, procedures, and references to support future SF operations. It also provides general UW guidance, mission procedures, and information ordered chronologically from receipt of the unit mission letter through postmission activities.

Users of this manual should adapt its content to meet their situation and mission requirements. The SFODs use the mission, enemy, terrain and weather, troops and support available—time available and civil considerations (METT-TC) analysis system.

Examples of specific UW techniques and procedures are provided in the appendixes. The appendixes let the users of this manual review the basics of UW mission performance from beginning to end. For users interested only in the details of specific techniques, the appendixes provide reference material keyed to the generic activities in the text.

Commanders and trainers should use this information and other related manuals to plan and conduct rehearsals of mission-specific training. They should also use command guidance and the Army Training and Evaluation Program (ARTEP). The key to assuring success is planning UW-related training before being employed with a specific UW mission.

The proponent of this manual is the United States Army John F. Kennedy Special Warfare Center and School (USAJFKSWCS). Submit comments and recommended changes to Commander, USAJFKSWCS, ATTN: AOJK-DT-SFD, Fort Bragg, NC 28310-5000.

Unless this publication states otherwise, masculine nouns and pronouns do not refer exclusively to men.

Chapter 1

Overview

FM 3-05.20 defines UW as a broad spectrum of military and paramilitary operations, predominantly conducted through, with, or by indigenous or surrogate forces organized, trained, equipped, supported, and directed in varying degrees by an external source. UW includes, but is not limited to, guerrilla warfare (GW), sabotage, subversion, intelligence activities, and unconventional assisted recovery (UAR).

UNCONVENTIONAL WARFARE ASPECTS

1-1. UW also includes interrelated aspects that may be prosecuted singly or collectively by predominantly indigenous or surrogate personnel. An external source usually supports and directs these personnel in varying degrees during all conditions of war or peace. The intent of United States (U.S.) UW operations is to exploit a hostile power's political, military, economic, and psychological vulnerability by developing and sustaining resistance forces to accomplish U.S. strategic objectives.

1-2. Regardless of whether UW objectives are strategic or operational, the nature of resistance and the fundamental tactics and techniques of UW operations remain unchanged. UW includes the following interrelated activities.

1-3. *Guerrilla warfare* consists of military and paramilitary operations conducted by irregular, predominantly indigenous forces against superior forces in enemy-held or hostile territory. It is the overt military aspect of an insurgency.

1-4. *Sabotage* is an act or acts with intent to injure or obstruct the national defense of a nation by willfully damaging or destroying any national defense or war materiel, premises, or utilities, including human and natural resources. It may also refer to actions taken to injure or obstruct the military capability of an occupying power. Sabotage may be the most effective or the only means of attacking specific targets beyond the capabilities of conventional weapon systems. Sabotage selectively disrupts, destroys, or neutralizes hostile capabilities with a minimum of manpower and material resources. SF conducts sabotage unilaterally through indigenous or surrogate personnel. Sabotage is also a form of effects-based targeting performed by SF personnel. FM 3-05.220, *(S) Special Forces Advanced Special Operations (U)*, Volumes I and II, provides detailed information on sabotage.

1-5. *Subversion* is any action designed to undermine the military, economic, psychological, or political strength or morale of a regime. All elements of the resistance organization contribute to the subversive effort, but the clandestine nature of subversion dictates that the underground will do the bulk of the activity. Subversion is a form of effects-based targeting on human terrain.

1-6. Effective SF targeting demands accurate, timely, and well-organized intelligence. SF personnel must develop good intelligence skills for overt collection, tactical reconnaissance, and the assembly of available intelligence for mission planning packets. Sound target analysis uses the criticality, accessibility, recuperability, vulnerability, effect, recognizability (CARVER) matrix; provides options to planners; satisfies statements of operational requirements (SOR); meets the commander's objectives; and reduces the risk to operators. FM 100-25 provides more detailed information on targeting.

1-7. *Intelligence activities* assess areas of interest ranging from political and military personalities to the military capabilities of friendly and enemy forces. SF must perform intelligence activities ranging from developing information critical to planning and conducting operations, sustaining and protecting themselves and the UW force, to assessing the capabilities and intentions of indigenous and coalition forces. These activities may be unilateral or conducted through surrogates. SF intelligence activities may require coordination with other government agencies (OGAs) and may involve national-level oversight.

1-8. *Unconventional assisted recovery* is a subset of nonconventional assisted recovery (NAR) and is conducted by special operations forces (SOF) (Department of Defense [DOD] Directive 2310.2). UW forces conduct UAR operations to seek out, contact, authenticate, and support military and other selected personnel as they move from an enemy-held, hostile, or sensitive area to areas under friendly control. UAR includes operating unconventional assisted recovery mechanisms (UARMs) and unconventional assisted recovery teams (UARTs). The UARM refers to an entity, group of entities, or organizations within enemy-held territory that operate in a clandestine or covert manner to return designated personnel to friendly control and most often consists of established indigenous or surrogate infrastructures. UARTs consist primarily of SOF personnel directed to service existing designated areas of recovery (DARs) or selected areas for evasion (SAFEs) to recover evaders.

1-9. UW has taken on new significance for several reasons. Historically, SF units have focused on UW as a part of general war. Now, the U.S. policy of supporting selected resistance movements requires SF to focus on UW during conflicts short of war. Also, global urbanization provides for a shift in emphasis from rural guerrilla warfare to all aspects of clandestine resistance including urban and border operations. Training and support for these operations may come from the joint special operations area (JSOA) or from an external training or support site. Some scenarios may dictate a traditional role reversal—the urban guerrilla may conduct most of the operations while supported by the rural guerrilla.

1-10. UW is the most challenging of SF missions because it involves protracted operations with joint forces, allied forces, indigenous or surrogate forces, U.S. agencies, or elements of all of these entities. UW involves detailed, centralized planning and coordination from the SFODA through the Secretary of Defense, and ultimately, decentralized execution. UW requires proficiency in other SF principal missions (foreign internal defense [FID], direct action [DA], and special reconnaissance [SR]) since, once deployed, the UW mission may include portions of those missions. Before the conduct of SF UW operations, a resistance potential should exist. SF personnel do not create this resistance potential. It is already present and has usually developed into a resistance movement or an organized effort by some portion of the civil population to resist the regime.

1-11. When UW operations support conventional military operations, the focus shifts to primarily military objectives. When a conventional force is committed and its area of interest nears the JSOA, resistance operations may expand to help the tactical commander. In addition, there are times (Operation ENDURING FREEDOM) when the introduction of conventional forces does not take the main effort away from unconventional operations; in fact, the conventional forces may support the unconventional forces. UW operations can—

- Delay and disrupt hostile military operations.
- Interdict lines of communication.
- Deny the hostile power unrestricted use of key areas.
- Divert the hostile power's attention and resources from the main battle area.
- Interdict hostile warfighting capabilities.

RESISTANCE AND INSURGENCY

1-12. A government's inability or unwillingness to meet the legitimate needs of its people may cause widespread frustration and dissatisfaction. People may lose their faith and confidence because the government lacks legitimacy. They may also simply recognize that the government is incapable of effectively providing internal security and development.

1-13. Resistance may be either nonviolent or violent. Nonviolent resistance involves acts such as ostracism, tax evasion, boycotts, strikes, or other types of civil disobedience. Violent resistance includes sabotage, subversion, and guerrilla warfare. People usually resist nonviolently at first. However, they may willingly take up violent resistance if a subversive cadre provides them with a cause they perceive to be both worthy and achievable. If the sociopolitical conditions are oppressive enough, resistance may develop into an organized resistance movement.

1-14. A resistance movement is an organized effort by some portion of the civil population of a country to oppose or overthrow the established government or cause withdrawal of an occupying power. The center of gravity in any resistance movement is the people's will to resist. The people bear the brunt of the established authority's retaliatory measures. Although armed resistance may be stability operations and support operations from the U.S. perspective, it is total war for those who take up arms.

1-15. An insurgency is an organized resistance movement that uses subversion, sabotage, and armed conflict to achieve its aims. It is a protracted politico-military struggle designed to weaken government control and legitimacy while increasing insurgent control and legitimacy—the central issues in an insurgency. Each insurgency has its own unique characteristics based on its strategic objectives, its operational environment, and available resources. Insurgencies normally seek to overthrow the existing social order and reallocate power within the country. They may also seek to—

- Overthrow an established government without a follow-on social revolution.
- Establish an autonomous national territory within the borders of a state.
- Cause the withdrawal of an occupying power.
- Extract political concessions that are unattainable through less violent means.

1-16. The structure of a revolutionary movement can be compared to a pyramidal iceberg, the bulk of which lies submerged with only its peak visible. In building a resistance structure, insurgent leaders give principal attention to the development of a support infrastructure—a task done by specially trained personnel. The resistance cadre organizes the support infrastructure, which in turn supports the guerrillas. This infrastructure works among the citizens in rural villages, towns, and urban cities; within the military, police, and administrative apparatus of government; and among labor groups and students.

DYNAMICS OF INSURGENCIES

1-17. Insurgencies arise when the government is unable or unwilling to address the demands of important social groups. These groups band together and begin to use violence to change the government's position. Insurgencies are often a coalition of different forces united by their common hostility for the government. To be successful, an insurgency must develop unifying leadership, doctrine, organization, and strategy. Only the seeds of these elements exist when an insurgency begins. The insurgents must continually nurture and provide the necessary care if the insurgency is to mature and succeed. Insurgencies succeed by mobilizing human and materiel resources to provide both active and passive support for their programs, operations, and goals. Mobilization produces workers and fighters, raises funds, and gets the necessary weapons, equipment, and supplies. Mobilization grows out of intense popular dissatisfaction with existing political and social conditions. In an insurgency, the active supporters consider these conditions intolerable. The insurgent leadership articulates the dissatisfaction of the people, places the blame on government, and offers an alternative. The insurgent leadership then provides organizational and managerial skills to transform disaffected people into an effective force for political action. Ultimately, the insurgents need the active support of most of the politically active people and the passive support of the majority.

1-18. A successful insurgency is the most important political power in a newly liberated country. Guerrillas, existing and fighting under conditions of great hardship, develop extremist attitudes and become very jealous of their prerogatives to determine the postwar complexion of their country. These attitudes may make it difficult or impossible to establish a government sympathetic to U.S. national interests. However, a nation that sponsors a successful insurgency generally has a political advantage at the close of hostilities.

1·19. There are seven dynamics that are common to most insurgencies. These dynamics provide a framework for analysis that can reveal the insurgency's strengths and weaknesses. Although the analyst can examine the following dynamics separately, he must study their interaction to fully understand the insurgency.

LEADERSHIP

1·20. Insurgency is not simply random political violence; it is directed and focused political violence. It requires leadership to provide vision, direction, guidance, coordination, and organizational coherence. The insurgency leaders must make their cause known to the people and gain popular support. Their key tasks are to break the ties between the people and the government, and to establish credibility for their movement. The leaders must replace the government's legitimacy with that of their own. Their education, background, family, social connections, and experiences shape how they think and how they will fulfill their goals. These factors also help shape their approach to problem solving.

1·21. Leadership is a function of both organization and personality. Some organizations deemphasize individual personalities and provide for redundancy and replacement in decision making. These mechanisms produce collective power and do not depend on specific leaders or personalities to be effective. They are easier to penetrate but more resilient to change. Other organizations may depend on a charismatic personality to provide cohesion, motivation, and a focal point for the movement. Organizations led in this way can produce decisions and begin new actions rapidly, but are vulnerable to disruptions if key personalities are removed or co-opted by the enemy.

IDEOLOGY

1·22. To win, the insurgents must have a program that explains what is wrong with society and justifies its actions. They must promise great improvements after the government is overthrown. The insurgency accomplishes this goal through ideology. Ideology guides the insurgents in offering society a goal. The insurgents often express this goal in simple terms for ease of focus. The insurgents' plans must be vague enough for broad appeal and specific enough to address important issues.

1·23. The ideology of groups within the movement may suggest differing views of strategic objectives. Groups may have ideological conflicts that need to be resolved before an opponent can capitalize on them. Ideology may suggest probable goals and tactics. It greatly influences the insurgent's perception of his environment. This perception of the environment in turn shapes the movement's organization and operational methods.

OBJECTIVES

1-24. Effective analysis of an insurgency requires interpreting strategic, operational, and tactical objectives. The strategic objective is the insurgent's desired end state; that is, how the insurgent will use the power once he has it. The replacement of the government in power is only one step along this path; however, it likely will be the initial focus of efforts. Typically, the strategic objective is critical to cohesion among insurgent groups. It may be the only clearly defined goal the movement presents.

1-25. Operational objectives are those that the insurgents pursue as part of the total process of destroying government legitimacy and progressively establishing their desired end state.

1-26. Tactical objectives are the immediate aims of insurgent acts. Some examples include the dissemination of psychological operations (PSYOP) products or the attack and seizure of a key facility. These actions accomplish tactical objectives that will lead to operational goals. Tactical objectives can be psychological and physical in nature. For example, legitimacy is the center of gravity for both the insurgents and the counterinsurgents. Legitimacy is largely a product of perception; consequently, it can be the principal consideration in the selection and attainment of tactical objectives.

ENVIRONMENT AND GEOGRAPHY

1-27. Environment and geography, including cultural and demographic factors, affect all participants in a conflict. The manner in which insurgents and counterinsurgents adapt to these realities creates advantages and disadvantages for each. The effects of these factors are most visible at the tactical level where they are perhaps the predominant influence on decisions regarding force structure, doctrine, tactics, techniques, and procedures.

1-28. UW in an urban environment presents a different set of planning considerations than in rural environments. These planning considerations impact directly on structure, doctrine, tactics, techniques, and procedures. Appendix A describes characteristics of cities and urban tactical operations.

EXTERNAL SUPPORT

1-29. Historically, some insurgencies have done well without external support. However, examples such as Vietnam and Nicaragua show that external support can accelerate events and influence the outcome. External support can provide political, psychological, and material resources that might otherwise be limited or totally unavailable. The types of external support involve the following:

- Morality—acknowledgement of the insurgents as just and admirable.
- Political issues—active promotion of the insurgents' strategic goals in international forums.
- Resources—money, weapons, food, advisors, and training.
- Sanctuary—secure training and operational or logistics bases.

1-30. Accepting external support may affect the legitimacy of both insurgents and counterinsurgents. It implies the inability to sustain oneself.

Also, the country or group providing support attaches its legitimacy along with that of the insurgent or the counterinsurgent group it supports. The consequences can affect programs in the supporting nation wholly unrelated to the insurgent situation.

PHASING AND TIMING

1-31. Successful insurgencies pass through common phases of development. Not all insurgencies experience every phase, and progression through all phases is not a requirement for success. The same insurgent movement may be in another phase in other regions of a country. Successful insurgencies can also revert to an earlier phase when under pressure, resuming development when favorable conditions return. The three phases of insurgency are explained below.

Phase I - Latent or Incipient Insurgency

1-32. During this phase, the resistance leadership develops the movement into an effective clandestine organization. The resistance organization uses a variety of subversive techniques to psychologically prepare the population to resist. These techniques may include propaganda, demonstrations, boycotts, and sabotage. Subversive activities frequently occur in an organized pattern, but no major outbreak of armed violence occurs. In the advanced stages of this phase, the resistance organization may establish a shadow government that parallels the established authority. Also during this phase, the resistance leadership—

- Recruits, organizes, and trains cadres.
- Infiltrates key government organizations and civilian groups.
- Establishes cellular intelligence, operational, and support networks.
- Organizes or develops cooperative relationships with legitimate political action groups, youth groups, trade unions, and other front organizations. This approach develops popular support for later political and military activities.
- Solicits and obtains funds.
- Develops sources for external support.

Phase II - Guerrilla Warfare

1-33. Phase II begins with overt guerrilla warfare. The guerrilla in a rural-based insurgency will normally operate from a relatively secure base area in an insurgent-controlled territory. In an urban-based insurgency, the guerrilla operates clandestinely using cellular organization. Subversive activities can take the form of clandestine radio broadcasts, newspapers, and pamphlets that openly challenge the control and legitimacy of the established authority. Recruiting efforts expand as the people lose faith in the established authority and decide to actively resist it.

Phase III - Mobile Warfare or War of Movement

1-34. The last phase starts the transition from guerrilla warfare to conventional warfare. If successful, this phase causes the collapse of the established government or the withdrawal of the occupying power. Without direct intervention, a Phase III insurgency takes on the characteristics of a civil war. The resistance organization could achieve legal belligerent status. As it gains control of portions of the country, the resistance movement becomes responsible for the population, resources, and territory under its control. Based on the conditions set earlier, an effective resistance movement will—

- Establish an effective civil administration.
- Establish an effective military organization.
- Provide balanced social and economic development.
- Mobilize the population to support the resistance organization.
- Protect the population from hostile actions.

Failure to achieve these objectives may cause the resistance movement to revert back to an earlier phase.

1-35. Some insurgencies depend on proper timing for their success. Because of their limited support, the insurgents must weaken the government's legitimacy so that it becomes ineffective. Then an opportunity to seize power exists. When the insurgents move to seize power, they expose their organization and intentions. If they move too early or too late, the government may discover their organization and destroy it.

ORGANIZATION AND OPERATIONAL PATTERNS

1-36. Insurgencies develop organizational and operational patterns from the interaction of various factors. The interactions cause each insurgency to be unique. The three general patterns that emerge—*foco*, mass-oriented, and traditional—are explained below.

Foco Insurgency

1-37. A foco (Spanish word meaning "focus" or "focal point") is a single, armed cell that emerges from hidden strongholds in an atmosphere of disintegrating legitimacy. In theory, this cell is the nucleus around which mass popular support rallies. The insurgents build new institutions and establish control based on that support. For a foco insurgency to succeed, government legitimacy must be near total collapse. Timing is critical. The foco must mature at the same time the government loses legitimacy and before any alternative appears. An infamous foco was led by Castro in Cuba. The strategy was very effective because the Batista regime was corrupt and incompetent. The distinguishing characteristics of a foco insurgency are the—

- Deliberate avoidance of preparatory organizational work. The rationale is based on the premise that most peasants are intimidated by the authorities and will betray any group that cannot defend itself.

- Development of rural support as shown by the ability of the foco to strike against the authorities and survive.
- Absence of any emphasis on the prolonged nature of the conflict.

Mass-Oriented Insurgency

1-38.   The mass-oriented insurgency aims to achieve the political and armed mobilization of a large popular movement. Mass-oriented insurgencies emphasize creating a political and armed legitimacy outside the existing system. They challenge that system and then destroy or supplant it. These insurgents patiently build a large armed force of regular and irregular guerrillas and construct a base of active and passive political supporters. The insurgents plan a protracted campaign of increasing violence to destroy the government and its institutions from the outside. Their political leadership normally is distinct from their military leadership. Their movement normally establishes a parallel government that openly proclaims its own legitimacy. Insurgents have a well-developed ideology and choose their objectives only after careful analysis. Highly organized, they mobilize forces for a direct military and political challenge to the government using propaganda and guerrilla action. Examples of this pattern include—

- The communist revolution in China.
- The Viet Cong insurgency.
- The *Sendero Luminoso* (Shining Path) in Peru.

NOTE: The following excerpts cite the success of the Sendero Luminoso and their heavy influence in the rural areas of Peru.

The government's failure to change conditions in the southern highlands made peasants question the relevance of the distant, culturally alien government which has little understanding of rural life. Sendero played on the frustration of the Andean peasants by proposing to entirely overthrow the "fascist" government in Lima. Not only did peasants have no viable alternative, but in fact, Sendero genuinely focused on their marginalized concerns.

Andrea Curtis, "Sendero Luminoso, A Study in Paradox,"
Latitudes, Volume 1, 1991-1992

The peasants support Sendero Luminoso because the movement supports their historical aspirations: for local control and for the right to pursue subsistence agriculture through ownership of plots of land.

Ronald Berg, "Sendero Luminoso and the Peasantry of Andahuaylas," Journal of
Inter-American Studies and World Affairs, 28 (1986-1987)

The slow and inadequate state response to the Sendero threat was augmented by the failure of military intelligence to comprehend the nature of the guerrilla movement. Sendero has a tight administration and its intelligence network is extensive and flexible. Sendero's guerrilla units are composed of cells of no more than five senderistas, thus creating a tightly controlled unit impervious to infiltration.

"War in Peru Gets Bloodier," Latin American Weekly Report,
25 October 1990

1-39. There are distinguishing characteristics of a mass-oriented insurgency. These characteristics include—

- Political control by the revolutionary organization that assures priority of political considerations.
- Reliance on organized popular support to provide recruits, funds, supplies, and intelligence.
- Primary areas of activity, especially in early phases, in the remote countryside where the population can be organized and base areas established with little interference from the authorities.
- Reliance on guerrilla tactics to carry on the military side of the strategy. These tactics focus on avoiding battle, except at times and places of the insurgents' choosing. They also focus on employing stealth and secrecy, ambush, and surprise to overcome the initial imbalance of strength.
- A phased strategy that first focuses on organizational structure in which the population is prepared for its vital role. Secondly, an "armed struggle" is launched and the guerrilla force gradually builds up in size and strength. The third phase consists of more mobile conventional warfare. Conceptually, this phase is accompanied by a popular uprising that helps overwhelm the regime. It is a concept of "protracted" war.

Traditional Insurgency

1-40. This insurgency normally grows from very specific grievances. At first it has limited aims. It springs from tribal or factional, racial, religious, linguistic, or other similarly identifiable groups. The insurgents perceive that the government has denied the rights and interests of their group and work to establish or restore them. They frequently seek withdrawal from government control through autonomy or semiautonomy. Insurgents seldom specifically seek to overthrow the government or control the whole society. They generally respond in kind to government violence. Their acts of violence can range from strikes and street demonstrations to guerrilla warfare. These insurgencies may cease if the government agrees to the insurgents' demands. However, the concessions the insurgents demand are so great that the government concedes its legitimacy along with them. Examples of this pattern include the—

- Mujahideen in Afghanistan before the Soviet withdrawal.
- Ibo revolt in Nigeria (Biafra).
- Tamil separatists in Sri Lanka.

Sri Lanka is a diverse nation. Sinhalese make up 74 percent of the population and are concentrated in the more densely populated southwest. Ceylon Tamils, whose South Indian ancestors have lived on the island for centuries, form around 12 percent of the population and live in the north and the east. Indian Tamils, a distinct ethnic group, represent about 6 percent of the population. Other minorities include Veddas, Muslims (both Moors and Malays), and Burghers who are descendants of European colonial settlers. Most of the Sinhalese community are Buddhist, most Tamils are Hindu. Most of the Muslims practice Sunni Islam. The different groups tend to lead highly segregated lives and live within their own communities, apart from in the capital, Colombo. Although Sinhalese are the clear majority they fear the influence of the huge Tamil population across the Palk Straits in the southern Indian state of Tamil Nadu.

The British colonial policy of divide and rule sowed the seeds of renewed tensions between the Sinhalese and Tamil communities after Independence. Tamils, although well educated, were given a dispro-portionate number of top jobs in the civil service by the British. Once the Sinhalese majority held sway, its politicians sought to redress the balance with populist but discriminatory policies against Tamils. In 1956, the victory of SWRD Bandaranaike on a platform of Sinhalese nationalism led to him declaring Sinhala to be the country's official language among other anti-Tamil measures. Communal tension and violence increased from 1956 onwards as Tamils became increasingly frustrated. By the mid-70s, Tamils were calling for a separate state in the north and east of the country. In the 1977 elections, the separatist TULF won all the seats in Tamil areas, while groups such as the Liberation Tigers of Tamil Eelam (LTTE) began to use violence for the same ends.

Barry N. Stein, "Tigers Seize Key Town as Death Toll Soars,"
1 October 1998

UNITED STATES SPONSORSHIP

1-41.   The United States cannot afford to ignore the resistance potential that exists in nations or countries that are our potential enemies. In a conflict situation or during war, SF can develop this potential into an organized resistance movement capable of significantly advancing U.S. interests. The strategic politico-military objective of UW during wartime is normally to influence conventional military operations. However, in stability operations and support operations the goals may range from interdicting foreign intervention in another country, to opposing the consolidation of a new hostile regime, to actually overthrowing such a regime.

1-42.   When directed, SF personnel support selected resistance organizations that enhance U.S. national interests. During a limited or general war, SFODs normally infiltrate hostile areas to organize, train, equip, and advise or direct an indigenous resistance organization. They may conduct UW internally in a JSOA or train an insurgent force at an external training site. The external element may be an indigenous force that will conduct UW inside its country or act as a surrogate for another internal or external mission.

1-43.   There are seven phases to a U.S.-sponsored insurgency (Figure 1-1, page 1-12). They are preparation, initial contact, infiltration, organization, buildup, combat employment, and demobilization. Although each insurgency is unique, U.S. sponsorship of a resistance organization generally passes through the seven phases. Each phase may not occur sequentially or receive the same degree of emphasis. The phases may occur concurrently or not at all, depending on the specific situation. A large and effective organization may only require logistics support, while a small or disorganized

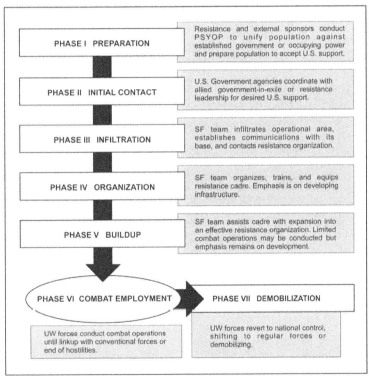

Resistance and external sponsors conduct PSYOP to unify population against established government or occupying power and prepare population to accept U.S. support.

PHASE I PREPARATION

U.S. Government agencies coordinate with allied government-in-exile or resistance leadership for desired U.S. support.

PHASE II INITIAL CONTACT

SF team infiltrates operational area, establishes communications with its base, and contacts resistance organization.

PHASE III INFILTRATION

SF team organizes, trains, and equips resistance cadre. Emphasis is on developing infrastructure.

PHASE IV ORGANIZATION

SF team assists cadre with expansion into an effective resistance organization. Limited combat operations may be conducted but emphasis remains on development.

PHASE V BUILDUP

PHASE VI COMBAT EMPLOYMENT   PHASE VII DEMOBILIZATION

UW forces conduct combat operations until linkup with conventional forces or end of hostilities.

UW forces revert to national control, shifting to regular forces or demobilizing.

organization might require more attention.

Figure 1-1. Seven Phases to a U.S.-Sponsored Insurgency

PHASE I - PREPARATION (FORMERLY CALLED PSYCHOLOGICAL PREPARATION)

1-44. The preparation phase must begin with a complete intelligence preparation of the battlespace (IPB). UW operations need to include, but are not limited to, a thorough analysis of the resistance force's strengths, weaknesses, logistic concerns, level of training and experience, political or military agendas, factional relationships, and external political ties. Along with this data, a thorough area study should be done of the target area. The area study should include, but is not limited to, political issues, religion, economics, weather, living standards, medical issues, education, and government services. This study is required to develop strong PSYOP and Civil Affairs (CA) plans that are crucial in the support of a strong UW plan.

1-45. The preparation phase includes CA and PSYOP support. CA units support SF in UW missions by providing advice and assistance relating to social, economic, and political considerations within the JSOA. PSYOP units prepare the resistance organization and civilians of a potential JSOA to accept U.S. sponsorship and the subsequent assistance of SFODs.

1-46. The nature of UW may limit the use of supporting CA units to outside the JSOA. CA personnel may accompany deploying SF units depending on mission requirements or METT-TC. CA personnel train insurgent military and political elements in CA activities and civil-military operations (CMO). The training focuses on the civil centers of gravity and gains momentum to mobilize the civilians towards the insurgents' goals. These activities must be coordinated with the JSOA PSYOP plan.

1-47. The United States Government (USG) begins PSYOP as far in advance as possible. PSYOP units prepare the resistance organization and the civilian population of a potential JSOA to accept U.S. sponsorship. PSYOP objectives in a UW operation include—

- Creating popular support for the insurgency movement.
- Developing support of the populace to allow the insurgents to avoid detection and move freely.
- Promoting the recruitment of others into the resistance movement.
- Discrediting the existing government and its programs.
- Informing the international community of the goodwill and intent of the United States and insurgents.
- Gaining support of the indigenous populace for U.S. support and presence.
- Countering hostile propaganda.
- Training members of the indigenous population or force in PSYOP (target audience analysis, local product development, targeting, dissemination, and analysis of impact indicators).
- Maintaining motivation among the insurgents.
- Passing information or instructions to the resistance organization or its subordinate elements.
- Providing a "link" between the resistance organization and foreign populations.
- Promoting reforms the insurgent organization will establish after the hostile government's overthrow.

1-48. CA planning teams may participate in the military decision-making process (MDMP) and analyze the JSOA to provide the SFOD commander with a perspective of the nonmilitary factors—civil areas, structures,

capabilities, organizations, people, and events (CASCOPE)—that shape the operational environment. CA planning team functions include—

- Establishing a civil-military operations center (CMOC) at the earliest opportunity to facilitate collaborative premission coordination with the nonmilitary agencies that will participate in or influence the outcome of the pending operation.
- Determining what, when, and why civilians might be encountered in the JSOA, what activities those civilians are engaged in that might affect the military operation, and how military operations might affect the lives of the civilians.
- Determining CA measures of effectiveness (MOEs) that generate the definition and conditions for success.
- Determining the orientation and requirements of a posthostilities infrastructure.
- Identifying and requesting United States Army Reserve (USAR) CA functional specialists who will provide a more comprehensive CA capability to facilitate the transition to stability operations.
- Developing a draft disengagement concept.

PHASE II - INITIAL CONTACT

1-49. Ideally, initial contact with the established or potential resistance movement should be made before committing SF units. This procedure allows for an accurate assessment of the potential resistance in the JSOA and arranges for the reception and initial assistance of the infiltrated element. Other USG agencies normally conduct the initial contact. During contact, SF personnel assess the resistance potential in the area of operations (AO) and the compatibility of U.S. and resistance interests and objectives. This phase also allows assessment planners to make arrangements for the reception and initial assistance of the SFOD. The special operations command (SOC) should arrange to exfiltrate an asset from the AO to brief the staff and SFOD while in isolation. Under certain circumstances, a small, carefully selected "pilot team" composed of individuals possessing specialized skills may make initial contact. This team's mission is to assess designated areas to determine the feasibility of developing the resistance potential and to establish contact with indigenous leaders. Once the theater command or SOC has determined the feasibility of developing the area, additional SF elements may be infiltrated. The pilot team may remain with the SFODs or be exfiltrated as directed.

1-50. During this phase, PSYOP units can develop themes, symbols, and programs that support the planned resistance operations. They can also prepare the local inhabitants to receive allied forces and actively assist in the UW mission to follow. PSYOP begins targeting the enemy and resistance forces with the need to adhere to the law of war, highlighting enemy violations. CA team members may continue to support SFOD assessments.

CA specialists can participate as members of the "pilot team" to assist in assessing the feasibility of developing the resistance potential in designated areas and establishing contact with indigenous leaders.

PHASE III - INFILTRATION

1-51. During the infiltration phase, the SFOD clandestinely or covertly infiltrates into the JSOA. Mission requirements, along with METT-TC, will determine the most desirable method of infiltration. After infiltration, the SFOD meets the resistance organization and moves to its secure area. Infiltration is not complete until the initial entry report is sent to the Special Forces operational base (SFOB) or forward operational base (FOB). The detachment submits the initial entry report as soon as possible upon infiltration. The report must be sent even if the SFOD does not contact the local resistance. Immediately upon infiltration, the SFOD begins a continuous area assessment to confirm or refute information received before infiltration. The detachment will continue to report all relevant operational information. If the mission warrants, selected CA and PSYOP team members may infiltrate into the JSOA with the SF detachment. Otherwise, CA and PSYOP team members support infiltration and subsequent phases as reachback assets from the SFOB or FOB.

PHASE IV - ORGANIZATION

1-52. The SFOD begins to establish rapport with the resistance leadership by showing an understanding of, confidence in, and concern for the resistance organization and its cause. The detachment explains its capabilities and limitations and begins to assist the resistance leadership with the development of the resistance organization. The SFOD must then prove its value in actual operations. Building rapport is a difficult and complicated process based on mutual trust, confidence, and understanding. It is not accomplished overnight.

1-53. Before a resistance organization can successfully engage in combat operations, the resistance leadership must organize an infrastructure that can sustain itself in combat and withstand the anticipated hostile reaction to armed resistance. During the organization phase, the resistance leadership develops a resistance cadre to serve as the organizational nucleus during the buildup phase. The SFOD assists the resistance leadership in conducting a cadre training program to prepare for the eventual buildup of the resistance organization.

1-54. The resistance leader and SFOD commander must agree upon command and control (C2) arrangements. Detachment members normally advise and assist counterpart resistance leaders. In some situations, SFOD members may actually direct some resistance activities.

1-55. The specifics of resistance organization depend on local conditions. UW requires centralized direction and decentralized execution under conditions that place great demands on the resistance organization and its leadership. Armed rebellion inherently creates an ambiguous and unstructured environment. No two resistance organizations need the same degree or level of organization. The SFOD commander should consider the following factors when advising the resistance leadership concerning organization:

- Effectiveness of existing resistance organization.
- Extent of cooperation between the resistance organization and the local populace.
- Hostile activity and security measures.
- Political boundaries, natural terrain features, potential targets, population density, and other characteristics of the JSOA.
- Religious, ethnic, political, and ideological differences among elements of the population and competing resistance organizations.
- Proposed type and scope of combat operations.
- Degree of U.S. influence with the resistance organization.

1-56. During the organization phase, PSYOP personnel can be used to promote the resistance movement's expansion and development by highlighting the enemy's weaknesses and countering the enemy's propaganda. PSYOP forces use themes to help the resistance organization influence attitudes and behavior to win the populace's support. PSYOP programs can support damage control and assist the development of a sound infrastructure. Such programs contribute to the overall attainment of the resistance movement's goals. PSYOP programs can cover the resistance movement's political, economic, and social goals; the resistance movement cadre's ideological indoctrination; the practical impact of tactical operations on the population; and the significance of and need for the resistance member's proper personal conduct with the populace.

1-57. CA team members can be used to assess the effect of the organization efforts on the political, economic, information (social and cultural), and humanitarian aspects of the JSOA. They can also screen the membership of the resistance cadre for potential positions in a posthostilities infrastructure. In future operations, CA team members may present redevelopment models illustrating the impact of posthostilities civil-military initiatives. CA team members can assist by helping indigenous people and their institutions, as may exist, and building a local capacity to survive ensuing conflicts or crises.

PHASE V - BUILDUP

1-58. The buildup phase involves expanding the resistance elements and their activities. Their tasks include infiltration or procurement of equipment and supplies to support the expansion and subsequent combat operations. During the buildup phase, the resistance cadre expands into an effective organization that can conduct combat operations. Recruitment increases due to successful missions. Guerrilla force missions and tactics dictate a simple, mobile, and flexible organization capable of rapid dispersion and consolidation in response to the tactical situation. Each unit must be self-contained with its own intelligence, communications, and logistics systems.

1-59. In this phase, PSYOP units can be used to focus on the resistance movement's full expansion and development. PSYOP programs enhance the resistance leadership's legitimacy and effectiveness, emphasize the rules of engagement (ROE), and identify targets whose destruction would impact adversely on the civilian populace. They highlight the government's actions taken against the population during its counterinsurgency campaign. PSYOP units can promote the uncommitted population's support for the insurgency and counter the enemy's propaganda. Unit members continue to stress and assure the success of the resistance movement and allied operations.

1-60. CA team members can continually assess the effect of the buildup efforts on the political, economic, information, and humanitarian aspects of the JSOA. CA team members can assist the SFOD in training insurgent military forces in CA activities and CMO. CA team members begin focusing on planning posthostilities transition operations that capitalize on the unique skills of the USAR CA functional specialists, to include training potential members of the posthostilities infrastructure separately and concurrently with the guerrilla force.

PHASE VI - COMBAT EMPLOYMENT

1-61. Combat operations increase in scope and size to support the objectives of the area command. During the combat employment phase, the resistance organization conducts combat operations to achieve its strategic politico-military objectives. The SFOD ensures that resistance activities continue to support the goals of the area command. Interdiction is the basic UW combat activity. These operations can drain the hostile power's morale and resources, disrupt its administration, and maintain the civilian population's morale and will to resist. Each target should contribute to destroying or neutralizing an entire target system.

1-62. In this phase, PSYOP units can exploit successful combat operations to attract more recruits. Unit members focus on themes and symbols of nationalism, success, and inevitability of complete victory. PSYOP units can also induce enemy defections or noncompliance with orders in an effort to protect themselves. They continue targeting the population to increase their support for the insurgency, the allied forces, and the eventual follow-on government. PSYOP units can assist in controlling or directing the dislocated civilian (DC) flow to facilitate the movement of combat forces and to minimize casualties. They continue to counter the enemy's propaganda.

1-63. CA teams analyze the civil component of the JSOA for CASCOPE to determine the impact of the civil environment on combat operations, as well as the impact of combat operations on the civil environment. CA teams anticipate, monitor, and conduct mitigating activities to reduce the negative effect of combat operations on the civil sector and vice versa, as well as to identify when the MOEs have been achieved. They assist the SFOD and area commander by fulfilling the command responsibilities inherent in CMO. They do this directly, by conducting CA activities and indirectly, by providing CA advisors. They assist the SFOD in continuing to apply mediation skills to possible and actual sources of indigenous tension.

PHASE VII - DEMOBILIZATION

1-64. Demobilization is the last, most difficult, and most sensitive phase of UW operations. Demobilization planning begins when the USG decides to sponsor a resistance organization and ends in the JSOA. Civilian USG agencies, along with international organizations and agencies such as the United Nations (UN) and the Organization of American States (OAS), normally conduct demobilization of the military groups. SF, PSYOP, and CA units help these agencies conduct demobilization using their knowledge of the terrain and the forces within the JSOA. The manner in which demobilization occurs will affect the postwar attitudes of the people and the government toward the United States. The greatest demobilization danger is the possibility that former resistance members may resort to subversion of the new government, factional disputes, or banditry. The new government brings arms and ammunition under its control to ensure public security and to return to a functional civil structure based on the rule of law. It helps resistance forces return to previous occupations and may integrate them into the new reconstituted national army. The new government must make every effort to reorient former resistance members into a peaceful society and gain their trust.

The most important phase is the one where successful accomplishment meets the U.S. government objectives.

COL John Mulholland, Commander,
5th Special Forces Group (Airborne), Afghanistan

1-65. PSYOP units help explain the demobilization process and promote the insurgent's orderly transition to peaceful civilian life. The primary aim is to prevent the formation of groups opposing the recognized government. Maintaining loyalty to the legitimate (newly established) government is the major concern. PSYOP units also conduct many direct and indirect activities that assist the new government's demobilization effort. PSYOP units—

- Help to secure lines of communications (LOCs).
- Control rumors by publishing and broadcasting the news.
- Assist the marshalling of available labor.
- Help to establish law and order.
- Continue to assist controlling DCs by directing them to available assistance.

1-66. CA teams support the SFOD and area commander by implementing well-planned and coordinated transition plans. CA teams draw upon civilian-attained skills in 16 functional areas to assist the SFOD and new indigenous civil authorities in returning affected areas to normalcy and establishing a sustainable, durable solution to the conflict. Through the CMOC, CA teams continue to facilitate interagency operations with USG agencies, nongovernmental organizations (NGOs), and other nonmilitary organizations during the transition of operations from military to indigenous authority, as well as from former to new regime. CA teams perform various roles in support to civil administration. They also support the conduct of DC operations. CA teams oversee programs designed to retrain former combatants to become productive members of civil society.

INFORMATION OPERATIONS IN UW

1-67. Information operations (IO) involve actions taken to affect adversary information and information systems, while defending one's own information and information systems to achieve information superiority in support of national military strategy. Information superiority is the capability to collect, process, and disseminate an uninterrupted flow of information while exploiting or denying an adversary's ability to do the same. IO applies across all phases of an operation, across the range of military operations, and at every level of war. Information warfare (IW) is IO conducted during time of crisis or conflict (including war) to achieve or promote specific objectives over a specific adversary or adversaries. The ultimate targets of offensive IO are the human decision-making processes. Defensive IO activities are conducted on a continuous basis and are an inherent part of force employment across the range of military operations. IO may involve complex legal and policy issues requiring careful review and national-level coordination and approval. Offensive and defensive IO should also be integrated with intelligence and other information-related activities, as well as those activities leveraging friendly information systems, including friendly decision-making processes. The IO cell on the joint special operations task force (JSOTF) staff is a critical element to ensure ARSOF plans and operations are integrated, coordinated, and deconflicted across the full spectrum of IO.

1-68. IO support the strategic, operational, and tactical levels of war, and the effective employment of IO is essential for meeting the JSOTF's objectives. As appropriate, IO target or protect information, information-transfer links, information-gathering and information-processing nodes, and the human decision-making process. Offensive and defensive IO are applied to achieve synergy through a combination of elements. JP 3-13, *Joint Doctrine for Information Operations*, provides additional information.

PSYCHOLOGICAL OPERATIONS IN UW

1-69. PSYOP units are a vital part of UW operations. When properly employed, coordinated, and integrated, they can significantly enhance the combat power of resistance forces. PSYOP specialists augmenting the SFOD can deploy into any JSOA and plan the propaganda themes, messages, media, and methods to be used, based on target audience analysis. PSYOP in contemporary and future UW become more critical as ideological and resistance struggles increase. A temporary tactical advantage may create a long-term psychological disadvantage. All actions must be reviewed, based upon their local, regional, or even international impact. PSYOP usually involve the following major target audiences in a JSOA.

ENEMY FORCES

1-70. These elements may represent the government forces, an occupying power, or one assisting the hostile government and may be of the same nationality as the local populace. In any case, PSYOP personnel wage campaigns against the members of the enemy forces to make them feel isolated and improperly supported, doubtful of the outcome of their struggle, distrustful of each other, and unsure of the morality of their cause.

ENEMY SYMPATHIZERS

1-71. This target audience consists of civilians in an AO who are willing enemy collaborators, unwilling enemy collaborators (will collaborate under duress), and passive enemy sympathizers. The goal of a PSYOP campaign aimed at this group is to identify and discredit the enemy collaborators and to weaken their belief in the enemy's military strength and power.

THE UNCOMMITTED

1-72. These members of the general population are neutral during the initial stage of hostilities or resistance movements. They may fear the aims of the movement or are uncertain of its success. To win over the uncommitted, PSYOP personnel must stress that the resistance shares and fights for the political and social goals of the population. The United States and its allies, in backing the resistance movement, support these same goals to ensure the resistance movement will be successful.

RESISTANCE SYMPATHIZERS

1-73. This target audience includes civilians and government, military, or paramilitary members who support the goals of the movement but who are not active members of the resistance force. PSYOP directed at this target audience stress themes that encourage the populace to support actively (though generally covertly) or cooperate passively with the resistance force in achieving common goals. These appeals ensure that the people, their sensitivities, cultures, customs, and needs are respected.

1-74. PSYOP advisors and the SFODs with whom they work exploit propaganda opportunities. The PSYOP teams attached to the SFOD help convince the guerrillas to conduct operations that create popular support for the resistance movement, both in and out of the JSOA. Indigenous personnel are trained in the effective conduct of PSYOP and then integrated into the political infrastructure and guerrilla forces. These forces then conduct PSYOP in support of the needs of the area commander. Those needs should relate to the goals of the unified commander, specific situation, or UW mission. Through face-to-face meetings with local indigenous leaders, SFOD personnel strengthen mutual respect, confidence, and trust. They also gain valuable insight into the guerrilla force's problems and gain rapport by sharing the same living and fighting conditions.

CIVIL-MILITARY OPERATIONS IN UW

1-75. CMO are inherent to UW. The UW environment contains both military and civilian components that are scattered and intertwined within the JSOA. Although the SFOD generally focuses its efforts on the military aspect of an insurgency, it must also consider the nonmilitary aspects of the JSOA. Natural, routine, planned, or unpredictable indigenous activities may hinder or help the activities of the guerrilla force during all phases of a U.S.-sponsored insurgency.

1-76. CMO are the commander's activities that establish, maintain, influence, or exploit relations between military (including guerrilla or insurgent) forces, government, and nongovernment civilian organizations and authorities, and the indigenous populace in the JSOA. These activities should facilitate military operations and consolidate and achieve U.S. objectives. In CMO, military forces may perform activities and functions normally the responsibility of local, regional, or national government. These activities will occur before, during, or after other military actions. They may also occur, if directed, in the absence of other military operations.

SPECIAL OPERATIONS IMPERATIVES

1-77. SOF commanders must incorporate the 12 special operations (SO) imperatives into their mission planning and execution to use their forces effectively. These imperatives, although developed to provide guidance to SOF, apply to any unit, organization, agency, or activity that may be involved in UW. They are discussed below.

1 - UNDERSTAND THE OPERATIONAL ENVIRONMENT

1-78. In UW, there are two aspects of the operational environment that SF must be familiar with—the internal and the external. The first aspect is critical to applying resources and skills effectively to accomplish the mission. The second aspect is critical to guiding actions in a very fluid and highly unstructured environment.

Internal Factors

1-79. SFOD members must know pertinent METT-TC as in any military operation. In addition, they must understand the insurgent movement, to include the underlying political and social causes, demographic composition of the movement's membership, history, goals, claims to legitimacy, methods, and any other pertinent information. SFOD members must have a thorough knowledge of the government, military, and other institutions that formally or informally exercise power normally associated with a functional government. This knowledge includes—

- Strengths, weaknesses, vulnerabilities, functions, and actual power centers (as opposed to what appears on organization charts) of the organizations.
- Interrelationships between these organizations.
- Goals and motivating factors for each organization.
- Relationships with the United States, other governments, international organizations, and NGOs.

1-80. The civilian population is the critical factor. SFOD members must understand the demography, culture, taboos, beliefs, customs, history, goals, ethnic composition, and expectations of the civilian population. Most important, they must be aware of the dynamics of the many correlations among these various aspects of a society. SFOD members must be aware of who can influence whom, and how that influence is achieved and exercised. They must also be aware of any incidental effect the actions with any one factor have on another.

External Factors

1-81. SFOD members must understand the U.S. Army command relationships, both military and interagency, that affect the individual guerrilla and the SFOD. In addition, SFOD members must understand the—

- Scope and limitations of each agency's influence and programs.
- Legal and political restrictions on SF activities.
- Sources and assistance available to SF to further assure mission accomplishment.
- Role of the U.S. media and the international press.
- Intent and goals of the USG.
- Intent and goals of NGOs, humanitarian relief organizations (HROs), and other key civilian agencies in the JSOA.
- Command relationships of international agencies and NGOs with representatives of the USG.
- Intent and goals of international agencies (United Nations, North Atlantic Treaty Organization [NATO]).
- Applicable ROE, to include their intent as well as the specifically enumerated provisions.

1-82. SFOD members must also be able to visualize and act on unforeseen circumstances. Therefore, they must have a clear understanding of the charter and goals of the total U.S. effort. It is impossible to predict every situation and write specific ROE or a course of action (COA) that addresses each and every situation. When the SFOD members understand the commander's intent, they can respond with rapid flexibility to the apparent unforeseen and unplanned circumstances.

2 - RECOGNIZE POLITICAL IMPLICATIONS

1-83. UW is essentially a political activity. Every act, from advising military activities to informal conversation, has a potential political impact. SFOD members should not anticipate a conventional environment where more traditional military concerns predominate. Whether conducting military operations independently or in conjunction with conventional forces, SFOD members must consider both the short- and long-term political implications of their acts.

3 - FACILITATE INTERAGENCY ACTIVITIES

1-84. UW, by definition, is an interagency effort in which military operations represent only one part (usually not the most important one) of the overall U.S. program. SF must be aware of all the agencies that comprise the UW effort. SF may also act as the liaison between the resistance force, U.S. agencies, and other DOD components to ensure that synergy is achieved. When participating in an interagency and often joint effort, SF must strive for unity of effort and recognize the difficulty in achieving it. SF must also anticipate ambiguous missions, conflicting interests and goals, and disunity of effort. When lacking unity of command, SF can promote unity of effort by—

- Requesting clear mission statements and the decision maker's intent.

- Actively and continually coordinating activities with all involved.

4 - ENGAGE THE THREAT DISCRIMINATELY

1-85. The SF commander must know when, where, and how to employ his assets based on short- and long-term objectives. This imperative contains three messages for SF involved in a UW effort.

1-86. The first message concerns the selection and distribution of resources for both personnel and materiel. Appropriateness, not mass, is the standard. SF commanders must ensure that SFODs selected for the mission are capable, qualified, trained, and necessary for the effort. Minimizing the U.S. presence while maximizing its impact is the desired outcome.

1-87. The second message relates to selection of training, advice, and assistance to be given. Resources are normally limited in a UW environment and must be used wisely for best effect. Based on SOF's understanding of their operational environment and its complex internal dynamics, SF must carefully select which particular training and advice to give. This impact is as much a consideration in selecting training and advice as are the political implications of the type of subject and assistance given.

1-88. The third message deals with tactical considerations. Tactical operations in UW must be carefully targeted to ensure success and avoid alienating the civilian population.

5 - CONSIDER LONG-TERM EFFECTS

1-89. UW efforts are inherently long-term. Tactical victories are of little value unless they contribute to the success of the overall operational scheme. The operational scheme may be nonmilitary in nature. Placing each problem in its broader political, military, and psychological context is the next consideration. SFOD members develop a long-term approach to solving the problem. They accept legal and political constraints to avoid strategic failure while achieving tactical success. They do not jeopardize the success of theater long-term goals by the desire for immediate or possible short-term success. Policies, plans, and operations must be consistent with U.S. national and theater priorities and the objectives they support.

6 - ENSURE LEGITIMACY AND CREDIBILITY OF SPECIAL OPERATIONS

1-90. Significant moral and legal considerations exist in a UW effort. Legitimacy is the most crucial factor in developing and maintaining international and internal support. Without this support, the United States cannot sustain assistance to a resistance movement. Without recognized legitimacy and credibility, military operations will not receive the support of the indigenous population, the U.S. population, or the international community.

7 - ANTICIPATE AND CONTROL PSYCHOLOGICAL EFFECTS

1-91. All operations and activities in a UW environment will have significant psychological effects. Combat operations and civic action programs are examples of the type of operations or activities with obvious psychological effects. Some operations and activities may be conducted specifically to produce a desired psychological effect. A tactical victory may be totally negated or overshadowed by negative psychological impact. Recognizing that perceptions may be more important than reality in this arena, SF must take care to ensure operations are understood by all audiences. Loss of control of perceptions may cause distortion of the facts and may even diminish or destroy the difficult gains of even the best-planned and executed missions.

8 - APPLY CAPABILITIES INDIRECTLY

1-92. The primary role of SF in UW is to advise, train, and aid resistance forces. The resistance area commander must assume primary authority and responsibility for the success or failure of this combined effort. Successful U.S.-advised operations reinforce and enhance the legitimacy and credibility of the area command and resistance movement.

9 - DEVELOP MULTIPLE OPTIONS

1-93. SFOD members engaged in a UW operation must be aware of and prepared for possible contingencies and follow-on missions. The SFOD members must plan to use their range of expertise even if not specifically tasked to do so. A change of operational environment may dictate a change of ROE or mission. SFOD members maintain operational flexibility by visualizing and developing a broad range of options and concept plans (CONPLANs). They can then shift from one option to another before and during mission execution.

10 - ENSURE LONG-TERM SUSTAINMENT

1-94. SFOD members involved in a UW effort must avoid advising or training the resistance forces in techniques and procedures beyond their capabilities to sustain themselves. U.S. tactics, techniques, and procedures (tactical communications, medic, demolitions, weapons, and logistics) may be modified to negate the threat. SF must recognize the need for training programs and equipment that are durable, consistent, and sustainable by the resistance movement and the USG.

11 - PROVIDE SUFFICIENT INTELLIGENCE

1-95. Intelligence forms the basis for all UW activities and programs. UW operations depend on detailed and comprehensive intelligence on all aspects of the operational environment and its internal dynamics. SFOD members establish priority of effort when they identify intelligence requirements. Effective operations security (OPSEC) requires an alert organization that can assess the hostile threat, warn the unit, and take timely action to penetrate and neutralize the hostile effort. SFOD members in a UW environment need intelligence that identifies the enemy locations and their intentions for force protection. However, not all threats may come from an identifiable enemy. SFOD members should consider the nonmilitary threats posed by the civil sector, such as criminal activities, hazardous materials, civil unrest, and disease. The knowledge they gain prepares them to effectively advise and train the guerrilla force.

12 - BALANCE SECURITY AND SYNCHRONIZATION

1-96. SFOD members performing a UW mission may be in a unique position to significantly help other SOF and conventional forces accomplish their missions. SO are often compartmented for security concerns, but compartmentation can exclude key personnel from the planning process. Insufficient security may compromise a mission, but excessive security will almost always cause the mission to fail because of inadequate face-to-face coordination. SF must resolve the dichotomy of mission planning synchronization and security.

Chapter 2

Premission Activities

SF commanders conduct both deliberate and time-sensitive mission planning and targeting. They receive their missions as a result of the joint strategic planning process. Strategies, policies, and SF missions are subject to continual change. This chapter describes how SF missions are identified and how SF battalions, companies, and SFODAs conduct mission analysis, feasibility assessments, and mission planning to perform UW missions. Ingredients of successful irregular warfare are as follows:

1. Patience to withstand protracted conflict. "Time works for us. Time will be our best strategist" – Truong Chinh.
2. Political awareness on the part of all ranks.
3. Intensive "wooing" of all the "little people" to the side of the insurgent.
4. The weakening of the enemy's morale by constant propaganda and harassment.
5. Constant offensive action against enemy personnel and sensitive points, but only when tactical advantage is on the side of the irregulars.
6. The avoidance of pitched battles with equal or superior forces.
7. Defense only when it is essential to survival or to aid another element to withdraw.
8. The consideration of the enemy's supply system as your own—making him haul the materiel to dumps, then seize it from him.
9. Constant striving to grow undercover forces into regular forces, once capable of meeting the enemy on his own ground when the time and circumstances make victory certain.

Findings From BG Yarborough's Study,
Circa 1961

MISSION ANALYSIS

2-1. In UW mission analysis, the battalion staff analysts view all sources of mission letters and taskings. They set priorities for resources and efforts through a clear statement of the battalion commander's intent and concept of operation. Mission analysis provides the basis for the battalion mission-essential task list (METL) preparation and, with the mission letter development, drives unit training for all the SFODs.

PROCEDURES

2-2. Home station mission analysis of UW follows a specific application of the deliberate planning process. This process assumes the SF battalion has more than one operation plan (OPLAN) it may have to execute. The deliberate planning process allows staff analysts to allocate resources and set priorities of effort. The analysts develop and refine draft METLs based on METT-TC planning. The bulk of the work on area studies is completed before beginning specific deliberate planning. Figure 2-1 summarizes the sources, processes, and products in mission analysis.

- **Study** purpose of higher headquarters mission (understand the why).
- **Determine** the higher commander's intent, two levels up. Review higher commander's overall deception plan.
- **Review** area of operations to understand higher headquarters mission and intent:
  - The command.
  - The environment.
  - The threat.
- **Identify** specified and implied tasks:
  - Consider the mission statement, purpose, and concept of the operation.
  - Develop a mental picture and outline the desired end state.
  - Consider limitations:
    8 Constraints (what must be done) imposed by the command, the environment, and the threat.
    8 Restrictions (what cannot be done) imposed by the command, the environment, and the threat.
- **Identify** mission-essential tasks.
- **Review** available assets.
- **Determine** acceptable levels of risks.
- **Conduct** detailed time analysis.
- **Restate** the mission.

Figure 2-1. Mission Analysis

2-3. An SF battalion is seldom activated to execute a mission from scratch; therefore, planning does not begin with a total absence of previous guidance or deliberate planning. By the very nature of UW, deliberate planning is mandated at home station due to the complexity and sensitivity of the mission. This planning results in a mission letter. Mission analysis, METL development, and mission letters are an integral part of the deliberate planning process. During time-sensitive crisis action planning, a tasking order (TASKORD) drives mission analysis and planning. Crisis action planning is an abbreviated version of the deliberate planning process conducted on a 96-hour timeline. The battalion normally modifies or updates previously completed plans developed at home station. Reviews of the battalion METL and mission letters should be done annually or when—

- Major changes in the political and social environment occur after receipt of the mission letter.
- Modified, improved, and enhanced METLs significantly alter the mission.
- A new or additional TASKORD is received in isolation.
- Supported OPLANs are significantly changed.
- Battle focus analysis (BFA), as outlined in the United States Army Special Forces Command (Airborne) (USASFC[A]) Regulation 350-1, *Component Training*, is conducted. Normally BFA occurs before and after the company and battalion commanders are briefed.

NOTE: BFA is the process of deriving peacetime training requirements from wartime missions. The correlation between BFA and the deliberate planning process at home station identify the specific unit mission, target organizations or countries, and the country study.

MISSION RECEIPT

2-4. Consistent with joint mission planning, mission analysis begins with the transmission of the mission tasking package (MTP) in accordance with (IAW) JP 3-05.5. Receipt of an MTP from the SOC or JSOTF, or a mission letter from the SF group initiates planning at the battalion level. The battalion staffs must analyze the mission letter along with many other documents. These documents include OPLANs, peacetime campaign plans (PCPs), and Joint Strategic Capabilities Plans (JSCPs). The staffs first look at developed war plans (OPLANs and CONPLANs) containing or implying mission requirements. They review the PCPs that outline major operations such as the overall counterdrug efforts for an area or region. The staffs also use the JSCPs to allocate missions and resources to unified combatant commanders. The JSCPs developed at the Joint Staff and the PCPs developed at unified levels are basic outlines of the "big picture" for regional U.S. efforts. In addition to external documents specifying potential missions, the battalion commander may deduce missions based on his evaluation of the assigned JSOA. The battalion commander must direct priority of effort first to externally directed missions and second to deduced missions. The battalion staff should forward mission requirements to the SF group for validation and inclusion in tasking documents. SFODA and B commanders must have a clear understanding of the intent of all the commanders involved, whether or not the mission is externally or internally developed. If any staff member notes a conflict or lacks understanding of the intent, he should resolve these problems at the highest level before mission analysis proceeds.

INFORMATION EXCHANGE

2-5. Staff representatives and commanders exchange information critical to initial mission analysis. Additionally, interagency information support may be obtained through the JSOTF. The battalion staff is the focal point for passing information. Therefore, battalion staff must ensure that all requests and responses are quickly and fully disseminated.

INITIAL MISSION ANALYSIS (DELIBERATE PLANNING)

2-6. The commander, selected staff representatives, and certain key support element leaders review the documents received during mission receipt and identify and list the specified and implied tasks. They must consider the relationship of UW to other missions and its status as a mission. At this point, they do not direct mission analysis against a specific target for execution by a specific SFODA. Rather, they direct analysis at allocating resources against projected requirements to best achieve the SF group commander's intent. The final products are the basis for routine personnel and administrative activities during garrison operations. These products are also used to develop specific battalion- and lower-level plans of execution (POEs). The result of this analysis is the battalion commander's restated mission and operational planning guidance. The restated mission must clearly identify the requirement to conduct UW, state the commander's intent, contain specific COAs, and provide general guidelines.

PREPARATION OF STAFF ESTIMATES

2-7. The staff may present staff estimates orally or in writing. The volume of UW material may dictate that such estimates be briefed to the commander orally with emphasis on the staff sections' conclusions and recommendations. The following paragraphs discuss the considerations that each staff section covers in its estimate.

S-1 - Personnel

2-8. In considering the battalion's overall UW requirement, the S-1 must evaluate battalion personnel strengths in terms of its capability to accomplish the mission. The S-1 presents the battalion commander with projected shortfalls in specific military occupational specialties (MOSs); individual qualifications; distribution of personnel; or projected losses, gains, and absences affecting overall readiness.

S-2 - Intelligence

2-9. Thoroughly reviewing available systems and identifying required intelligence support are keys to developing the intelligence estimate. The S-2 section identifies and produces intelligence estimate requirements as soon as possible to ensure mission success. As the S-2 and other staff members review available data, such as area studies, after-action reports (AARs), and area assets, they must also consider alternate means of gathering the required information. These may include requesting aerial overflights, imagery, or exploiting sources within the JSOA. S-2 personnel review all available information related to the priority intelligence requirements (PIR), commander's critical information requirements (CCIR), and information requirements (IRs) passed by deployed SFODs to gain current information and adjust established POEs. They should also request and review information gathered by other group and battalion assets such as the military intelligence (MI) detachment and its special operations teams A (SOT-As).

S-3 - Operations

2-10. The S-3 section's estimate shows the recommended number of subordinate units needed to meet requirements. The operations estimate must identify general requirements for UW-related schooling, such as the Combat Diver Qualification Course (CDQC); military free-fall (MFF), advanced special operations (ASO), operations and intelligence (O&I), and survival, evasion, resistance, and escape (SERE) training; language courses; and training with an evaluation of the SFOD's current status and capabilities. Considerations for UW involvement include the—

- Number of SFODAs and SFODBs dedicated to preparing for UW as a primary mission.
- Feasibility of functionally aligning SFODAs within the companies with all UW-tasked teams in one company or the preferability of having them decentralized.
- Requirements to deploy an FOB, advanced operational base (AOB), or special operations command and control element (SOCCE) and, if so, the number required.

S-4 - Logistics

2-11. The logistics section analyzes the logistics needs to support the required type and number of missions. This estimate may drive the acquisition of certain types of items, revision of the modified table of organization and equipment (MTOE), and budgeting for expendables and air items to support UW. Supplies may also be acquired by battlespace recovery and through indigenous sources in the JSOA.

Other Staff Elements

2-12. Special staff sections that involve CA, PSYOP, signal, medical, and legal personnel may also be required to provide estimates. These estimates must, as a minimum, enable the UW-tasked teams to—

- Evaluate the adequacy and compatibility of the type and density of communications systems available versus mission requirements (Appendix B).
- Identify special medical requirements to support the types and numbers of missions to be performed in a given JSOA (Appendix C).
- Evaluate the legality of the general type of missions proposed, particularly that of battalion-generated functional requirements (Appendix D).

PRODUCTS

2-13. Once the staff sections prepare the estimates, they present them to the commander. Based on the information contained in the estimates, the commander, aided by the battalion executive officer (XO), command sergeant major (CSM), and S-3, prepares his estimate. This estimate contains information on UW requirements, priorities, and other missions. The commander then formulates a clear statement of intent or concept of operations (CONOPS) that lists his priorities concerning UW operations (Figure 2-2). He further translates his CONOPS into a written mission letter to the SFODs A and B. These products drive several activities for the battalion staff and subordinate units. Although these actions begin during product development, they will not be finalized until after completion of premission activities and the deliberate planning process at home station.

Figure 2-2. Military Decision-Making Process

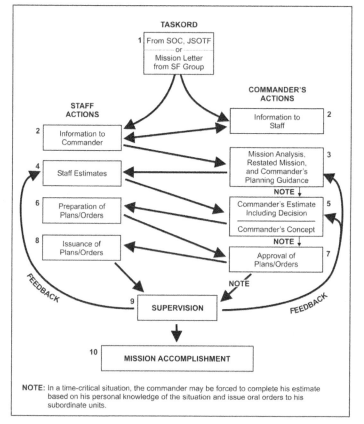

NOTE: In a time-critical situation, the commander may be forced to complete his estimate based on his personal knowledge of the situation and issue oral orders to his subordinate units.

STAFF ACTIVITIES

2-14. As a result of the commander's statement of intent, mission letters, and guidance to battalion staff sections, various actions begin. The goal of these actions is to aid the preparation, conduct, and support of UW operations. These actions normally parallel actions taken in support of other missions. However, each staff element fulfills the following UW-specific considerations.

PERSONNEL

2-15. Based on the general guidance contained in the commander's statement of intent and guidance to the battalion, the S-1 conducts a comprehensive review of personnel resources, assignments, and procedures. Working closely with the S-3, battalion CSM, company commanders, and sergeants major (SGMs), the S-1 determines the adequacy of assigned personnel to meet the specific mission requirements. If he identifies shortfalls in MOSs or specific qualifications, the S-1 forwards personnel requests to the SF group. If he finds that authorizations under the current MTOE do not support requirements, he works with the S-3 in submitting MTOE changes. If the S-3 detects shortfalls in training, he corrects the MTOE or obtains schooling as required. The S-1 maps the location of personnel with mission-essential skills, experience, and abilities. For example, certain missions may call for a native speaker, a member of a given ethnic group, or an individual with in-country experience.

2-16. Although identifying requirements is not the S-1's responsibility, he does identify and find the assets. Based on requirements identified by the SFODs A and B, S-3, commanders, and SGMs, the S-1 matches available personnel who have UW-related skills with existing mission profiles. Working with the SF group S-1 and the battalion CSM, the battalion S-1 requests appropriate personnel and advises the commander on the most appropriate assignment of incoming personnel. After mission-specific planning is completed, the battalion S-1 and company staffs monitor the profiles for individual positions to assign incoming personnel accordingly.

INTELLIGENCE

2-17. During all stages of the mission, the S-2 section, more than any other staff section, must be proactive. Given the commander's intent, the S-2 should anticipate the IRs and generate the appropriate requests for intelligence information (RIIs) and specific requests for information (RFIs). When a UW mission is identified, the S-2 section—

- Collects all available information on the JSOA.

- Supports the deployment of pilot teams to collect current information. FM 3-05.220 provides more information on pilot team support.

- Sends RFIs to all available sources and agencies to gain current material and information about the JSOA.

- Reviews on-hand information including a detailed review of the intelligence summaries (INTSUMs) reflecting information about the JSOA.

- Reviews current map coverage requirements for the JSOA.

OPERATIONS

2-18. When acting as the operations center (OPCEN) director, the S-3 reviews specific skill qualifications and asks for required school quotas. Working with subordinate element commanders and SGMs, he sets priorities for allocations to UW-related schools. The S-3 drafts and presents the battalion METL, which must reflect requirements of subordinate units. He synchronizes specific mission planning with other elements participating in the supported OPLAN. When missions are to be performed in support of conventional forces, the S-3 requests direct liaison authority during plan development. Based on the draft METL and commander's concept of the operation, he drafts the battalion commander's training guidance and begins work on the battalion's long-range training plan. He matches resource forecasts to UW-specific requirements. He coordinates plans for PSYOP and OPSEC. He must also be alert to training opportunities that are relevant to METL requirements.

LOGISTICS

2-19. The S-4, like the S-2, must anticipate SFOD requirements. The S-4 section orders, purchases, or identifies specialized equipment (Appendix E). When the current MTOE does not support the requirements, the S-4 submits MTOE changes.

CIVIL-MILITARY OPERATIONS

2-20. The S-5 plans section must ensure all CMO plans related to UW missions are made readily available. CMO considerations are analyzed using the acronym CASCOPE. The six characteristics of CASCOPE are—

- *Civil Areas.* Key civilian areas or aspects of the terrain within a commander's battlespace, which are not normally thought of as militarily significant.
- *Structures.* Determine the location, functions, capabilities, and application of all structures in support of military operations, to include weighing the cost of their use.
- *Capabilities.* Determine assistance needs by evaluating the capabilities of the populace to sustain themselves.
- *Organizations.* Identify all organized groups that may or may not be affiliated with government agencies.
- *People.* Includes all civilians one can expect to encounter in an AO, as well as those outside the AO whose actions, opinions, or political influence can affect the military mission.
- *Events.* Analyze all events occurring in the AO, both civilian and military, that will impact the lives of the civilians.

2-21. Based on the civil centers of gravity, the CMO section coordinates with supporting CA elements to determine possible (positive and negative) impacts of the mission on noncombatants and enemy forces. It then relays this information to the tasked SFODs. The S-5 is the principal staff officer for all CA activities and CMO matters. Employing the principles of CASCOPE, he supplies data on politico-military, economic, and social matters. He identifies possible surplus or shortage of supplies and estimates the effects of military operations on the local populace, international organizations, and NGOs operating in the AO. The S-5 establishes the CMO center as required.

COMMUNICATIONS

2-22. The signal section analyzes the requirements for UW-unique communications capabilities and evaluates the battalion's ability to support the mission with organic assets. Considerations for UW communications are generally the same as those for other missions; however, certain UW-specific aspects require special consideration. Planning for UW communications requirements is vital to mission success. Redundancy and reliability of all communications become imperative. The section must seek the best compromise between the equipment weight, compatibility, and capabilities for mission support. Appendix B provides further information.

SUBORDINATE OPERATIONAL ELEMENTS

2-23. The transmission of mission letters to the SF companies begins their direct involvement in the mission analysis process. The SF battalion support company receives a mission letter at home station. The following paragraphs discuss each element and specific personnel duties.

SFODB

2-24. The SFODB commander is the company commander. One of the SFODB's missions is to support the SFODAs in their UW mission. The SFODB begins mission analysis upon receipt of the company mission letter. Based on the letter and deliberate planning, the battalion commander determines the UW-related SFODB team's missions. The SFODB commander's dual role is to keep his assigned SFODAs trained for their missions and to prepare for the SFODB mission. He may also—

- Support an area assessment (pilot) team.
- Support a SOCCE for a UW mission.
- Establish an AOB to support a UW mission.
- Establish and run an isolation facility (ISOFAC).
- Augment and reinforce the FOB.

2-25. Based on the company mission letter, the battalion commander designates primary missions for each SFODA and SFODB. He provides them with a mission letter clearly stating the commander's intent. The battalion commander and staff analyze the abilities of the SFODAs and SFODBs, ensuring they can accomplish the mission.

SFODA

2-26. The SFODA manages the operations journal and monitors incoming and outgoing message files. Detachment members continue with OPSEC measures to include controlling entry into their working area. They identify the tasks for which they have functional area planning responsibility by reviewing the higher commander's operation order (OPORD) or OPLAN and the mission briefing. By requesting clarification and additional guidance from higher headquarters (HQ), the SFODA clarifies all questions it has about the mission concerning—

- Risk assessment.
- Specified and implied tasks.
- Resistance force training and its present status.
- ROE, which include—
  - Area studies.
  - Cross-training plan development based on METT-TC.
  - Other operational objectives, such as the threat and civilian welfare.

2-27. Based on the specified and implied tasks, the SFODA selects and lists the mission-essential tasks (to include contingencies) for each of the following phases of the mission:

- Predeployment.
- Deployment.
- Employment.
- Redeployment.
- Postdeployment.

2-28. SFODA staff members begin initial planning estimates of tentative COAs for the mission-essential tasks based on the commander's intent, the restated mission, and S-3 guidance.

2-29. SFODA staff sections list CCIR in descending order of criticality based on their functional areas and information gaps in the higher commander's peacetime OPLAN. SFODA staff sections submit their functional area CCIR to the S-3 and submit their IRs to the S-2. The S-3 develops a consolidated list of all CCIR by collating the CCIR submitted by other staffs and the PIR or IRs submitted by the S-2. The staff sections coordinate with the S-2 for the dissemination of intelligence information to all SFOD members and, as applicable, to subordinate and attached elements.

SFODA Commander

2-30. The SFODA's mission analysis will normally begin after it has been alerted and received a mission briefing in isolation. The SFODA commander leads and provides guidance during the mission analysis. He establishes his intent, which clearly states what the SFODA is to achieve, including the specific objectives of the mission. He states the priority of effort and the most likely contingencies and follow-on operations. The commander restates external command, control, communications, and intelligence (C3I), combat support (CS), and combat service support (CSS) relationships for all phases of the mission identified in the higher commander's OPORD or OPLAN and the mission briefing. He establishes an event time schedule for the remainder of the mission analysis. The schedule will include—

- Maintaining OPSEC.
- Requesting an asset.

- Conducting the mission concept (MICON).
- Performing briefback planning.
- Performing rehearsals.
- Performing other mission activities as per the isolation schedule.

2-31. The planning and preparation phases are based on the METL and the higher commander's OPLAN or CONPLAN.

Assistant Detachment Commander

2-32. The SFOD warrant officer (WO) is the assistant detachment commander (ADC) who supervises and directs all staff functions. He is the acting SFOD chief of staff. The ADC identifies the legal status of forces conducting operations in the JSOA. He ensures the SFOD understands the legal category of the armed conflict within the JSOA and the ROE. He ensures all detachment members understand the U.S. policy regarding prisoners. The ADC updates the CCIR relating to operational legal questions. He coordinates for the submission of any additional METL items to the SFOD's METL. He also performs all CA and PSYOP functions for the team, if there are no attachments.

Operations Sergeant (18Z)

2-33. The SFOD S-3 restates the mission to the SFOD in concise and accurate terms of who, what, when, and where as per the higher commander's OPORD or OPLAN. He submits the restated mission to the SFOD commander for approval. The S-3 gives the approved mission statement to all SFOD members and subordinates. He produces a single list of SFOD mission-essential tasks by collating the task lists submitted by the other staff sections. He determines the tentative contents for the SFOD's OPLAN to include the necessary annexes to cover all phases of the mission IAW FM 5-0, *Staff Organization and Operations* (currently published as FM 101-5), and the consolidated METL. He develops planning guidance for the other staff members based on the tentative contents of the SFOD's OPLAN. This list has specified and implied tasks. From these tasks, he develops the mission METL from other team members and distributes the developed planning guidance to the applicable staff sections.

Assistant Operations and Intelligence Sergeant (18F)

2-34. The SFOD S-2 reviews all submitted RFIs. He coordinates these and any special staff section requests as separate requests. Also he reviews the higher commander's PIR and coordinates with the S-3 to identify other IRs. He develops a tentative list of SFOD PIR and IRs based on the commander's intent, the SFOD mission, the criticality of specific staff IRs, the higher commander's PIR, and anticipated intelligence requirements to support operations. The S-2 submits the tentative PIR and IR list to the S-3 for incorporation into the SFOD CCIR. The CCIR are prioritized for his use in developing his timely information management, tactical decision process, and his actions and reactions that affect successful mission accomplishment. He also coordinates for the inclusion of additional mission-essential tasks into the SFOD's METL.

SF BATTALION SUPPORT COMPANY

2-35. To best support the SFODs, the battalion support company must have a clear picture of mission requirements. The company provides intelligence and electronic warfare (IEW) support, CSS, and signal support to an FOB and their deployed SFODs. The first source of these requirements is the mission letter. Working with other primary and special staff sections, the S-3 section prepares this mission letter, which the battalion commander issues. The mission letter contains general guidance as to the types and quantities of support the company will be required to provide. The mission letter must alert the signal detachment to any unusual signal requirements and include other UW-specific taskings. The mission letter serves as a basis for METL development for the SF battalion support company commander. The second means of identifying support requirements are the briefbacks conducted by the employed SFODs. Representation of all concerned staff sections at this mostly oral presentation enhances mission success more than almost any other briefing. The briefback is normally the last chance for the S-3 and S-4 representatives to brief the SFOD; commanders present any last minute changes and updates.

2-36. Upon completion of specific mission planning, the support company commander revises the draft METL. Working with the appropriate staff section, the support company commander issues guidance to each of his subordinate elements in a mission letter. The letter includes a statement of intent and CONOPS. This letter provides a start point for developing the battalion METL. Subordinate elements then draft specific and related tasks from this general analysis.

MISSION PLANNING

2-37. FM 3-05.20 and Graphic Training Aid (GTA) 31-1-3, *Detachment Mission Planning Guide*, outline specific SFODA mission planning procedures to include deliberate and time-sensitive (crisis action) planning. Deliberate (peacetime) planning is based on projected political and military situations that are applicable to a UW environment. The objective of this process is to develop an OPLAN with CONPLANs to provide for flexible execution. A crisis is fluid by nature and involves dynamic events, making flexible planning a priority. Deliberate planning supports time-sensitive (crisis-action) planning by anticipating potential crises and developing CONPLANs that assist in the rapid development and selection of a COA.

DELIBERATE PLANNING PROCESS

2-38. The deliberate planning process begins with receipt of the TASKORD and target intelligence package (TIP). The process (Figure 2-3, page 2-13) will ultimately result in a completed special operations mission planning folder (SOMPF). A mission letter and TIP are needed to begin a feasibility assessment (FA) or develop a POE. Each TIP contains the SOC and group commanders' operational intent. It also contains a specification of premission constraints and considerations that will hamper the assessment and planning process. The group commander and staff review the TIP and SOMPF to determine the general shortcomings and requirements inherent in the TASKORD. They then assign a battalion to assess the mission's feasibility and to begin planning the mission. Although the group passes the action to the battalion for more detailed analysis, group staff elements must continue their own analysis and coordinate the known and anticipated shortfalls.

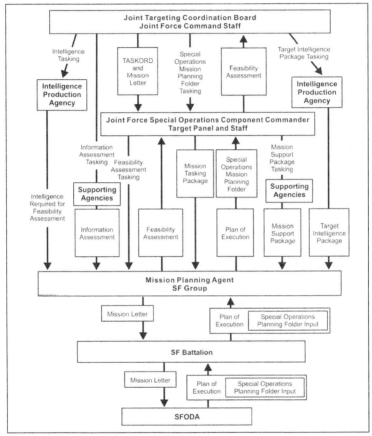

Figure 2-3. Deliberate Planning Process

FEASIBILITY ASSESSMENT PROCESS

2-39. Upon receipt of the TASKORD, the SF battalion begins the FA process. This assessment determines the ability of the SFODA to perform the mission and the abilities of the battalion or SFODB to support the mission. The battlefield operating systems (BOS) and SO imperatives are the guides to use for conducting an FA. The FA process requires direct involvement of the battalion or FOB staff, the SFODB staff, and the SFODA. Each has specific degrees of concern and areas of responsibility (AORs) that, when addressed, will accurately reflect mission feasibility. Reviewing these items ensures unity of effort of all units in the JSOA and avoids conflict among friendly units. When determining mission feasibility for a preconflict mission assignment at home station, planners must forward to the isolated SFOB detailed mission shortfalls in training or resource requirements that are beyond the battalion's capability to fix, such as school quotas and mission-specific equipment. Once completed, the FA must clearly show whether mission feasibility is conditional upon the resolution of identified shortfalls. The battalion commander translates training deficiencies into additions to the SFOD METL for training. He then tasks his staff elements to coordinate the resolution of materiel or personnel shortfalls.

BATTALION FEASIBILITY ASSESSMENT ACTIVITIES

2-40. The battalion commander and his staff consider the specific mission requirements in the context of overall group and battalion plans. They must assess the battalion or FOB staff's ability to prepare, support, sustain, command, and control UW elements once they are committed to an operation. The SF battalion has two principal roles in the FA process, to guide and support the SFOD's efforts. In the deliberate planning process at home station where time is not a critical factor, the battalion will not find a mission infeasible without allowing the tasked SFOD to conduct its assessment. If the SFOD's and the battalion staff's assessments conflict, the battalion commander makes the final determination. The battalion operations staff serves as the focal point for coordinating infiltration and exfiltration feasibilities. SFODs and battalion staffs must consider all methods of infiltration and exfiltration during FA. Infeasible or inappropriate methods of infiltration or exfiltration are excluded from future consideration. A mission becomes infeasible when all potential infiltration and exfiltration methods are infeasible. The battalion or FOB staff forwards to the tasked SFODA and SFODB known constraints, available information, and the commander's intent, which become their basis for assessment.

COMPANY FEASIBILITY ASSESSMENT ACTIVITIES

2-41. A battalion gives missions directly to each of its 3 SFODBs and 18 SFODAs. This tasking does not imply that the company HQ does not participate in tasking its organic SFODAs. Unless there are security reasons for compartmentalizing the mission, the company receives the TASKORD from the battalion commander and staff. The battalion then tasks one of its SFODAs or SFODBs and supervises its assessment activities. The SF battalion commander has three reasons to pass the TASKORD through the company commander. First, the SFODB (company) manages the day-to-day activities of the SFODA and SFODB. Second, operational experience of the

SF company HQ normally exceeds that of the SFODA; the company staff mentors the SFODA. Third, after deployment, the most common missions for an SFODB will be that it is independently deployed into the JSOA or deployed to support the SFODA as an AOB or as a SOCCE. For UW, the company's FA concerns include—

- Communications means and schedules.
- Emergency exfiltration requirements.
- Emergency resupply considerations.
- Preliminary contact and link-up plans.

2-42. The SFODA or SFODB performing FAs for specific missions does not develop plans at this time. Either detachment can determine mission requirements and examine applicable tactics, techniques, and procedures. It identifies interagency coordination, required resources, training beyond its organic capability, and augmentation needs. It must include these requirements as conditions in the final FA. FAs are stated as either—

- Affirmative—trained, equipped, and routinely supported.
- Conditional—we can do it, but the following conditions or requirements exist.
- Negative—we cannot accomplish this mission because of a clearly stated reason.

SUPPORTING AGENCY FEASIBILITY ASSESSMENT ACTIVITIES

2-43. Aviation assets conduct FAs for aircraft availability and compatibility with mission guidelines and routes for infiltration and exfiltration. Technical augmentees conduct FAs to ensure compatibility with the mission. This FA should include—

- Capability to execute the selected infiltration and exfiltration.
- Emergency resupply.
- Fire support.
- Other mission-specific skills necessary for mission success.

FIRE SUPPORT ASSESSMENT

2-44. Joint fires, close air support (CAS), naval gunfire, fire support types, availability, limitations, and requirements need to be identified early in the mission planning sequence. During planning, the commander—

- Establishes restricted fire areas (RFAs), no-fire areas (NFAs), and fire support coordination lines as needed.
- Develops fire support coordination measures that protect deployed SFODs and are not unnecessarily restrictive on the conventional or supporting forces.

NOTE: FM 3-05.20 and JP 3-09, *Doctrine for Joint Fire Support*, provide detailed fire support information.

POSTFEASIBILITY ASSESSMENT ACTIVITIES

2-45. Once a mission is determined feasible or conditionally feasible, the FOB staff or SFOD anticipates actual TASKORD. The battalion or FOB staff immediately identifies requirements for schooling, training, and equipment. Modifying MTOEs or task-organizing early to meet mission requirements are examples of long-term fixes that should begin during FA. The battalion staff and the SFOD retain all documentation and working papers from the FA since they form the basis for subsequent POE development.

PLAN OF EXECUTION DEVELOPMENT

2-46. The POE is the final element of the SOMPF. It shows how the SFODA intends to carry out the assigned mission. Specific mission preparation begins when the battalion receives the tasking to prepare a SOMPF to accomplish a tasked mission. This tasking takes the form of a SOMPF "shell" containing all elements developed to that point. FM 100-25 and JP 3-05.5 provide information on SOMPF contents. Options for conducting specific mission planning include—

- Activating the FOB for training and isolating SFODAs so that they may accomplish their detailed planning.
- Conducting planning as part of the routine training day.

BATTALION ACTIVITIES

2-47. The battalion commander and staff plan for support of the overall operation. In addition, the battalion has activities that support SFOD POE development. Building upon the analysis conducted during the FA, the battalion staff uses the military decision-making process as described in FM 5-0 (currently FM 101-5). For planning that is not time-critical, the staff prepares formal written estimates that identify anticipated mission-specific requirements of the SFODs. They also address planning options available to the tasked SFOD. For example, the signal section addresses available communications capabilities and procedures for transmitting data without undue risk of compromise. At the battalion level, the commander directs the decision-making process toward—

- Developing estimates to be used in preparation of the battalion order and SFOD planning guidance.
- Developing the commander's intent into a feasible CONOPS.
- Planning for FOB activities required to support the employed SFODs.

Battalion Order

2-48. The battalion planning process produces the battalion order. The battalion order encompasses all missions the battalion's SFODs will accomplish. SFODAs and SFODBs will normally receive information on their JSOA only.

2-49. Once completed, the coordinated battalion order or plan becomes a supporting plan to the group or SFOB OPLAN. The revised or new mission letter normally requires the staff to review previous home station analysis and coordination.

Commander's Intent

2-50. The commander's intent serves to communicate guidance in the absence of specific orders. The commander's intent must be stated clearly. It must be brief and to the point. The commander must include a separate statement of intent for each specific TASKORD. The intent directs MICON development at the SFOD level. The order must contain sufficient detail to guide the SFOD commander's mission analysis and decision-making process without limiting the SFOD's flexibility during the planning options.

Mission Letter

2-51. The battalion commander issues a mission letter to the SFODAs and SFODBs. He then provides the battalion OPLAN and SOMPF to the SFODA. The SFODA needs time to review the information before receiving the mission briefing from the battalion commander and staff. The mission briefing consists of battalion staff officers, mission operation cell (MOC), and noncommissioned officers (NCOs). They summarize their specific areas and elaborate on data or changes in the OPLAN that impact on the SFODA's mission. The SFODA does not leave the briefing until it understands the commander's intent and has asked all the questions generated by its review of the battalion OPLAN and SOMPF. The battalion staff answers all questions concerning, for example, infiltration platforms, support equipment availability, and rehearsal areas available to the SFOD.

COMPANY ACTIVITIES

2-52. The SFODB may also prepare for its own follow-on area command mission in the future. When the SFODB is not compartmentalized from the SFODA receiving its mission, the SF company commander and staff monitor the mission briefing with the SFODA. This practice ensures the SFODB—

- Is available to the SFODA during the planning process.
- Understands the training and resource requirements related to the mission.
- If tasked to act as an AOB or as FOB augmentation, understands the missions it is supporting or controlling.

2-53. Deliberate UW planning during isolation prepares the SFODA for a hypothetical crisis based on the most current intelligence. This assumption allows for the preplanned use of resources and personnel projected to be available when the plan becomes effective. The assumptions make it improbable that any CONPLAN the SFODA has implemented will be totally usable without modifications. The detailed analysis and coordination that was accomplished during the time available for deliberate planning will expedite effective decision making as the crisis unfolds. At this time, assumptions and projections are replaced with hard data. Once the FOB commander selects an SFODA to execute the mission, the detachment moves into an ISOFAC, receives the OPORD and mission brief, and begins its mission preparation as follows.

Step 1: Receive the Mission

2-54. The SFOD and its MOC receive the battalion staff's planning guidance. This guidance may come in a mission letter from the group during normal peacetime operations, or it may come in the form of an OPLAN and SOMPF during hostilities (TASKORD). The company passes command guidance to the SFODA. The SFOD commander reviews this planning guidance and activates the staff sections within the SFODA. Unit standing operating procedures (SOPs) designate SFODA members for each staff section according to their MOSs and assigned staff responsibilities. Each SFOD member reviews his portion of the OPLAN. When review of the OPLAN is complete, the SFOD discusses the battalion commander's intent. Each member voices his concerns and develops questions to be answered in the mission briefing to the team. The SFOD develops RFIs and puts them in writing. These RFIs address unanswered questions and unclear points in the commander's intent. These RFIs are forwarded to the battalion staff and a mission briefing is scheduled. The battalion staff presents the mission briefing, during which it answers as many RFIs as possible and provides a working status on the others. The SFOD questions each staff member as required. The SFODA commander ensures the perception of the commander's intent is correct through face-to-face discussion with the battalion commander.

Step 2: Exchange Information

2-55. After the mission briefing is complete and all questions have been answered or noted for further research and coordination, the SFOD commander conducts a mission analysis session with the SFOD. This session ensures SFOD members understand PIR, ROE, intelligence indicators, legal and political constraints, and the role of CA and PSYOP. In this session, the SFOD reviews all available information to ensure that all SFOD members agree on what has been presented. SFOD members with specialized skills or experience (either for the mission or in the JSOA) provide information on their unique perspectives or requirements. If confusion over information or interpretations of information exists, the SFOD develops and forwards additional RFIs to the battalion for clarification.

Step 3: Restate Commander's Intent and Produce Planning Guidance

2-56. After exchanging information, the SFOD commander, ADC, and the SFOD operations sergeant (or company operations WO or SGM if an SFODB) meet to develop the restated mission and intent to produce OPORD planning guidance. Here, the SFOD leaders—

- Review the specified and implied tasks from the OPORD.
- Review the battalion mission statement and commander's intent.
- Consider the information received to date.
- Review the feasible infiltration and exfiltration means.

2-57. Based on this information, the SFOD leaders review and develop a comprehensive list of specified and implied tasks, and the commander develops a restated mission. The wording of the task in the OPORD does not need to be rearranged. The restated mission specifically identifies the task as the "what" of the who, what, when, where, and why. Based on the knowledge of the skills, capabilities, current and achievable standards of training of the SFOD, and available resources, the SFOD leaders develop numerous COAs for consideration.

2-58. Planning responsibilities different from, or not covered by, unit SOPs are also clearly stated. When the SFOD leaders have completed the analysis, they pass the findings out to the entire SFOD. Normally, information is given orally; however, written guidance or training aids (for example, flip charts) are preferable where guidance is complicated. As a minimum, the SFOD leaders must usually present three COAs in writing.

Step 4: Prepare Staff Estimates

2-59. Based on the planning guidance and unit SOPs, the SFOD members prepare estimates for their AORs. These estimates are not limited to those of the traditional staff AORs. PSYOP and CMO estimates will always be prepared for UW operations. At home station, SFOD's planning (where time is not a factor) includes written estimates. Written estimates provide needed continuity for replacements when SFOD members rotate. Staff estimates must identify support requirements for each COA. Once completed, the detachment commander briefs the staff estimates to the SFOD. The briefing serves the purpose of exchanging information between SFOD members.

Step 5: Prepare Commander's Estimate and Decision

2-60. After the staff estimate briefings, the SFOD commander reassembles the SFOD leaders and, with their assistance, prepares the commander's estimate. A critical portion of this step is finding and weighing the factors to be used in evaluating the COAs. The SFOD leaders select the specific factors for the mission based on the commander's intent and the specified and implied tasks. The commander's estimate must include specific factors for each of the functional areas in the BOS. The SO imperatives should be translated into specific factors related to the mission. The commander's estimate is prepared in written form. Based on his estimate, the commander decides which COA the SFOD will plan to execute. The product of this step is a statement of the SFOD commander's intent and a concept of the operation. The SFOD commander briefs them to the entire SFOD. This briefing serves to answer any questions the SFOD may have and serves as the SFOD "murder board" for the concept. After briefing the battalion, the commander schedules an informal MICON briefing with the SFOD and the battalion commander.

Step 6: Present MICON Briefing

2-61. The MICON briefing is an informal briefing presented to the battalion commander to ensure the planning efforts meet his intent. The MICON allows approval of the SFOD's concept of the operation before expending time in detailed planning. The goal of the MICON is to get the commander's approval for a COA. MICON briefings have no specific format but normally include the—

- Mission.

- Higher commander's intent.
- Concept of the operation.
- COAs considered.
- Factors used to evaluate the COA, risk assessment, and METT-TC.
- Specific UW tasks.
- Task organization (to include requests for required attachments).
- Infiltration, contact, and exfiltration means.
- Identification of external support required (such as interagency approval of special activities and nonstandard equipment).
- General statement of the commander's CONOPS.
- Mission-essential personnel and equipment problems not previously addressed.

2-62. Visual aids should be those that the SFOD is already using for mission planning. The MICON briefing should not be so formal the "event" hinders the SFOD's planning activities. The battalion commander approves the concept, modifies it, or directs the SFOD to return to Step 3, providing additional guidance to clarify his mission intent. Key battalion staff members may accompany the battalion commander to the MICON briefing and familiarize themselves with the approved mission concept.

2-63. Based on the approved concept, the battalion staff anticipates the SFOD's support requirements. For example, if the MICON calls for high-altitude low-opening (HALO) infiltration of a 12-man SFOD, the S-4 does not wait for a support request for HALO air items for the infiltration. The selected concept drives intelligence requirements. Because of the generally repetitious IR, intelligence personnel can anticipate and deliver many of their requirements. However, the SFOD is still responsible for all details of the UW operation.

2-64. Approval of the MICON ends the concept development phase for this planning session. Responsibility for the concept now rests with the battalion commander, and the SFOD continues with their planning.

Step 7: Prepare OPLAN

2-65. Upon approval of the MICON, the SFOD leaders produce the body of the OPLAN. The written OPLAN specifies tasking to subordinate elements and individual members of the SFOD. Annexes are not included at this point; they are produced during the detailed planning phase. The plan must be in keeping with the battalion commander's guidance and understood by all members of the SFOD. When these criteria are satisfied, the battalion commander approves the plan after completion of the briefback.

Step 8: Conduct Detailed Planning

2-66. The SFOD organizes for planning the same as it would for mission execution. When the mission does not require the entire SFOD, nonessential members help subordinate elements in the mission planning process. Compartmentation within the SFOD is generally counterproductive. Each

SFOD member or element completes a detailed plan for the execution of assigned tasks. Members of the SFOD brief their respective areas, while other members provide an appropriate critique. The battalion staff should be available to provide the same service with the added advantage of greater experience and objectivity.

2-67. In UW, certain aspects of the mission may be beyond the experience of any of the planners. In these circumstances, rehearsals are excellent mission planning tools. New or unfamiliar employment techniques may be tested by realistic rehearsals of portions of the plan during its development. Often, walking through an action will reveal the need for changes to the plan. In any case, before an SFOD briefs a POE to its battalion commander, SFOD members should physically confirm the viability of the plan under the most realistic circumstances possible. Formats for specific subelements of the detailed plan that support the POE vary with the mission. Some portions of the POE may require annexes; others only require mention in a larger section. The POE should relate how the exceptional activity contributes to collecting and reporting requirements or how it enhances the survivability of the SFOD. Alternate plans and CONPLANs are also considered. The POE lists all mission-essential equipment and accounts for the disposition of that equipment in SFOD packing and resupply plans. The SFOD leaders ensure that all supporting subplans are consistent and mutually supportive. They also must ensure that specialized equipment used for one activity can also be used for another. Upon completion of all supporting subplans, the SFOD leaders supervise the preparation of the formal POE. It includes all the annexes, notes, narratives, and graphics essential to conduct the mission.

Step 9: Conduct Briefback

2-68. The briefback serves a distinct purpose. Although the POE details what an SFODA intends to accomplish, the briefback explains to the battalion commander how the SFODA will execute the assigned tasks. All information is contained in the commander's folder and must be able to stand alone. The SFODA is now ready to accomplish its mission. The battalion commander's last effective influence on these activities is through guidance given at the briefback.

2-69. The briefback format is driven by the plan, not the reverse. Several mission briefback formats are available that provide general guidance. There is no "best" format or checklist for UW. The SFODA prepares the briefback using the completed detailed plan. Existing formats are useful as a means to organize the presentation (in general terms) and as a checklist to look for obvious areas that were overlooked during planning. Briefback preparation often reveals gaps in planning. In adapting the format, the following principles apply:

- The format must provide a detailed description of the activities of each SFODA member throughout the execution of the mission. This description provides a mental picture of the operation for the commander receiving the briefing.

- The briefing uses visual aids only if they help to clarify the briefing.

- Briefers must avoid constant reference to the commander's folder as it denies the staff access to necessary information (use charts instead).
- The briefing must provide the commander with adequate information to judge the efficacy of the plan.

2-70.   The SFODA presents its briefback in the ISOFAC where the planning was conducted. This practice enhances OPSEC and reduces both administrative and support requirements. Each SFODA member briefs his own responsibilities. The staff members focus questions on areas where they did not hear adequate information to judge the completeness or viability of the plan. However, all staff elements should have thoroughly coordinated their input during the mission-planning phase. The traditional habit of quizzing SFODA members' memory of mission-essential details is appropriate for this briefback since mission preparation and training will continue. The purpose of the briefback is for the commander and staff to judge the merits of the plan. For example, if the battalion communications representative hears reference to a communications system that he cannot personally verify as available, he questions the SFODA on the availability of that system. If he hears discussion on the use of an antenna that appears inappropriate, he confirms the reason for that selection. The briefback is intended to show any weaknesses in the plan while they can still be corrected. If the SFODA cannot justify any action, no matter how minute, that action needs to be reconsidered, corrected, and then implemented.

2-71.   Once the battalion commander is confident the plan is workable and is delegated the authority by the group commander, he approves the POE. If further work is still required, he gives specific guidance and returns the SFODA to the planning phase. The commander determines the extent of revision and whether another full briefback is required. As a minimum, he should require the appropriate staff officer to personally brief him on any changes. Once the plan is approved, the SFODA commander is responsible only for the preparation of the SFODA and execution of its mission. The battalion commander assumes responsibility for the viability of the plan. He should withhold final approval of plans until all support requests are confirmed and the TASKORD authority approves the POE.

Step 10: Obtain POE Approval

2-72.   Once the POE is completed and approved by the battalion commander, the S-3 forwards it through the SF group to the tasking agency. The tasking agency then compiles the SOMPF by obtaining the mission support package (MSP) and other supporting documents. The S-2 or S-3 secures the basic folder and returns a copy to the mission planning agent (MPA). This procedure constitutes POE approval.

MISSION PREPARATION

2-73.   Mission preparation must predate isolation and the deliberate planning process. During mission preparation, specific mission employment is not required. SFODs tasked to conduct a specific type of mission or use a specific means of infiltration continue to support their METL through scheduled training. Mission preparation, which is best done at the unit's home station, includes METL, individual, and mission-specific training.

2-74. Based on the group commander's training guidance, the battalion commander assigns the missions and approves the draft SFOD's METL that supports the assigned missions. The company commander must plan, conduct, and evaluate company and SFOD training to support this guidance and the approved METL for the mission.

PREMISSION TRAINING

2-75. The SFOD commander ranks the tasks that need training. Since there will never be enough time to train in every area, he focuses on the METL tasks that are essential for mission completion. He emphasizes building and maintaining proficiency in those tasks that have not been performed to standard and sustaining proficiency in those tasks that are most difficult. He will rank those tasks during training meetings with the SFODAs and SFODBs.

2-76. Once the tasks for training are selected, the SFODA commander builds a training schedule and plans on those tasks. He provides the previous training requirements to the battalion commander. The battalion commander approves the list of tasks to be trained, and then the SFODA commander includes them in the training schedule.

2-77. The company commander coordinates the support and resource requirements with the battalion S-3 well before the scheduled training to allow S-3 personnel sufficient time to coordinate for them. He ensures that tasks, conditions, and standards are enforced and conducted IAW principles outlined in FM 7-0, *Training the Force*.

2-78. In UW, the SFOD must know the operational environment. The SFOD often deploys to the actual AO, even when the activities in the potential JSOA are not directly related to the TASKORD. The opportunity to survey the climatic, geographic, cultural, and other environmental factors must not be lost. Where it is impossible to deploy to the actual area and conduct offset training, the S-3 coordinates with the battalion S-2 to identify accessible locations for training that replicate each detachment's AO. The SFOD trains to exercise its mission plans as carefully and realistically as possible while always maintaining OPSEC.

INTELLIGENCE

2-79. The battalion S-2 is responsible for all intelligence-related matters. He is responsible for keeping the commander and his staff informed on all UW security matters, to include hostile and indigenous force activities. Due to the nature of UW, the battalion S-2 must play a key role in mission success. All mission planners will understand the PIR and IR goals. The S-2 must ensure the collection plan PIR and IRs on which the mission is based have not been nor can be satisfied by other sources. If the S-2 identifies other mission-capable sources, he informs the battalion commander through the S-3, and the support is requested. The SF group commander determines minimum-essential preparation tasks. He then modifies the deliberate planning process to do those tasks in the time available. The SF group commander must inform the SOC or JSOTF when he cannot accomplish these tasks with an acceptable degree of risk for mission success.

TARGET INTELLIGENCE PACKETS

2-80. Intelligence is perishable over time. The battalion S-2 has the primary responsibility for keeping the intelligence database current. The S-2 requests additional information from higher and adjacent HQ to meet and monitor PIR and IRs. The S-2 section conveys changes to the situation and to TIPs that affect mission accomplishment for the appropriate SFOD. The S-2 section must provide liaison with local intelligence forces to maintain the command's security. The S-2, with S-5 input, also provides current situation updates and INTSUMs to the SFOD and responds to intelligence-related questions and requests.

AREA STUDIES

2-81. At the company and SFOD level, the country area study is the primary tool for tracking intelligence over time. The SFOD continually updates the area study at home station. The battalion S-2 provides the database for updating the study by using all available sources, to include the Special Operations Command, Research, Analysis, and Threat Evaluation System (SOCRATES) and the open-source intelligence system.

PERSONNEL

2-82. The S-1 section provides for and coordinates personnel service support (PSS). Its primary combat duties focus on strength management, casualty management, and replacement operations. Other responsibilities include mail, awards, pay, Uniformed Code of Military Justice (UCMJ), enemy prisoners of war (EPWs), and soldier readiness processing. The section takes part in the operations order process by developing administrative annex material, preparing personnel estimates, and recommending replacement priorities. In the PSS coordination role, S-1 serves as the focal point for personnel, administration, financial, religious, medical, public affairs, and legal activities.

LOGISTICS AND COMMUNICATIONS

2-83. All levels of command review the UW-specific requirements for logistics. The S-4 must redistribute the available supplies and equipment within the battalion and make inventory adjustments. In UW, communications requirements are usually long term and unique. The signal section must review the compatibility and type of equipment to ensure all requirements can be met. Battery inventory is particularly critical. The annual budget must include projections for training requirements. Where nonstandard equipment is used, the signal officer and his staff must identify reliable internal sources for prescribed load list (PLL) repair parts and batteries.

PREEMPLOYMENT PREPARATION

2-84. The S-3 must periodically review and update mission SOMPFs. This review and update should take place whenever—

- There is a significant change in the situation (intelligence).
- The supported plan or basic tasking has major revisions.
- Personnel turnover affects mission readiness.

2-85. After the battalion has been alerted to execute a mission, it activates the FOB. Normally, the FOB will operate from a forward secure area, but it may also operate from home station. The deliberate planning process and isolation procedures apply to the UW mission.

TIME-SENSITIVE (CRISIS-ACTION) PLANNING PROCESS

2-86. The time-sensitive (crisis-action) planning process continues the sequence begun during the deliberate planning process with receipt of the mission letter and continues with receipt of the TASKORD and TIP. Deliberate planning presumes that the SFOD has completed a SOMPF for the mission and conducted its mission preparation at home station. Time-sensitive tasks, such as reviewing the current INTSUM for changes and confirming infiltration and exfiltration means, are critical and timely activities. Failure to allow the SFOD to complete these activities in the 96-hour time-sensitive planning process decreases the probability of mission success.

EMERGING MISSIONS

2-87. Emerging missions are those other missions for which a requirement was not anticipated and no TIP or SOMPF has been prepared. The time-sensitive planning process for such missions involves a 96-hour cycle. At the FOB, the SFOD uses the first day to prepare orders and may dedicate the last 3 days to the deliberate planning process, rehearsals, inspections, and rest during the SFOD isolation. As with any such procedural guide, the time frames are approximate and planners can adjust them as required. The 96-hour time frame obviously does not permit the type of meticulous, METL-driven mission preparation described in the previous paragraphs of this chapter. If, however, the battalion has done a thorough job of mission analysis for its assigned JSOA, the general conditions of the emerging mission will parallel other missions for which it has previously prepared its SFODs. The JSOA may be similar (if not the same) as will the threat and other factors of the operational environment. The battalion and company commanders must make every effort to assign the emerging mission to the SFOD that has most closely prepared for the similar operation. During time-sensitive planning, staffs must anticipate mission requirements and staff-to-staff coordination. Planners must consider the transportation and information needs commonly requested for the type target being considered. Some specific areas that are particularly critical to time-sensitive planning are communications, intelligence, operations, map coverage, logistics, and infiltration and exfiltration methods.

2-88. Significant planning cannot begin without adequate and current map coverage. The FOB S-2 must supply current maps to the SFOD. Quality imagery will significantly enhance the probability of mission success. Detailed planning for infiltration and exfiltration is critical. Compromise of the SFOD on infiltration can indicate the mission will be a failure. Since infiltration and exfiltration usually involve joint external assets, coordination is more difficult in this short time period. Face-to-face coordination between the SFOD and the supporting asset (for example, pilot, boat operator, or ship captain) is crucial.

2-89. Supplies from the FOB support center (SPTCEN) are usually the only logistic support available. This situation highlights the need for the battalion S-4 to plan and deploy with a large assortment of equipment and supplies rather than just the minimum required for the preplanned missions.

DETAILED MISSION PREPARATIONS

2-90. After developing the OPLAN, the SFOD members continue detailed preparations for the mission. OPSEC measures remain important. SFOD members obtain supplies, equipment, and training materials and prepare for infiltration and mission accomplishment. SFOD members hone their military skills through mission rehearsals, conduct extensive area and language orientation, obtain input from various staff elements, and receive an asset debriefing that also enhances detailed planning.

STAFF ACTIVITIES

2-91. The SFOD staff sections follow up on previous requests for additional resources and support not already delivered. They contact supporting agencies IAW established procedures to find the status of their requests. SFOD staff sections consider alternate COAs when supporting agencies fail to provide the required resources and support. They route functional area information requests to the other staff sections through the SFOD S-3 and route IRs through the SFOD S-2. SFOD staff sections modify previously developed estimates and plans IAW the latest information available. They also update, through the SFOD S-3, the CCIR list IAW the latest information available and their needs for additional CCIR arising from modified estimates and plans. The actions of the SFOD staff members are listed below.

Commander

2-92. The commander commands and controls the SFOD. He ensures the SFOD completes mission preparation IAW the higher commander's OPORD or OPLAN and the SFOD's OPLAN. The commander ensures all SFOD members know and understand the SFOD's OPLAN. He approves tentative changes to the OPLAN if the changes satisfy requirements IAW his intent, identify mission objectives, and follow the higher commander's OPLAN or OPORD. The commander ensures all legal questions have been clarified and all operational plans are IAW applicable legal guidance and directives.

Assistant Detachment Commander

2-93. The SFOD ADC ensures mission preparation is IAW the event time plan. He supervises and directs all staff functions acting as the SFOD chief of staff. He is responsible for coordinating all staff efforts, identifying critical preparatory planning shortfalls, and evaluating all regional implications of the mission. He assists and supervises in the areas of operations, intelligence, CA, and PSYOP.

S-1

2-94. The S-1 ensures preparation for movement with soldier readiness processing (SRP) and the requirements are met IAW Army Regulation (AR) 600-8-101, *Personnel Processing (In-and-Out and Mobilization Processing)*, and the unit's SOP. He follows up all previous PSS requests IAW the SFOD OPLAN. He informs the commander of any problems in the administrative preparation of the SFOD for infiltration. He establishes procedures for personnel accountability and strength reporting in support of the SFOD.

S-2

2-95. The S-2 supervises SFOD requests for, and dissemination of, intelligence IAW the commander's PIR and IRs and the intelligence collection plans. He updates the enemy situation using the latest available information and intelligence. The S-2 informs the entire SFOD of changes in the situation that will affect planned mission execution. He monitors the implementation of the SFOD's intelligence collection plans to include updating the commander's PIR and IRs, conducting an area assessment, and requesting additional intelligence support. The S-2 also monitors the SFOD's OPSEC measures and plans to ensure they effectively counter the anticipated threat IAW the current situation. He then recommends appropriate actions.

S-3

2-96. The S-3 primarily controls OPSEC as he disseminates the SFOD's OPLAN, or applicable portions of it, to higher HQ staff for tentative approval. He distributes the SFOD's plan to SFOD members and, as required, to subordinates. The S-3 coordinates deception, PSYOP, CA, and fire support needed in the JSOA. He incorporates any approved changes into the SFOD's OPLAN and disseminates all approved OPLAN changes to the SFOD. He assigns mission briefback tasks to SFOD members. The S-3 ensures SFOD predeployment training and rehearsals are IAW the SFOD's OPLAN, the resistance training program of instruction (POI) in the language spoken within the JSOA, the unit's SOP, and the time event plan. He ensures weapons are test fired. The S-3 coordinates the theater combatant commander's directives and policies for preparation and use of the Special Forces evasion and recovery plan (SFERP).

S-4

2-97. The S-4 inspects, accounts for, and ensures the serviceability of required supplies and equipment (less medical and communications supplies and equipment) in the SFOD's custody. He stockpiles additional required supplies and equipment IAW the SFOD's OPLAN, to include the basic load of ammunition to support follow-on or contingency missions. The S-4 follows up all previous requests for additional logistics resources or support IAW the SFOD's OPLAN. He informs the SFOD ADC of any logistics problems in preparing the SFOD for infiltration.

S-5

2-98. The S-5 analyzes the civil component of the JSOA using CASCOPE and ensures civil considerations and CA team activities are integrated into the plans and activities of all other staff sections. He updates the civil situation using the latest available information. The S-5 monitors the activities of the SFOD and anticipates future requirements for CMO based on current and planned operations, as well as the results of completed operations.

Signal Section

2-99. The SFOD signal staff obtains the cryptographic materials, signal operating instructions (SOI), and additional related materials IAW the higher commander's OPLAN or OPORD and the SFOD's OPLAN. They conduct inspections to account for required communications equipment. The staff conducts function tests of communications equipment and systems as required by the higher commander's OPORD or OPLAN, the SFOD's OPLAN, and the unit's SOP. The signal staff informs the SFOD XO of any communications problems in preparing for the SFOD's mission.

Medic (18D)

2-100. The SFOD medical staff (usually two 18Ds) ensures the SFOD members meet medical and dental SRP requirements IAW the unit's SOP. They ensure the SFOD's required immunizations are current IAW AR 40-562, *Immunizations and Chemoprophylaxis*, and the unit's SOP contains information published by the Center for Disease Control and the World Health Organization. This information comes from the Armed Forces Medical Intelligence Center. The medical staff also ensures the SFOD members receive any required medical or dental treatment identified during SRP. They follow up all previous requests for additional medical resources or support IAW the SFOD's OPLAN. The medical staff account for and inspect the serviceability of the required medical supplies and equipment. They also inform the SFOD ADC of any health services problems in preparing for the SFOD's mission.

Instructors

2-101. Each SFOD instructor prepares his training materials in the resistance force's language, if possible. He prepares a lesson outline for each period of instruction IAW the POI, the tentative training schedule, and other assigned classes. The instructor includes in each lesson outline, as a minimum, the task, conditions, standards, performance measures, required training aids, manuals, and handouts.

ASSET DEBRIEFING

2-102. The purpose of an asset debriefing is to provide the SFODs firsthand and timely information that will allow them to prepare and plan a more detailed mission. The asset should have comprehensive background knowledge of the objective area. The preferred asset is indigenous to the JSOA or AO and is the designated representative of the area commander. He is a person who has been security-screened but is not a prisoner. U.S. security personnel will have already cleared him. In addition, he will have—

- Recently exfiltrated from the area.
- Been thoroughly interrogated for any intelligence information.
- Volunteered or have been recruited to assist in the SF mission.

2-103. The SF debriefer should quickly establish and maintain rapport, gain the asset's confidence, and question him as a friend, not as an enemy prisoner. Information needed from an asset should include, but not be limited to, the following:

- Current background information on the asset (experience, history).
- His method and reasons for assistance to the United States.
- The resistance force goals (past, present, and future).
- Local and regional combat and support power of the enemy security force.
- General and specific JSOA intelligence needed for initial contact, infiltration, operations, sustainment, and exfiltration.

Chapter 3

Employment

Employment of SFODs in UW encompasses several of the seven phases of a U.S.-sponsored insurgency. The phases are preparation, initial contact, infiltration, organization, buildup, combat operations, and demobilization. Although each resistance movement is unique, U.S.-sponsored resistance organizations generally pass through all seven phases. The phases may not occur sequentially or receive the same degree of emphasis. They may occur concurrently or not at all, depending on the specific situation. This chapter covers infiltration through combat operations by addressing the following steps: infiltration, area assessment, development of the JSOA, development of a resistance organization, training the guerrilla force, combat operations, and combatting counterguerrilla operations.

Rules of Conduct:

1. There shall be no confiscation whatever from the poor peasantry.

2. If you borrow anything, return it.

3. Replace all articles you damage.

4. Pay fairly for everything that you purchase.

5. Be honest in all transactions with the peasants.

6. Be courteous and polite to the people and help them when you can.

Mao Tse-tung, 1928

INFILTRATION

3-1. Infiltration follows initial contact with the resistance organization or government in exile. Normally, OGAs conduct initial contact and make an assessment of the resistance potential. Part of the initial contact phase also involves making arrangements for reception and initial assistance of the infiltrating SFOD or pilot team. Successful infiltration into the JSOA requires detailed planning and preparation at the joint level. Several methods are considered based on METT-TC. Appendix F provides additional information.

AREA ASSESSMENT

3-2. The SFOD members and the commander begin an area assessment immediately after entry into the JSOA. This assessment is the collection of special information and serves as the commander's estimate of the situation. The area assessment is a continuous process that confirms, corrects, refutes, or adds to previous intelligence acquired before commitment. The area assessment also serves as a basis for changing premission operational and logistic plans. There are no fixed formulas for doing an area assessment.

Each commander has to decide for himself what should be included and what conclusions may be drawn from the information he collects.

3-3. When making an area assessment, the SFOD commander considers all the major factors involved, including the enemy situation, security measures, and the many aspects of the civil component as defined by CASCOPE. The SFOD should only disseminate new intelligence information that differs significantly from the intelligence received before commitment. Area assessment is either initial or principal, depending on the urgency involved. Appendix G contains a sample format for an initial and principal area assessment.

INITIAL ASSESSMENT

3-4. Initial assessment includes those requirements deemed essential to the pilot team or SFOD immediately following infiltration. The mission of the team is to assess designated areas to determine the feasibility of developing the resistance potential and to establish contact with indigenous leaders. These requirements must be satisfied as soon as possible after the team arrives in the AO. Much of this initial assessment may be transmitted in the initial entry report (IER) (ANGUS) or situation (CYRIL) report. Once the theater command or JSOTF has made a determination as to the feasibility of developing the area, additional SF elements may be infiltrated. The assessment team may remain with the operational element or be exfiltrated as directed. FM 3-05.220 provides further information on pilot team support.

PRINCIPAL ASSESSMENT

3-5. Principal assessment forms the basis for all other subsequent UW activities in the JSOA. It is a continuous operation and includes those efforts that support the continued planning and conduct of operations. It should be transmitted using the format planned during isolation. This format may be abbreviated by deleting information already confirmed. This report should include new or changed information.

AREA ASSESSMENT IN AN URBAN ENVIRONMENT

3-6. What makes urban guerrilla warfare so different from rural guerrilla warfare or conventional military contest is the presence of a large audience to the struggle. Unlike rural guerrillas, urban guerrillas cannot withdraw to some remote jungle where they are safe from observation and attack. They must be able to live in the midst of hundreds of witnesses and potential informers.

3-7. Appendix A provides guidance for the planning and conduct of UW in an urban environment. The appendix describes characteristics of cities and urban tactical operations, and provides an urban operations survey checklist. Users of Appendix A should already have had sufficient exposure to ASO and therefore amplifications and definitions of specific terms are unnecessary (FM 3-05.220 provides further information).

DEVELOPMENT OF THE JSOA

3-8. The organization and development of the JSOA or region involves early marshalling of the resistance command structure and the subsequent buildup of the resistance force. A well-organized JSOA allows close coordination between the SFOD and the resistance element. The SFOD gains a thorough knowledge of the AO through extensive area studies. These studies include history, economy, religion, infrastructure, ethnic groups, needs of the populace, customs, taboos, and other data that will affect the organization; C2; and selection of leaders within the resistance force. Appendix H provides an area study outline format.

OBJECTIVE

3-9. After infiltration, the major task facing the SFOD is to develop all resistance elements into an effective force able to achieve U.S. and the area commander's objectives. To the area command, the SFOD is the direct representative of the U.S. Government. The SFOD members must be diplomats as well as military advisers and establish a good working relationship with the resistance organization. This relationship develops from acceptance of U.S. sponsorship and operational guidance. The SFOD and guerrillas are united with a common goal against a common enemy.

DEVELOPMENT

3-10. Politics, ideology, topography, security, communications, and many other factors govern the shape, size, and ultimate organization of the JSOA or region. The operational areas of guerrilla forces must have clearly defined boundaries. These limits simplify coordination and C2 and reduce friction between adjacent units. The operational areas should conform to the existing spheres of influence of the established commanders. History demonstrates that areas with basic religious, ethnic, or political differences should not be included in the same area command.

3-11. JSOAs should not be larger than the communication and logistics capabilities can effectively support. JSOA is the largest territorial organization commanded by an overall area commander who is within enemy territory. The JSOA should include enough dense terrain for the operation, security, training, and administration of the guerrilla forces.

3-12. A country may be divided into several JSOAs based on administrative units or natural geographic boundaries. Administrative units include counties, districts, provinces, departments, and states. This system is satisfactory when guerrilla missions include sabotage, propaganda, and espionage conducted by small cellular units. One negative aspect of this method is that by following the present government's established unit of administration, the resistance is indirectly aiding the government's control and coordination efforts.

3-13. Countries divided by natural geographic boundaries are superior for military and overt operations on a large scale. Each major operational area should include difficult terrain or uncontrolled areas suitable for area complexes and guerrilla operations. Each JSOA and subordinate sector command may also include food-producing areas that will support the guerrilla force in the area. These considerations may only be ignored when logistics support from external sources is available regularly and on a very substantial scale.

3-14. The establishment of rapport between the SFOD and the resistance element is a vital first requirement for the SFOD. An effective working and command relationship helps develop a high degree of cooperation and influence over the resistance force. This influence is ensured when resistance leaders are receptive to the SFOD's suggestions to accomplish the mission. The command structure and the physical organization of the area are priority tasks of the SFOD. In some situations, the resistance organization may be well established, but in others, organizational structure may be totally lacking. In all cases, some improvement in physical area organization will probably be necessary. Tasks and requirements dictate the organization of the JSOA, but organization also depends on local customs and conditions more so than on any fixed set of rules.

GOVERNMENT-IN-EXILE

3-15. A government-in-exile does not exist in every UW situation. Where it does, the leader may be a "figurehead" for the resistance. He may be a deposed former leader of the country or a prominent person of society who commands the respect of his fellow citizens. A highly structured resistance organization might report to a national government-in-exile or, if one does not exist, to a shadow government in-country. The leader of the area command may declare himself the leader of a "shadow government." If the enemy government usurped power against the wishes of the people, the USG may instead recognize the government-in-exile as the official government of the country.

AREA COMMAND

3-16. An area command is a combined (indigenous and SF) command, control, communications, computers, and intelligence (C4I) structure that directs, controls, integrates, and supports all resistance activities in the JSOA or region. The size of the area command is dependent on METT-TC. The area commander is the resistance leader. Selected SFOD members serve as advisors to the area commander and his staff. Small and mobile, the HQ size is limited because of meager communication capabilities. Functions and forces must be decentralized due to the ever-present possibility of the area command being destroyed by enemy action. The area command, with the underground, auxiliary, and other support systems, should be organized prior to Phase II (Guerrilla Warfare). They all conduct centralized planning but give maximum latitude for decentralized execution to their subordinate sector commanders. This policy supports the utmost latitude allowing subordinate commanders to determine the "how to" in planning and executing their missions. Mutual confidence, cohesion, and trust must exist between the area commander, subordinate commanders, and the SFOD for each to be effective.

3-17. The area commander should be located where he can safely control the resistance movement and its activities. Flexibility, intelligence, mobility, and OPSEC are the keys to survival and success. The area commander or his designated representatives should make frequent visits to subordinate units, both for morale enhancement and to become acquainted with the local situation. Where personal visits are not possible, the commanders should communicate with each other frequently.

AREA COMMAND ELEMENTS

3·18. There are no rigid patterns for the structure and function of an area command. The area command is compartmented but should include representatives from all elements of the resistance movement. Regardless of the level of organization, the basic elements of the area command are the command group and the resistance forces. Figure 3·1 shows the JSOA command structure.

Command Group

3·19. The command group consists of political leaders or their representatives from the exiled or shadow government, the area commander as the resistance leader, the commander's staff, and key members of the SFOD.

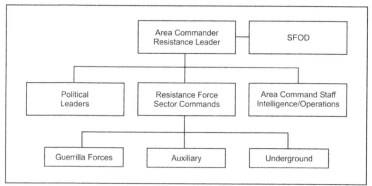

Figure 3-1. Area Command Structure

Resistance Forces

3·20. Sector commanders or resistance element leaders from each sector in the JSOA represent the resistance forces. Historically, U.S. UW doctrine has made a clear distinction among elements of the resistance movement— guerrilla forces, the auxiliary, and the underground. The composition and duties of these elements forming the resistance force will depend on factors unique to each JSOA and resistance organization.

AREA COMMAND MEETING

3-21. The area command meeting is the primary method of conducting business within an area command. The SFOD must thoroughly plan and rehearse its agenda for the meeting. Personnel must analyze information from the area study, operational area intelligence study, and area assessment to determine the main points for discussion. The meeting is not a confrontation between the area commander and the SFOD. Seating arrangements should integrate the area commander, his staff, and the SFOD among each other to form a large team. Planning considerations for the area command meeting include—

- Security measures.
- Key issues to be discussed.
- Personnel who should attend.
- Location of meeting site.
- Length of meeting.

3-22. METT-TC is the basis for an area command or sector meeting. Suitable locations for the site should be in a secure and isolated location, either rural or urban. When indigenous or enemy government-imposed population control measures are in effect, it may be easier for meetings to be held in rural or guerrilla-controlled territory. The initial meeting should be conducted as soon as possible after the SFOD infiltrates. During the meeting, SFOD members should—

- Establish personal and professional relationships with the resistance.
- Discuss guerrilla and SFOD abilities and limitations.
- Discuss procedures for developing the resistance cadre.
- Establish centralized planning and decentralized execution.
- Establish security measures and discuss threat activity.
- Discuss political boundaries, terrain features, targets, density of population, and other JSOA- and region-specific information.
- Establish positive U.S. influence with the resistance organization.
- Establish type and scope of combat operations.
- Organize the resistance infrastructure to survive in a nonpermissive environment.
- Organize cooperation between the resistance and local civilians.
- Establish necessary documentation, cover stories, and proper clothes.
- Discuss ROE.
- Emphasize unity of effort with open dialogue.
- Always plan for contingencies.

3-23. The SFOD advises and assists with security for the meeting in a similar manner to that of the area complex. Outer and inner security zones are formed. The outer security ring consists of observers strategically placed (determined by METT-TC) away from the meeting place. Members of the outer security zones observe avenues of approach and provide early warning.

They may use handheld radios or telephones to provide early warning of enemy threats, which are passed using code words or messages. The inner security zones surround the meeting place itself and consist of enough personnel to allow for the escape of the resistance leadership in case of compromise. Before the meeting convenes, those present must decide on the actions to take in case of a compromise. They must consider escape plans and routes. A security element, usually members of the inner security zones, serves as a rear guard while key personnel, equipment, and documents are removed and quickly evacuated.

Intelligence Section

3-24. During the initial organization of an area command, the intelligence section of the staff is given special emphasis. Throughout all phases of the organization of a resistance force, the intelligence net is expanded progressively until the intelligence requirements for the area command HQ can be fulfilled. The functions of an area command intelligence section are to—

- Collect, record, evaluate, and interpret information of value to the guerrilla forces. It distributes the resulting intelligence to the area commander and staff and to higher and lower commands.
- Organize, supervise, and coordinate, together with the operations section, special intelligence teams (airfield surveillance, air warning, and coast watcher).
- Plan and supervise the procurement and distribution of maps, charts, photos, and other materiel for intelligence purposes.
- Recommend intelligence and counterintelligence (CI) policies.
- Collect and distribute information on evasion and recovery (E&R), to include instructions for downed aircrews, evaders, and escapees.
- Establish liaison with the intelligence staffs and lower commands.
- Provide intelligence personnel for duty at lower commands.
- Conduct training to carry out intelligence functions.

3-25. The intelligence section is organized into a forward and rear echelon to provide continuous operation when enemy pressure forces the area command HQ to move to alternate locations. When these moves are anticipated, the forward echelon sets up and begins operations in the prepared alternate site before the rear echelon moves. During large-scale overt operations, the forward echelon provides an intelligence section for an advance command post organized to direct the operations of two or more sector commands. A guerrilla area command must produce the intelligence needed for its own security and for local operations against the enemy. It must also gather the information required by higher HQ. Although supervised by the area command intelligence section, information collectors are decentralized as far as practicable to subordinate sector commands.

Sector Commands

3-26. Large area commands may establish subordinate sector commands. Sector command meetings are conducted after the initial area command meeting. Sectors are formed to simplify C4I operations and to provide a mechanism to promote centralized planning and decentralized execution. If the area command is subdivided into sector commands, its component units are the subordinate sector commands. The sector command is the command element of the resistance in a given sector. The same factors that define the boundaries of area complexes define the boundaries of sectors. The kinds and disposition of facilities within a sector are the same as those for an area complex. The sector command performs the same functions as the area command, except within the limits of its own boundaries. The component elements of a sector command are the functional components of a resistance movement.

AREA COMPLEX

3-27. An area complex is a clandestine, dispersed network of facilities to support resistance activities. It is a "liberated zone" designed to achieve security, control, dispersion, and flexibility. To support resistance activities, an area complex must include a security system, base camps, communications, logistics, medical facilities, supply caches, training areas, and escape and recovery mechanisms. The area complex may consist of friendly villages or towns under guerrilla military or political control.

3-28. According to Mao Tse-tung in *On Guerrilla Warfare*, a guerrilla base may be defined as an area, strategically located, in which the guerrillas can carry out their duties of training, self-preservation, and development. The ability to fight a war without a rear area is a fundamental characteristic of guerrilla action, but this does not mean that guerrillas can exist and function over a long period of time without the development of base areas. There is a difference between the terms base area and guerrilla base area. An area completely surrounded by territory occupied by the enemy is a "base area." On the other hand, a guerrilla base area includes those areas that can be controlled by guerrillas only while they physically occupy them.

3-29. Within the area complex, the resistance forces achieve security by—

- Establishing an effective intelligence net.
- Using the early warning with listening posts (LPs), observation posts (OPs), and security patrols.
- Practicing CI measures.
- Rehearsing withdrawals and CONPLANs.
- Employing mobility and flexibility.
- Using rapid dispersion techniques for personnel.
- Camouflaging and adhering to noise and light discipline.
- Organizing the active support of the civilian population.

3-30. The C2 base camp is in the heart of the area complex. Specially trained and equipped guerrilla forces control and defend this camp. A special guerrilla security detachment provides the internal protection for the area commander, his staff, and the SFOD. Key personnel, critical equipment, and sensitive information are based from there and may include the following:

- The area commander and staff.

- The SFOD and support personnel.
- Communication equipment.
- Controlled medical supplies and treatment facilities.
- Supply caches of weapons, ammunition, and explosives.

3-31. An area complex can be subdivided into two security zones: outer and inner (Figure 3-2, page 3-10). There are no clear-cut boundaries between zones, and security responsibilities can overlap. Each zone is the responsibility of a specific guerrilla element whose mission is to provide for the security and defense of the zone in the area complex to achieve total and overlapping security coverage.

Outer Security Zone

3-32. The outer security zone is vitally important to a guerrilla force. The local guerrilla forces and the civilian support infrastructure are organized and developed in the outer security zone. This area serves as the primary source of recruits for the guerrilla force. The outer zone also serves as the first line of in-depth security and defense for the area complex. Resistance elements in this area are responsible for providing the area command with timely and accurate information on enemy activities within the zone. Local guerrillas are the resistance element responsible for the zone's control and defense. This element is also responsible for the conduct of operations within the zone. The local guerrilla forces organize, employ, and serve as part of the civilian support element. The civilian support element gathers current intelligence information and provides logistic, PSYOP, and operational support to the regular guerrilla forces and the area command. The initial screening, selection, and training of new resistance members takes place in this zone. The most promising and trusted recruits are then selected for membership in the regular or full-time guerrilla forces.

Inner Security Zone

3-33. The inner security zone encompasses the base camp of the regular or full-time guerrilla forces. These forces defend and control the zone and are constantly mobile within the area. The primary mission of the guerrilla forces operating in this zone is to temporarily delay any penetration made by the enemy. They watch trails and avenues of approach. They use OPs or LPs, fixed fighting positions, and pre-positioned obstacles such as bunkers and minefields to delay enemy forces. They employ harassment, ambushes, sniping, and other interdiction tactics and practice rapid withdrawal procedures. These tactics increase the in-depth defense of the area complex. They should also use command-detonated antivehicular and antipersonnel mines on a permanent basis. Guerrilla forces may place mines along probable enemy vehicular and personnel avenues of approach, such as trails, creeks, and riverbeds. The guerrillas must avoid, at all costs, becoming decisively engaged while carrying out their delaying and defensive mission. Civilians do not normally occupy the inner security zone; therefore, it may serve as an area of food cultivation for the guerrilla population.

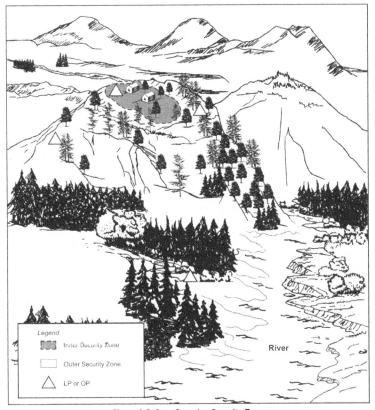

Figure 3-2. Area Complex Security Zones

GUERRILLA BASES

3-34. A guerrilla base is HQ for any size guerrilla force. A base may be temporary or permanent, depending on the guerrilla's stage of development. Guerrilla C4I, support, facilities, and operational units are located within the base. LOCs connect the base and facilities within the area complex. The installations and facilities found within a guerrilla base are the command posts, training areas or classrooms, a communications facility, and medical services. The occupants and facilities must be capable of rapid displacement with little or no prior warning. There is usually more than one guerrilla base within a sector or JSOA. They are in remote, inaccessible areas and their locations are revealed only on a need-to-know basis. Personnel must use passive and active security measures to provide base security, employing overhead cover, concealment, and escape routes. A mandatory requirement for a guerrilla base camp is a source of water. Wells may be dug where permanent bases are established. Ideally, there will be an abundance of water sources to choose from in the area. All base camps should have an alternate location for contingency use. In case the enemy overruns the base, all personnel should plan for and rehearse rapid withdrawals.

TYPES OF BASES

3-35. There are three types of guerrilla bases. In order of development, they are mobile, semipermanent, and permanent. Initially, all guerrilla base camps are mobile, and as the JSOA matures, semipermanent camps are constructed. When the JSOA matures enough to conduct battalion combat operations, the semipermanent camps become permanent. Normal occupation time is based on METT-TC.

Mobile

3-36. Full-time guerrillas and local guerrilla forces establish mobile bases. These bases are at the periphery of their zones of responsibility. Mobile bases are normally occupied for periods ranging from 1 to 7 days.

Semipermanent

3-37. HQ elements or sector commands establish semipermanent bases in the inner security zones. These bases are in areas that provide a tactical advantage for the guerrilla. Semipermanent bases are normally occupied for periods ranging from 1 to 2 weeks.

Permanent

3-38. This base is within the rear security zone of the area complex. The guerrilla command element, SFOD, and key installations and facilities are located here. Adequate training areas are established to support all the training activities. The guerrilla force protects the training areas, and an SFOD member, who is the subject-matter expert (SME), monitors the training. When needed, personnel secure drop zones (DZs) and landing zones (LZs) to receive supplies and equipment. An SFOD member accounts for supplies. These DZs and LZs must be accessible to the appropriate aircraft and be a safe distance from the guerrilla base camp. Permanent bases may normally be occupied for periods ranging from 1 to 2 months.

BASE SECURITY MEASURES

3-39. The defense of any base includes strict adherence to camouflage, noise, and light discipline. Defense measures should also include inner security posts, LPs and OPs, security and tracking patrols, antipersonnel mines, and other obstacles to concentrate, impede, or stop the enemy (Figure 3-3). Personnel should plan contingencies for rapid withdrawal from the area before any enemy attack.

Figure 3-3. Permanent Base Security

Inner Security Posts

3-40. Inner security posts are normally established within 100 meters of the main body. The mission of the inner security posts is to delay a small reaction force that has penetrated the base perimeter and is closing in on the main body. This delay allows the main body to break out. During low visibility, inner security posts are closer, about 25 meters from the main body. A challenge and password system should be implemented.

Listening and Observation Posts

3-41. LPs and OPs are established in unit SOPs and based on observation and fields of fire, avenues of approach, key terrain, obstacles, and cover and concealment (OAKOC). At a minimum, LPs and OPs will be located on the most likely avenues of approach. They should be located on high and commanding ground surrounding the base, as per unit SOP. The mission of the posts is to detect and report in a timely manner enemy air and ground movement that threatens the guerrilla base. If the enemy is detected, post personnel may not fire on the enemy but radio a size, activity, location, unit, time, and equipment (SALUTE) report. This tactic saves giving away their position and possibly the position of the base. These posts are normally within 400 to 800 meters from the base.

Security and Tracking Patrols

3-42. Security and tracking patrols may be carried out at dawn and dusk to provide security and early warning for the base. Each patrol should carry a frequency modulated short-range radio, similar to an AN/PRC-77, enabling the patrol to relay information to the base in a timely manner. Patrols must search all areas, but give priority of search to the high ground surrounding the base and to creek and riverbeds in the area. Patrols also search roads and trails for tracks or signs of enemy presence. If there are friendly civilians in the area, they may be questioned regarding enemy activity. Civilians unfamiliar to the patrol may be a threat or sympathizer. Information provided by the friendly civilians is critical to the security of the guerrilla base camp. The mission of the security patrols is to detect signs or other indicators of enemy presence or activity. These indicators include—

- Tobacco, candy, gum, and food wrappers.
- Human excrement or other waste products.
- Tracks made by bare feet or boots on recently used trails.
- Broken branches and bent twigs suggesting direction of travel.
- Discarded rations, containers, and equipment.

3-43. Passive security measures that can be taken include camouflaging dwellings and hutches with vegetation. Personnel should change vegetation daily. They can also camouflage trails and erase tracks. Personnel should avoid smoke from cooking fires, especially during daylight hours, and maintain noise and light discipline at all times.

Antipersonnel Mines

3-44. SFODs may temporarily use antipersonnel mines along likely avenues of approach into the base. Creeks, riverbeds, and the surrounding elevations are good locations for placing antipersonnel mines. Personnel will warn the civilian population about the use of mines to preclude unnecessary civilian casualties. They may temporarily employ antipersonnel mines in the following areas not used by civilians:

- Near running water sources.
- Around fruit and shade trees.
- On little-used roads and trails.
- In and around abandoned fighting positions or around abandoned uninhabited dwellings.

3-45. Minefield reports should be submitted by the fastest secure means available and are classified Secret when complete. Exact format may be specified by local command SOP. FM 5-34, *Engineer Field Data*, or FM 20-32, *Mine/Countermine Operations*, provides more information on reporting and recording minefield information.

MISSION SUPPORT SITES

3-46. A mission support site (MSS) is a temporary operational and logistics base for guerrillas who are away from their main base camp for more than a few days. It extends the range of guerrillas in the JSOA by permitting them to travel long distances without support from their base camps. The guerrillas should not occupy them for more than 24 hours. Guerrillas should always reconnoiter and surveil the MSS before occupying it.

3-47. Personnel establish an MSS to support a specific mission and should not use it more than once. Using the MSS only once protects the force from setting up repeated patterns of movement. However, it may be used before and after a mission, based on METT-TC. The MSS may contain food, shelter, medical support, ammunition, demolitions, and other operational items. To preclude unnecessary noise and movement in and out of the MSS, auxiliary personnel may establish supply caches in the surrounding vicinity before the combat force arrives.

3-48. When selecting the location for an MSS, personnel must consider the following:

- Proximity to the objective.
- Level of enemy activity.
- Cover and concealment.
- Preplanned routes of withdrawal.
- Tribal or factional and religious issues.

METT-TC is very important when selecting the MSS. MSSs must not be near LZs, DZs, or any other sites of heightened activity. Further information on MSSs is provided in Appendix E.

DEVELOPMENT OF THE RESISTANCE ORGANIZATION

3-49. The primary technique or type of recruitment used in the early stages of a resistance movement is selective recruitment. As security is emphasized, recruitment is highly selective. Many tasks of the resistance force require no qualification for its recruits beyond a certain degree of intelligence and emotional stability. Since some activities require special qualifications, recruiters must look for individuals who can perform leadership duties, intelligence collection, and other special tasks. The screening process includes surveillance and background checks. The recruiters use the following methods to ensure loyalty: loyalty checks, oaths, and probationary periods. Once the resistance cadre is established and the resistance movement is successful, mass recruitment begins. Recruiters seek a base of support among large segments of the indigenous population. Auxiliary members are excellent recruiters because they can move easily through denied areas. The resistance movement must rely on mass support if it is to survive and expand (Figure 3-4, page 3-16). Recruiting techniques include appeals, coercion, and suggestion, as well as playing on an individual's feelings of governmental alienation.

3-50. Recruitment is difficult in the early phases of the operation and easier after the resistance establishes its credibility. If the resistance recruits too many civilians, enemy reprisals against the remainder of the community are very possible. The number of base camps and the quantity of supporting logistics stock limit the number of potential armed guerrilla recruits.

ADMINISTRATIVE PROCEDURES

3-51. As development of the resistance organization progresses, documentation and record keeping of mission functions is vital to maintaining a well-organized force. This information also enables the SFOD commander to conduct effective C2, pay, rewards, and eventually demobilization measures. The SFOD must establish administrative procedures early on to facilitate a well-organized guerrilla force. Appendix I addresses detailed administrative issues.

COMMANDERS

3-52. The most delicate part of an SFOD's duty is to ensure that competent indigenous personnel occupy key leadership positions. If leaders and staff members of the resistance organization do not appear qualified to fill positions held, the SFOD should try to increase their effectiveness. Increasing the effectiveness of these personnel will normally enhance the influence of the SFOD. The personality and characteristics of the area commander are extremely important. His ability must extend beyond military and technical fields. Successfully commanding a guerrilla force with all its diverse elements requires psychological and political skills. The area commander should have distinction among the civilian population and the confidence of his followers.

3-53. The area commander influences others to accomplish the mission by providing purpose, direction, and motivation. Purpose gives the guerrillas the reason why; direction shows what must be done; and motivation gives his guerrillas the will to do everything they are capable of to accomplish their mission.

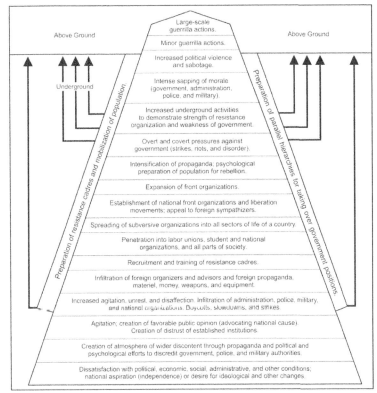

Figure 3-4. Building a Resistance Movement

3-54. A combat-tested leader demonstrates his tactical and technical proficiency and uses initiative to exploit opportunities for success. He accomplishes this process by taking calculated risks within the commander's intent. He leads by example (from the front) and not by fear and coercion. Successful leadership in combat enables a leader to—

- Never underestimate his enemy.

- Consider the civil component in all operations.
- Understand basic weapons and demolitions.
- Understand both conventional force and guerrilla tactics.
- Appreciate and understand the strategy of war.
- Respect and anticipate the objectives and campaign goals of conventional forces.
- Be able to task-organize himself and others.
- Be able to recognize and appoint good leaders.
- Improvise on short notice.
- Allow the use of initiative.
- Employ and exploit all types of intelligence-gathering opportunities.

3-55. Historically, the sector leaders have been recognized as commanders within their spheres of influence. In the organization of a command, every effort is made to assist and recognize a local guerrilla leader as the overall area commander. This concept must not be violated just because the local commander may lack the requisite military service or qualifications. If he can command the respect of the people and subordinate commanders in the area, the SFOD should tutor him in carrying out his area commander functions. Replacing locally developed leaders with area commanders from external (out-of-country) sources, even though the new area commanders are native-born, may create personal or political rivalries and alienate the area commanders already in existence. The recognition of commanders, especially the overall area commander, must not be arbitrary or hasty. Recognition should be based on a careful assessment of the existing political conditions and social attitudes within the JSOA. If a resistance movement has failed to develop due to serious personal rivalries or political differences, the concept of recognizing a popular local leader as the overall commander may in fact be violated. In this case, a leader who commands respect and can unify the efforts of the opposing factions is then appointed or infiltrated into the JSOA.

3-56. The local area commander is responsible for the organization, training, administration, and operations of guerrilla forces within his area. Specifically, the duties of the guerrilla area commander are operations of the forces under his command and coordination of operations between subordinate forces and allied forces. He continuously determines the resources, combat strength, dispositions, movements, and capabilities of the enemy that will affect completion of his mission. He also—

- Appoints or recognizes subordinate sector commanders.
- Prepares plans to accomplish assigned missions and contemplated missions.
- Prepares and assigns missions to subordinate sector commanders.
- Establishes adequate communication systems between the various forces of his command.
- Organizes and operates CI and intelligence nets.
- Plans security and defensive measures within the area command and the area complex.

- Guides general administrative policies.
- Establishes morale and welfare measures.
- Ensures the care and handling of all EPWs are IAW all the applicable Geneva Accords and Conventions.
- Plans, prepares, and employs PSYOP.
- Guides training for individuals and units.
- Requisitions and collects supplies from local sources.
- Requisitions supplies and equipment from outside the JSOA.
- Allocates and disburses equipment and supplies to subordinate sector commands.

3-57. The area commander ensures the reception, support, and protection of SFOD personnel in the JSOA. He accounts for key EPWs, prominent civilians, and for the rescue and exfiltration of downed aircrews. He is also responsible for the civilians in the area. Initially, his responsibilities are for the safety and welfare of those noncombatants within the JSOA. As the JSOA matures, he may actually supervise the organization of a civil administration capability among the populace using promising members of the resistance movement. The SFOD supports him in these requirements by employing CA assets, first as planners and advisors to the SFOD (including using reachback capabilities to CA specialists in rear areas or the continental United States [CONUS]), then as core advisor teams to fledgling civil administrators, and finally as fully staffed teams capable of providing support to civil administration. The organization and employment of these CA assets is based on U.S. policies and objectives in the JSOA and METT-TC.

ELEMENTS OF THE RESISTANCE

3-58. The resistance organization consists of three elements. They are the guerrilla force, the auxiliary, and the underground. The guerrilla force is the overt military or paramilitary arm. The auxiliary is the clandestine support element of the guerrilla force. The underground is a cellular organization that conducts clandestine subversion, sabotage, UAR, and intelligence collection activities. FM 3-05.220 contains additional information on resistance organization and structure.

GUERRILLA FORCE

3-59. Guerrillas are a decisive combat force. They conduct tactics, techniques, and procedures employed in the United States during the French and Indian Wars. They continued to have success during the American Revolution and during the American Civil War for both the Federal and Confederate troops. During World War II, a classic example of a decisive combat force was Merrill's Marauders and their use of raids, ambushes, and to a lesser extent, offensive and defensive maneuvers to defeat the Japanese in Burma.

3-60. The organization of a guerrilla force from the resistance movement or the reorganization of existing guerrilla forces into a combat command is a time-consuming process. The organization must follow a definite plan, phased and coordinated with the SFOB. Directives from outside the JSOA to the guerrilla area commanders prescribe the general COAs. Based on detailed reports and recommendations of the SFOD, the commander issues more specific orders much later to reach the desired organizational level. Then, the highly organized guerrilla force may be employed in overt combat operations.

3-61. Guerrilla forces are organized in a similar manner to conventional units. Since guerrilla operations normally do not exceed the equivalent of battalion-level operations, most guerrilla forces are organized only to that level. In the later stages of a successful UW situation, guerrilla forces conceivably could conduct coordinated regimental or higher operations against the enemy forces.

3-62. The progressive organization of a guerrilla force in an AO works in three general phases. These phases are not specific periods but normally overlap and merge into one another. The typical organization and functions of each phase are as follows.

Organization - Phase I

3-63. In the first phase of organization, individuals band together under local leadership (Figure 3-5, page 3-20). Their main concern is survival. They have a basic need for shelter, food, water, and weapons. Appropriate terrain and friendly villages on the outer limits of enemy-controlled areas offer shelter. These small bands obtain food, water, and weapons locally. The activities of these small bands are limited to the organization and establishment of a support infrastructure within the local civilian population to obtain information, recruits, and logistic assistance. They may also conduct political work, small-scale attacks, and sabotage. The area commander locates his HQ where he can directly influence organization and operations in the most important sectors of his JSOA. His HQ is in a secure area where access is limited or uncontrolled by the enemy. The surrounding terrain should not favor large-scale, enemy-mounted, or dismounted operations. Logistic concerns and health conditions in the area are further considerations. Also, just in case, the area commander selects two or more alternate sites and prepares them for emergency use.

3-64. The area commander appoints a second-in-command and organizes a staff to accomplish military staff functions. The staff is kept small and mobile. It places special emphasis on the organization of the intelligence section. HQ units carry out the administrative functions. Based on advice from the SFOD, the area commander makes an estimate of the situation, formulates tentative organizational and operational plans, and issues directives to place them into effect. This effort should focus on—

- Division of the JSOA into sectors.
- Appointment of sector commanders.
- Assignment of missions to sector commanders.
- Organization in each sector: designation of units and authorized strengths.
- General operating principles and procedures.
- Communications system and responsibilities.

3-65. In areas that have no guerrilla forces or strong resistance movement, the area commander may appoint a sector commander for the exploitation and organization of the area. This support may consist of assigning cadre personnel for a sector commander's HQ, combat units to provide security, and a nucleus around which he may organize and expand his local forces. The area commander helps the sector commanders obtain the support of the indigenous population by visiting the sector and employing CA activities, such as HA, emergency services, military civic action (MCA), and support to civil administration. The effectiveness of CA activities may be enhanced by a strong public information campaign supported by PSYOP.

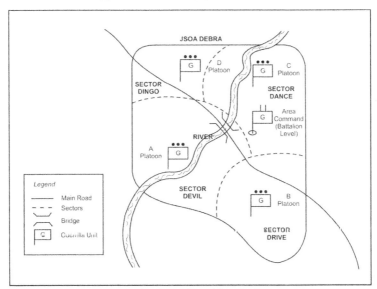

Figure 3-5. Typical Phase I Organization

3-66. In areas where many independent guerrilla forces exist, the area commander gives the appointed sector commander the necessary support to bring about unity of command. He gives this support through personal contact with the various local guerrilla leaders. The area commander may apply drastic measures to influence independent leaders and units that resist integration into the overall command. Withholding logistic support from outside the JSOA to those elements resisting integration is normally sufficient to encourage their willing compliance. The SFOD commander should be prepared to advise the area commander on the possible repercussions of the area commander's actions.

3-67. Normally, a skeleton organization is formed during Phase I. Also established are—

- A command HQ in each subordinate sector.
- A communication system linking the area command HQ with sector HQ.
- An extensive intelligence and CI net covering the entire JSOA. Establishment of this net is extremely important.

3-68. The overall strength of the command and the component units may be kept as low as one-third of the potential strength to be developed. Premature expansion and buildup of strength during this phase can cause undue strain on local resources, create hardships, and result in dissension among the civilian population.

Organization - Phase II

3-69. In the second phase of organization, the number and size of units increase (Figure 3-6, page 3-22). Small units unite under common leadership; volunteers, individual soldiers, or deserting army units further strengthen their ranks. When a tested local leader emerges as a commander, command and leadership improve. Personnel work diligently to establish contact with external support sources or with a sympathetic national government. These external support sources, along with battlefield recovery efforts, increase the quantity of war materiel. Greater enemy pressure results in widespread sabotage, raids, and ambushes. Political and administrative considerations, policies of the sponsor supporting the resistance movement, and METT-TC determine the extent to which unified commands develop. During Phase II, the commander modifies or adopts the tentative plans prepared in Phase I and places them into effect. He makes continuous assessments and considers additional COAs to further expand and build up forces. The expansion that takes place during this phase directly relates to the amount of logistic support from sources outside the JSOA. Missions and internal functions in the operational area also lead to expansion. This organizational expansion may include—

- Increasing the strength of the skeletonized command, combat, and service support units up to 50 percent of their potential strength.
- Organizing additional guerrilla units.
- Expanding the communication system within the AO and with subordinate sector commands.
- Expanding the intelligence and CI nets.
- Emphasizing the organization of the civilian population.

3-70. Phase II is normally the most critical period in the organization of a guerrilla force. The commander must ensure the guerrilla organization and its infrastructure (supporting civilian population) is well organized and strong enough ideologically to withstand heavy enemy political and military pressure.

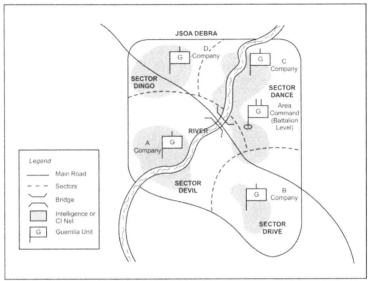

Figure 3-6. Typical Phase II Organization

Organization - Phase III

3-71. During the third phase of organization (Figure 3-7, page 3-23), a unified command is established over some areas, often because of a strong and competent leader emerging as the recognized commander. Increased communication and liaison enhance control and coordination among the various guerrilla forces and external sources. Based on the mission assigned by higher HQ (input from the SFOD is a critical factor), the area commander makes an estimate of the situation and plans the mission. The decision to conduct an operation results in an OPLAN that states requirements for the area command staff, sector commands, and logistic elements. Portions of these tentative plans are then sent to subordinate commands. The subordinate commanders determine the area commander's intent and prepare their own plans accordingly. Also during Phase III, command personnel—

- Methodically develop and expand effective CI and intelligence nets.
- Observe and enforce strict OPSEC measures.
- Determine what control measures the enemy has imposed on the civilian population.

- Develop and implement programs of benefit to the populace (for example, developmental MCA projects), supported by PSYOP efforts to counter enemy propaganda and help elevate the morale of guerrillas and loyal civilians.
- Execute training and well-planned operations to improve the effectiveness of individuals and units.
- Infiltrate supplies from external sources to augment existing military equipment.

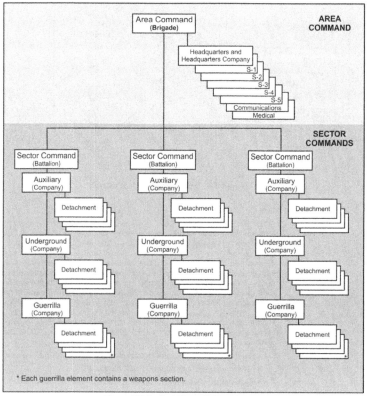

Figure 3-7. Typical Phase III Organization

3-72. In addition, the guerrilla force, supported from an external source, develops a cohesive military establishment able to firmly defend and strike with substantial force at selected targets. General directives normally control guerrilla activities during this phase. Typical organizational expansion during Phase III may include—

- Building existing units up to authorized strength.
- Activating additional units.
- Pre-positioning units closer to their tentative operational areas.
- Increasing efforts to organize the civilian population into an effective support mechanism.

3-73. The joint commander makes every effort to develop a balanced guerrilla force, trained and ready to negate the threat and carry out these activities assigned by the area command. The organization of the guerrilla force depends on existing threat conditions and operational considerations within the JSOA. If the threat is armor, then the force should task-organize as an antiarmor force. When practical, the organization of the guerrilla force should closely parallel the organization of a conventional force to enhance mission C2. The single most important point about guerrilla forces is that they cannot be arbitrarily located or pinpointed due to their use of tactics, flexibility, and knowledge of the area. In turn, available guerrilla manpower and material assets influence these missions and tactics. They must also be careful not to reduce the inherent flexibility that the force requires.

Membership

3-74. The guerrilla force consists of people in different social classes and ethnic groups, some of whom are often antagonistic toward each other. They reflect a variety of educational and aptitude categories with different interests and inclinations. The guerrilla leader depends on volunteers to increase the size of his force. If he is incompetent or unpopular, or if the guerrillas suffer tactical reversals, he will have difficulties in getting more recruits. The following quote serves as a good representation of the underground, auxiliary, and guerrilla force relationship.

The people are the sea; the revolutionaries are the fish. The sea supports the fish. It also hides them from predators. The revolutionaries only want to show themselves when they are not themselves vulnerable. Then they fade back into the sea, or the mountains, or the jungles.

Mao Tse-tung

AUXILIARY

3-75. The success or failure of the guerrilla force depends on its ability to maintain logistic and intelligence support. The auxiliary fills these support functions by organizing civilians and conducting coordinated support efforts. Its organization and mission depend upon METT-TC. The assistance of the civilian population is critical to the success of the resistance movement. Auxiliary units have their own combat, support, and underground units. The auxiliary primarily provides security, intelligence, and logistic support for the guerrilla force by using civilian supporters of the resistance. The auxiliary conducts clandestine support functions by organizing people on a regional, district, or sector basis depending on the degree to which guerrilla forces are organized. The auxiliary members screen all new potential underground members. For OPSEC reasons, all auxiliary functions must first section off from each other and from the guerrilla forces they support through dead-letter drops and other clandestine communications. The guerrilla force needs the following clandestine support functions to supplement its own capabilities:

- Air, land, or maritime reception support.
- Internal systems for acquisition of supplies.
- Internal systems to acquire operational information and intelligence.
- Medical facilities for hospitalization, treatment, and rehabilitation of sick and wounded.
- CI systems to deter enemy penetration attempts.
- Outer zone security for early warning to guerrilla forces.
- Systems and procedures for recruitment of personnel.
- Compartmented communication systems for various support functions.
- Current information on terrain, weather, civilians, and local resources.
- Direct intelligence support, especially in the outer security zone of the guerrilla base camp.
- Deception operations support.
- Manufacture and maintenance of equipment.
- Transportation systems.

Organization

3-76. An auxiliary command committee organizes civilian sympathizers into subordinate elements or uses them individually. When possible, the committee organizes subordinates into a functionally compartmented structure (Figure 3-8, page 3-26). Historically, each subordinate auxiliary has had to perform several functions because of a shortage of loyal personnel.

3-77. The auxiliary normally organizes to coincide with or parallel the existing political system or administration. This system ensures that an auxiliary unit assists each community and the surrounding countryside.

3-78. Organization of auxiliary forces starts at any level or at several levels simultaneously. It is either centralized or decentralized. The auxiliary establishes commands at each administrative level; for example, at the regional, county, district, local community, or village level.

3-79. A command committee at each level controls and coordinates auxiliary activities within its AOR. In this respect, the committee resembles the command group and staff of a military unit. At the lowest level, one individual may perform two or three duties. Members of the command committee are assigned specific duties, such as—

- Security.
- Intelligence.
- Operations.

- Communications.
- Transportation.
- Supply.
- Recruiting.

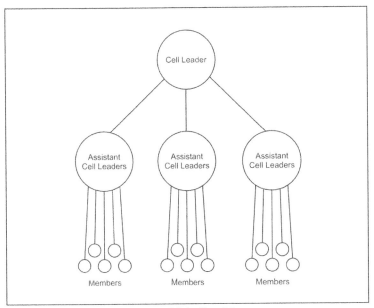

Figure 3-8. Auxiliary Cell

Membership

3-80. Members of the auxiliary are people who maintain a permanent residence in the denied sector or AO and have identifiable and legitimate means of livelihood. The auxiliary members must appear in all respects to be "average citizens." They must be loyal to the resistance cause. People who are simply coerced or duped into supporting the resistance are not considered auxiliary members. Auxiliary components in a sector or AO are normally satellites of local guerrilla forces. They also provide support to other guerrilla forces that normally do not operate within this JSOA or region.

3-81. Guerrilla forces depend on the civilian population for recruits to replace operational losses and to expand their forces. Auxiliaries spot, screen, and recruit personnel for active guerrilla forces. If recruits are provided from reliable auxiliary sources, the enemy's chances of placing agents in the guerrilla force are greatly reduced.

3-82. The two most important keys to the survival and effectiveness of auxiliary members are maintaining an "average citizen" image and being extremely cautious about confiding in others. Examples of "what not to do" include—

- Failing to maintain an "average citizen" image.
- Being repeatedly absent from work without good explanations.
- Showing an unusual concern about enemy activities.
- Failing to account for missing supplies.
- Appearing unusually nervous or habitually tired.
- Confiding too freely in strangers.
- Asking questions and unusual favors of people of questionable loyalties.
- Being too eager to recruit people without adequate security checks.

Security Support

3-83. Auxiliary members and units derive their protection by two principal means—their compartmented structure and their mode of operation (under cover). While enemy counterguerrilla activities often force the guerrillas to move temporarily away from given areas, the auxiliaries survive by remaining in place and conducting their activities to avoid detection. Individual auxiliary members carry on their normal, day-to-day routine while secretly carrying out the many facets of resistance activities. Auxiliary units frequently use passive or neutral elements of the population to provide active support to the common cause. They usually use such people on a one-time basis because of the increased security risks involved.

3-84. The demonstrated success of the friendly forces further enhances the ability of auxiliary forces to manipulate large segments of the neutral population. The organization and use of the auxiliary varies from country to country or AO. Security must be the first thought when the auxiliary is organized. The resistance movement depends heavily on the logistic support and early warning systems the auxiliary provides. The resistance movement cannot survive without the support of its greatest asset—the civilian population.

3-85. Auxiliary members continue participating in the life of their community. To all appearances, they present no break from their daily routines and, at the same time, engage in resistance activities and operations. Such personnel are, in fact, leading double lives, and their success in the resistance depends on their ability to keep that side of their lives secret from all, including family and friends. The "farmer by day, supporter by night," commonly called a "part-time guerrilla," often is the forerunner to the full-time guerrilla.

3-86. The auxiliary leader assigns tasks to groups or individuals according to their capability, dependability, and the degree to which they are willing and able to participate. Those who unwittingly give support or are coerced into giving support are not considered auxiliaries. Personnel who sympathize strongly with the resistance movement but may be under surveillance by the enemy provide little value as auxiliary members. Other examples of personnel who might prove more dangerous than profitable are former political leaders or technicians employed by the enemy. Functions that require travel or transportation might be performed by such persons as foresters, farmers, fishermen, or transportation workers. In addition, these functions should, if possible, be covered by routine daily activities. Other duties, such as security and warning, require a valid reason for remaining at a given location over an extended period.

Intelligence Support

3-87. Auxiliary members can give considerable intelligence support due to their at-home status and their freedom of movement throughout the AO. The auxiliary organizes an extensive system of civilians who can keep enemy forces under surveillance and provide early warning of their movements. Individuals are selected because of advantageous locations that permit them to monitor the enemy.

3-88. When engaged in specific intelligence operations, select personnel and informants, because of their locations, can surveil virtually every overt enemy activity. The auxiliary also aids the area command CI effort by maintaining watch over transitory civilians, by screening recruits for guerrilla forces, and by monitoring refugees and other personnel not indigenous to the area. Due to their intimate knowledge of the civilian population, auxiliaries can identify attempts by enemy agents and local civilians sympathetic to the opposition or enemy forces in the area. They can also name those civilians whose loyalty to the resistance might be suspect. Auxiliary units collect information to support their own operations and those of the area command. This information provides direct intelligence support to guerrilla forces operating within the AOR.

3-89. Because the auxiliary members live and work among the civilian population at large, they can inconspicuously observe enemy movements and activities. They report sightings of interest to the guerrillas. Observers must have good reasons to justify their activities. Simply loitering in an area where the enemy is draws suspicion and causes the observer to be arrested and interrogated. The best justification for an observer's activities is that he or she works in the area. Examples are a sales clerk in a store near an enemy facility, a gas station operator in a gas station used by the enemy, a street cleaner near an enemy facility, and a farmer working in a field beside a road where enemy convoys are moving. The auxiliary can be sensitive to CI operations of the enemy, such as the attempt to infiltrate the guerrillas with recruits who are actually spies.

3-90. The area command controls auxiliary activities. The auxiliary members' responsibilities relate to their civilian occupations, such as construction workers with access to explosives and related supplies, doctors, medical assistants, pharmacists, hardware store managers, transportation workers, and communications technicians.

3-91. Also, civil service employees are excellent sources of information. Functions are compartmented so that if a member of the auxiliary is compromised, the information that he can reveal is limited and not time sensitive.

3-92. The auxiliary also provides the guerrillas goods and services that relate to their civilian occupations. It provides guerrilla recruiters with the names and addresses of prospective new guerrillas. It can also tell the guerrillas of homes and places in the community that favor the resistance and can give support.

Logistic Support

3-93. Most missions of the auxiliary support the guerrilla forces in its area. There are two methods—direct support or area command-directed support. Normally, the auxiliary provides direct support missions for the guerrilla forces in its area. The auxiliary supports guerrillas in all phases of logistic operations. The auxiliary—

- Provides transportation for supplies and equipment.
- Cares for the sick and wounded.
- Provides medical supplies.
- Arranges for doctors and other medical personnel.
- Collects food, clothing, and other supplies through a controlled system of levy, barter, or contribution.
- Sometimes provides essential services such as repair of clothing, shoes, and other items of equipment.
- Supplies personnel to help at reception sites.

3-94. The extent of the logistic support given by the auxiliary depends on the resources of the area, the degree of influence it exerts on the population, and enemy activities. When requisitioning support, the auxiliary must emphasize the righteousness of the resistance objectives and the commonality of resistance or population goals. The resistance depends on the goodwill of the population and the steady "I don't know" replies to enemy interrogators. In cases where the population acts only halfheartedly for the resistance, some civilians are willing to help by being observers, scouts, or messengers.

Home Guard

3-95. The home guard is the paramilitary arm of the auxiliary force. The various command committees control home guards. All auxiliary elements do not necessarily organize home guards. Home guards perform many missions for the auxiliary forces, such as tactical missions, guarding of caches, and training of recruits. Their degree of organization and training depends upon the extent of effective enemy control in the area.

Psychological Operations

3-96. A very important mission in which auxiliary units assist is PSYOP, which must be integrated and synchronized at all levels to achieve its full force-multiplier potential. The spreading of rumors, leaflets, and posters is timed with guerrilla tactical missions to deceive the enemy. The spreading of conveyed selected information usually involves little risk to the disseminator and is very difficult for the enemy to control.

Populace and Resources Control

3-97. The auxiliary employs populace and resources control (PRC) measures to minimize or eliminate black marketing and profiteering and to demonstrate to the enemy the power of the guerrilla movement. PRC consists of the following two distinct, but related, concepts:

- *Populace controls* provide security for the populace, mobilize human resources, deny personnel to the enemy, and detect and reduce the effectiveness of enemy agents. Populace control measures include curfews, movement restrictions, travel permits, registration cards, and resettlement of villagers. DC operations and noncombatant evacuation operations (NEO) are two special categories of populace control that require extensive planning and coordination among various military and nonmilitary organizations.
- *Resources controls* regulate the movement or consumption of materiel resources, mobilize materiel resources, and deny materiel to the enemy. Resources control measures include licensing, regulations or guidelines, checkpoints (for example, roadblocks), ration controls, amnesty programs, and inspection of facilities.

3-98. To perform PRC and give the enemy an impression of guerrilla power, the auxiliary establishes a legal control system to help prevent black marketing and profiteering. The auxiliary may use subtle coercion or other stricter means to control collaborators.

Evasion and Recovery

3-99. The auxiliary is ideally suited for the support of E&R mechanisms. Contact with, and control over, segments of the civilian population provide the area commander a secure means of aiding evaders.

3-100. The auxiliary members receive, conceal, and transport resistance personnel who are infiltrating into, or exfiltrating out of, the JSOA. They also receive and conceal guerrillas who have been wounded or separated from their units during hostilities.

Other Support Missions

3-101. The auxiliary may be called upon to perform several other guerrilla support missions, such as coordinating actions with the guerrillas against their targets. For example, the auxiliary may conduct minor acts of sabotage, such as cutting telephone lines, reversing street signs, giving false information, and obstructing troop movements. It may also support guerrilla missions by—

- Furnishing guides.
- Operating courier systems.
- Conducting active guerrilla-type operations on a limited basis.
- Raising funds.

UNDERGROUND

3-102. The underground supports the area command, auxiliary, and guerrilla force, based on METT-TC. These personnel commit sabotage, intelligence gathering, and acts of deception through the action arm, intelligence, supply, and personnel sections. Trainers develop a guerrilla METL after mission analysis and apply it to METT-TC.

Organization

3-103. The underground organizes into compartmented cells (Figures 3-9 and 3-10, page 3-32). It forms these cells within various political subdivisions of the sector or area, such as the U.S. equivalents of counties, towns, and neighborhoods. The underground environment may be urban or rural. FM 3-05.220 includes further discussion on cell organization.

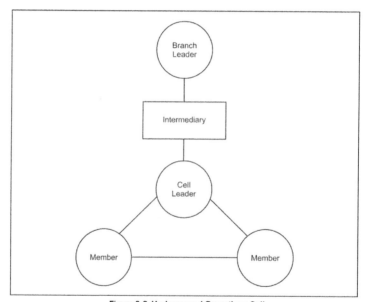

Figure 3-9. Underground Operations Cell

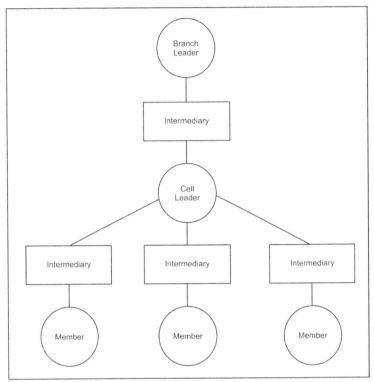

Figure 3-10. Underground Intelligence Cell

3-104. If a member of the underground is compromised, the information that he can reveal is limited. A command committee organizes and controls underground activities. The committee members perform duties and responsibilities based on their skills and the degree of risk they are willing to accept.

3-105. For security reasons, the size of the underground is kept as small as possible. The underground receives evaders, downed pilots, and other key people. It hides people and moves them as needed or moves them out of the JSOA entirely. The auxiliary also moves and hides people within its sector of operation. However, the underground can move people across the entire area complex. It has a system of "safe houses" that have been carefully selected and prepared to hide these people. It develops procedures so that people can be moved along selected routes at the best times to avoid detection. The underground moves them in false-bottom containers to include laundry carts, fish crates, vehicles, furniture, and caskets. It also moves sensitive documents and equipment in a similar manner.

3-106. To support other operations, particularly those involving the smuggling of personnel and materials, the underground commits acts of deception to steal bonafide documents (identification [ID] cards, passes, ration coupons, money, and passports) and use them under false pretenses. If the underground cannot obtain the bona fide documents, it prepares facsimiles.

Membership

3-107. The underground member needs to apply traditional behavior patterns to create a positive image. He is frequently prohibited from taking anything from the people without paying for it. He may even have to befriend certain segments of the population to influence them in support of the movement. He strives to conform to the normal behavior and daily activities of his neighborhood. By appearing conventional and inconspicuous, he makes it difficult for the security force to detect, identify, or find him. Without records or physical evidence, he is difficult to link to the organization. Contact and communications between members are key survival and critical points of subversive operations.

3-108. The underground normally contains more specialists and technicians than either the guerrilla or auxiliary components. Ideally, they are able to conduct combat operations in SR, DA, and UW. Also, they should possess the ability, experience, and equipment necessary to prepare all types of counterfeit documents and be able to produce counterfeit money.

3-109. To survive and be effective, a member of the underground must exhibit many positive personality traits necessary to endure hardship and he must be highly self-motivated. Among these traits, he must—

- Be technically and tactically proficient in combat skills, stealth, and self-discipline.
- Maintain and display an inconspicuous, "average citizen" image toward the enemy.
- Be very cautious about confiding in others. Secrecy and dedication to the cause come before any personal benefit, allowing for greater longevity.

Nature of Operations

3-110. Underground operations can be clandestine, covert, and overt. These operations have major similarities with those of both the guerrillas and the auxiliary. Some involve overt and violent actions and others are passive. The following paragraphs discuss the underground's relationship to other elements of the resistance.

3-111. Underground cells support the operations of the guerrillas and auxiliary (within their sector commands) with acts of deception, sabotage, and movement of personnel and equipment. Underground cells cooperate closely with other underground counterparts in their sectors and throughout the area complex. Cooperation enables successful movement of personnel and equipment in and out of the JSOA.

3-112. The guerrillas and auxiliary are more independent. Only in rare, coordinated operations does the underground work with its counterparts in other sectors.

3-113. The underground may commit acts of violence or sabotage to interdict enemy operations and movements.

3-114. The underground may publish a resistance newsletter or newspaper promoting the resistance cause among the civilian population. In countries with a controlled media system, a private publication of this nature will be of high interest. However, the underground must anticipate enemy reprisals for possession of the paper. Also, the enemy will probably search for the printing press. A defense against this threat is to print the paper outside the JSOA and smuggle it into the country, storing the supply in various locations.

3-115. The underground may engage in covert operations to disseminate embarrassing or incriminating information about the enemy or its officials. These revelations may inflame existing problems in sensitive areas and degrade the enemy's rapport with the civilian population or cause dissension in the enemy's ranks.

TRAINING THE RESISTANCE ORGANIZATION

3-116. A major part of the SFOD's mission is to plan, organize, conduct, and evaluate training of selected resistance cadre. This work prepares the SFOD to be trainers and force multipliers for the resistance organization. During premission planning, the SFOD develops a tentative training plan based on METT-TC. The SFOD members prepare the training plan, POI, and training aids in the indigenous language, if possible. They include sand tables with toy soldiers and vehicles as instruction aids. After commitment into the JSOA, SFOD members evaluate the present level of the resistance forces' training and update the initial training plan or modify it to ensure its effectiveness.

TRAINING PLAN

3-117. The training plan outlines how the SFOD will best accomplish its training objective. SFOD members develop the training plan in isolation based on an estimate of the training situation by the pilot team. Important factors in developing the training plan are mission, personnel, time, facilities, and organization for training. Other considerations are weather, climate, and the enemy situation.

MISSION

3-118. Based on operational directives from higher HQ, the SFOD determines the specific tasks, conditions, and standards the resistance forces must accomplish. If the resistance force has to conduct multiple missions, the SFOD must set up priorities for training. Because a guerrilla travels primarily on his feet, he must undergo rigorous physical training and numerous cross-country marches.

TIME

3-119. The available training time is a critical factor. The shorter the training time, the more time is taken to define the training objectives. SFOD personnel will lose training time because of operational requirements. They must include makeup training as an integral part of the training program.

FACILITIES

3-120. The SFOD will advise the area command and resistance force on selecting and establishing ranges, training areas, improvised classrooms, training aids, and other training facilities. Security is of prime importance. The SFOD locates ranges and training areas away from the base camp. It can make a small valley with aerial concealment or a man-made tunnel into single-lane ranges. Air and BB rifles are excellent alternate, inexpensive, training aids in lieu of full-caliber marksmanship training.

POLITICAL TRAINING

3-121. Politically or religiously extreme insurgents use frequent criticism and self-criticism sessions as a form of catharsis (venting). These sessions allow members to voice fears and problems and to hear from other members. An individual who is disillusioned with the resistance movement will find it difficult to conceal his true feelings in these sessions. He will become influenced by what his friends and comrades think of him. Ideologically oriented unit leaders are more cohesive and effective in their training. Cadres in each unit must set the "politically correct" example during these daily training sessions. They must continually reinforce rank-and-file members, assuring them that what they are doing is needed to carry out the will of the people. Such confidence will elevate morale and fighting spirit.

Equal importance should be attached to the military and political aspects of the one-year consolidation and training program, which has just begun, and the two aspects should be integrated. At the start, stress should be placed on the political aspect, on improving relations between officers and men, enhancing internal unity and arousing a high level of enthusiasm among the masses of cadres and fighters. Only thus will the military consolidation and training proceed smoothly and attain better results.

Mao Tse-tung, 1945

TRAINING THE GUERRILLA FORCE

3-122. SFOD members evaluate how well the guerrillas are trained through personal observations and inspections and the results of limited (easy) combat missions. Characteristics of the guerrilla force that may present obstacles to training include—

- A wide range of education and military experience.
- Different personal motivation for joining the force.

- Possible language and dialect barriers requiring training through interpreters.

TRAINING ORGANIZATION

3-123. The requirements for physical security in the JSOA dictate that guerrilla forces be dispersed over a wide area. Consequently, the system and organization for training are decentralized and "hands-on" training is emphasized. The SFOD must train the guerrilla cadre and later help this cadre in additional training and combat employment. Throughout the organization, development, and training phases of guerrilla activities, the guerrillas conduct limited combat operations. These actions support training, instill confidence, and test the readiness of the force. The goals of these combat operations are to—

- Attract additional recruits to the guerrilla force.
- Assist in gaining popular support from the civilian population.
- Allow the area command and SFOD an opportunity to evaluate the training.
- Increase the morale and esprit de corps of the guerrilla forces with initial successful combat operations.

TRAINING METHODS

3-124. The SFOD generally uses the three-tier concept for training. This concept is similar to the U.S. Army red, green, and amber training cycle. It allows for one-third of the guerrilla forces in training, one-third providing security for the training, and one-third providing support or doing small-scale operations. The three-tier concept accommodates the training of any size unit.

3-125. Generic POI development is the same anywhere. Trainers base all training (basic, advanced, and specialized) on METT-TC and the current combat skills of the guerrillas. They modify the training after contact with the guerrilla force. Appendix J outlines a generic guerrilla POI.

3-126. Trainers base all training (basic, advanced, and specialized) on METT-TC and the current combat skills of the guerrillas. They may modify the training after contact with the guerrilla force.

As for the training courses, the main objective should still be to raise the level of technique in marksmanship, bayoneting, grenade-throwing and the like and the secondary objective should be to raise the level of tactics, while special emphasis should be laid on night operations.

Mao Tse-tung, 1946

Basic Training

3-127. METT-TC determines the need for base camps within the JSOA. All guerrillas including the area command may receive basic training. Each base camp may conduct its basic training in sectors independent of the other two, or it may conduct a part of basic training and rotate to another camp for more training. Either the SFOD or guerrillas may rotate. The base camps may construct ranges and training areas for their use, or one base camp may construct a range and teach all marksmanship classes. Another base camp may construct training areas for raids, and the other may construct areas for ambushes and reconnaissance. The present combat abilities of the guerrillas and the threat determine how much basic training is needed.

3-128. Basic training contains subjects on small arms, first aid, land navigation, and political or PSYOP classes. The time allotted for training needs to be flexible—between 21 and 31 days, depending on the knowledge and abilities of the force.

Advanced Training

3-129. Each base camp conducts some advanced training or rotates to other base camps for additional training. This concept is similar to basic training, and the guerrillas or SFOD may rotate. Trainers can conduct medical and demolitions training in one base camp; communications and intelligence in another; and tactics, operations, and heavy weapons in the third. At the end of the advanced training period, the guerrillas or SFOD would rotate to another base camp for a new training cycle. For security reasons, all the engineer, communications, medical, and intelligence sergeants should not be in the same sector base camp at the same time.

3-130. Advanced training may last from 40 to 80 days. This phase consumes the most time, but it also pays the most dividends. Some subjects covered in greater depth include combat orders, machine guns, tactics, survival, and MOSs of medical, communications, weapons, and demolitions.

Specialized Training

3-131. Specialized training is broadly subdivided into elementary and advanced specialized training. Personnel and units assigned to the theater SF may have received elementary specialized training. If not, such training becomes a responsibility of the theater SF commander. Specialized training, elementary and advanced, is conducted by a training center operated by the theater SF.

3-132. Elementary specialized training consists of training individuals and teams to carry out their assigned functions. Intensive courses are conducted and include the following:

- Map reading and sketching.
- Patrolling.
- Close combat.
- Physical training.
- Fieldcraft.
- Tactics of both regular and guerrilla forces.
- Demolitions and techniques of sabotage.
- Use and care of weapons, including those of the enemy forces.
- First aid.
- Use of enemy and civilian motor transportation.

- Enemy organization and methods.
- Methods of organizing and training guerrillas.
- Security information.
- Methods of supply to guerrilla forces.

3-133. Advanced specialized training prepares qualified individuals and teams for specific missions in enemy territory. During this training, individuals are organized into the teams in which they will be employed. Thereafter the group trains, lives, and operates as a unit under simulated conditions of the area where they are to be employed. Special techniques, skills, and orientation are stressed to enable them to carry out their mission and to weld them into efficient, mobile, and self-sufficient teams. Parachute or amphibious training is given, depending on the contemplated means of entering enemy territory.

3-134. Besides the training outlined above, technical training is given to radio operators, medical technicians, demolition experts, and other specialists.

TRAINING STAFF AND AUXILIARY OR UNDERGROUND PERSONNEL

3-135. While the SFOD members are training the guerrilla force, the SFOD commander, ADC, and team sergeant are training the area command and staff, sector commander and staff, and selected members of the auxiliary or underground. The area commander and his staff may train in the same base camp with his guerrillas. Although the area command and auxiliary or underground may be trained anywhere in the JSOA, it should be compartmented for security reasons. FM 3-05.220 provides more information on training the auxiliary and underground in advanced SO techniques.

TRAINING THROUGH INTERPRETERS

3-136. Historically, SFOD members in a UW environment have been faced with a social and political power struggle when they tried to select an interpreter to work with them. The struggle has not always been to their advantage. The next few paragraphs discuss some tips on how to select an interpreter and avoid some of the often-repeated pitfalls.

Native Speaker

3-137. The ideal interpreter would be a native speaker from the AO who knows most of the area dialects. His speech, grammar, background, and social mannerisms should be understandable to the students. If he fits this ideal description, the students will listen to what he says, not how he says it. The students will understand the interpreter.

Social Status

3-138. An interpreter often is limited in his effectiveness with students if his social standing is considerably lower than that of his students. There may be significant differences among the students and the interpreter in military rank or memberships in ethnic or religious groups. When students are officers, it may be best to have an officer or civilian act as an interpreter. On the other hand, if students are enlisted personnel, an officer interpreter might intimidate the students and stifle class participation. An enlisted interpreter would be the best choice in this case. Most cultures recognize technical competence and international differences in military structure, so there should be no problem for the SFOD. Despite personal feelings on social status, the instructor's job is to train all students equally, not act as an agent of social reform in a foreign land. The instructor must accept local customs as a way of life.

English Fluency

3-139. If the SFOD instructor and interpreter can communicate with each other in English, the interpreter's command of English is adequate. The instructor can check the interpreter's level of "understanding" by asking him to paraphrase in English what the instructor has just said. If the interpreter restates the comments correctly, both are "reading off the same sheet of music."

Intelligence

3-140. The interpreter should be quick, alert, and responsive to changing conditions and situations. He must be able to grasp complex concepts and discuss them without confusion in a logical sequence. Education does not equate to intelligence, but better educated interpreters will be more effective due to experience and maturity.

Technical Ability

3-141. If the interpreter has technical training or experience in the instructor's subject area, he will be more effective since he will translate "meaning" as well as "words." A doctor could interpret for a medic, and former military personnel could interpret best for the weapons and intelligence sergeants.

Reliability

3-142. An instructor must be leery of any interpreter who arrives late for the class. Many cultures operate on a "flexible clock," where time is relatively unimportant. The interpreter must understand the concept of punctuality. Also, it is safe to assume that any interpreter's first loyalty is to his country, not to the United States. The security implications are clear; the instructor must be very cautious in explaining concepts to give the interpreter "a greater depth of understanding." Also, some interpreters, for political or personal reasons, may have a "hidden agenda" when they apply for the job.

Compatibility

3-143. The instructor must establish rapport with his interpreter early in their relationship and maintain compatibility throughout their joint effort. Mutual respect and understanding are essential to effective instruction. Some rapport-building subjects to discuss with the interpreter are history, geography, ethnic groups, political system, prominent political figures, monetary system, business, agriculture, exports, and hobbies. The SFOD member is building a friendship on a daily basis.

3-144. If several qualified interpreters are available, the instructor should select at least two. The exhausting nature of the job makes a half-day of active interpreting the maximum for peak efficiency. One interpreter, however skilled, will seldom be enough except for short-term courses conducted at a leisurely pace. If two or more interpreters are available, one of them can sit in the rear of the class and provide quality control of the instruction by crosschecking the active interpreter. Meanwhile, additional interpreters can conduct rehearsals, grade examinations, and evaluate the exercises. Mature judgment and a genuine concern that the students are learning important skills go a long way toward accomplishing the mission.

3-145. Good instructors will tactfully ask about their interpreters' background. With genuine concern, they ask about the interpreter's family, aspirations, career, and education. They can start with his home life; it's very important to him and is neutral territory. Instructors can follow up with a discussion of cultural traditions to find out more about him and the land he lives in.

3-146. The instructor should gain his interpreter's trust and confidence before embarking on sensitive issues such as sex, politics, and religion. He must approach these areas carefully and tactfully. They may be useful and revealing in the professional relationship between instructor and interpreter. Once this stage is reached, the two are well on their way to a valuable friendship and a firm, professional working relationship.

TRAINING THE INTERPRETERS

3-147. Very early on, the instructor conveys to the interpreter that he will always direct the training. However, he must stress how important the interpreter is as a link to the students. He can appeal to the interpreter's professional pride by describing how the quality and quantity of learning are dependent on his interpreting skills and his ability to function as a conduit between instructor and students. The instructor must also stress patriotism, that the defense of his country is directly related to his ability to transfer the instructor's knowledge to the students.

3-148. Because of cultural differences, interpreters may attempt to "save face" by concealing their lack of understanding. They may attempt to translate what they think the instructor "meant" without asking for a clarification. Disinformation and confusion result for the students. Ultimately, when the students realize they have been misled, they question the instructor's credibility, not the interpreter's. If the instructor has established rapport with his interpreter, he is in a better position to appeal to the interpreter's sense of duty, honor, and country. A mutual understanding allows for clarification when needed, leads to more accurate interpretation, and keeps the instructor informed of any student difficulties.

Conducting the Training

3-149. To prepare for teaching, the instructor must have initial lesson plans available for basic, advanced, and specialized training. He must also have on hand the available supporting documentation, such as FMs. When the class begins, the instructor should—

- Express the training objective in measurable performance terms.
- Outline the course content with methods of instruction and the various training aids to be demonstrated and then used by the students.
- Supply and circulate all class handout material when needed.
- Modify the training schedule to allow more time to train foreign students due to language and translation constraints.

3-150. A glossary of terms is a valuable aid for the instructor and the interpreter. Many English words and phrases do not translate literally into many foreign languages. Technical terms need to be clearly defined well ahead of class. A listing of the most common terms and their translated meaning will be a useful product.

3-151. The instructor presents bite-sized information tailored to the student audience. He talks directly to the students in a relaxed and confident manner. The interpreter watches the instructor carefully and emulates his style and delivery as he interprets for the students. During the translation, the instructor observes the interpreter to detect any problems. The interpreter will do some "editing" as a function of the interpreting process, but it is imperative that he transmits the instructor's meaning without additions or deletions. A well-coordinated effort is the key to success.

3-152. Although maximum improvisation must be used in all phases of operations, the following items accompanying deployed detachments may prove useful in conducting training:

- Grease pencils and colored chalk.
- Target cloth or ponchos (blackboard substitutes).
- Basic manuals on weapons generally found in the area (in the language of the country, if possible).
- Graphic training aids improvised from parachutes or other such material.

Student Questions

3-153. Whenever students have questions, the interpreter immediately relays them to the instructor for an answer. The students then realize the instructor, not the interpreter, is the SME and is in charge of the class. When a problem occurs, neither the instructor nor the interpreter corrects each other in front of the students. They must settle all differences in a professional manner.

3-154. Rapport is as important between student and instructor as it is between interpreter and instructor. When the interpreter and instructor treat the students as mature, valuable people capable of learning, rapport will build easily between the students and the instructor.

Communication

3-155. An instructor learns by experience that a way to communicate is through an interpreter. Use of profanity, slang, colloquialisms, and military jargon with students is harmful. Often, these expressions cannot be translated and do not come out with the desired meaning. If he must use a technical term or expression, the instructor makes sure the interpreter conveys the proper meaning in the indigenous language.

Transitional Phrases

3-156. Transitional phrases tend to confuse the learning process and waste valuable time. Expressions such as "for example" and "in most cases" or qualifiers such as "maybe" or "perhaps" are difficult to translate. Many native interpreters have learned much of their English from reading rather than hearing English spoken. The instructor keeps the class presentation as simple as possible, using short words and phrases.

Taboo Gestures

3-157. Social and cultural restrictions will manifest themselves during class. Gestures are learned behavior and vary from culture to culture. If the instructor doesn't know, he should ask the interpreter to relate the cultural taboos before class and avoid them. The instructor should know before class—

- When it is proper to stand, sit, or cross legs.
- If the index finger, chin, or eyes may be used for pointing.
- If nodding of the head means yes or no.

Manner of Speaking

3-158. The instructor should try to look at the students and talk directly to them, not the interpreter. He speaks slowly and clearly and repeats himself as needed. The instructor should not address the students in the third person through the interpreter. Instead, he should say something like, "I'm glad to be your instructor," and not "Tell them I'm glad to be their instructor."

3-159. The instructor must speak to the students as if they will understand every word he says. He must convey enthusiasm and use all of the gestures, movements, voice intonations, and inflections he would use for an English-speaking audience. The students will reflect the same amount of energy, interest, and enthusiasm that the instructor conveys to them. The instructor must not let the interpreter "sabotage" training with a less than animated delivery and presentation of the material.

3-160. When the interpreter is translating and the students are listening to get the full meaning of the translation, the instructor should do nothing that could be distracting. These distractions might be pacing the floor, writing on the blackboard, drinking water, or carrying on with other distracting activities.

3-161. The interpreter should be checked periodically to make sure the students understand the instructor's meaning. A cadre member, qualified in the native language, may observe and comment on the interpreter's knowledge, skills, and abilities. When the instructor has been misunderstood, the point needs to be made clear immediately. If further clarification is needed, the instructor should phrase the instruction differently and illustrate the point as necessary.

COMBAT EMPLOYMENT

3-162. North Vietnamese General Giap wrote in his book, *The Military Art of People's War,* "We strike to win, strike only when success is certain; if it's not, then don't strike." This simple, straightforward idea for conducting combat operations is the key concept an SFOD advising guerrillas should never disregard.

OPERATIONS

3-163. The guerrilla force should carefully select, plan, and execute UW combat operations to ensure success with a minimum number of casualties. A combat defeat in the early stages of training demoralizes the guerrilla force. Combat operations should be commensurate with the status of training and equipment available to the resistance force. As training is completed and units are organized, guerrilla forces with SF assistance can plan and execute small-scale combat operations against "soft (easy) targets," an important confidence builder. Later, they progress to larger and more complex targets.

PRINCIPLES FOR SUCCESS

3-164. Successful UW combat operations depend on five principles. Those principles are speed of movement, surprise, low enemy morale, security, and collaboration with the local population.

Speed of Movement

3-165. To achieve speed, guerrillas practice rapid force concentration and rapid deployment from march formations. They also practice movements and attacks during periods of limited visibility, pursuit of disorganized enemy units with little time wasted on reorganization after an engagement, and fast withdrawals. Guerrillas use an MSS and travel light to increase their element of speed and surprise.

Surprise

3-166. To surprise the enemy, guerrillas plan to conduct and integrate deception operations into every UW mission.

Low Enemy Morale

3-167. Guerrillas take advantage of every opportunity to undermine enemy morale by including PSYOP.

Security

3-168. Guerrillas prepare the battlefield as far in advance as possible. Reconnaissance elements gather all available information on the terrain, installations, enemy units, and civilian activities. They also reconnoiter escape and withdrawal routes well in advance.

Collaboration With the Local Population

3-169. The auxiliary in the area provides the guerrillas information, transportation, supplies, hideouts, and guides familiar with the objective.

SECURITY WITHIN THE AREA OF OPERATIONS

3-170. The AO requires special security measures that apply particularly to insurgent forces. The survival of the insurgents depends upon constant vigilance on the part of every member of the organization, plus the ability to transmit warnings. Effective CI is also essential. Security measures must prevent losses by enemy action, ensure freedom of action, and minimize interruption of insurgent activities. Dependable security can be achieved by intensive training in security discipline, establishment of warning systems, and extensive CI.

Responsibility

3-171. The area commander is responsible for the overall security of the insurgent forces, although commanders of subordinate units must take individual measures for their own local protection. The chief of the security section of the area command controls all security operations, except CI. He prescribes necessary measures and coordinates those adopted by subordinate commanders. CI is the responsibility of the chief of the intelligence section of the area command. Again, subordinate commanders must establish local CI for their own security.

Factors Affecting Security

3-172. Security measures developed by the chief of the security section of the area command are affected by the following factors:

- Mission.
- Local situation of individual units.
- Physical characteristics of the AO.
- The enemy situation.
- Capabilities and limitations of the insurgent forces.
- Considerations affecting the civilian population.
- Operations of conventional and coalition forces.

3-173. During the early phases of insurgent warfare, the mission of insurgent forces will necessitate organization of a CI system alongside the intelligence system, development of a communications system that will facilitate warnings, and establishment of physical security for installations. Particular attention should be directed toward the enemy's state of internal security formations and their intelligence and communications systems.

3-174. Military actions against the enemy initiated during the early phases of operations should be planned and executed in such a way that they will not lead to wholesale enemy anti-insurgent activity, reprisals against the civilian population, or compromise of external logistical support in the latter stages of insurgent warfare. Operations are not curtailed for security reasons, because the established security system provides greater protection for the insurgents. Also, insurgent control over the area may rival the enemy's own influence.

Principles of Security

3-175. **Dispersion.** Insurgent forces avoid a large concentration of troops. Even though logistical conditions may permit large troop concentrations, commands should be broken down into smaller units and widely dispersed. The dispersion of forces facilitates concealment, mobility, and secrecy. Large forces may be concentrated to perform a specific operation, but on completion of the operation, they should again be quickly dispersed.

3-176. The principle of dispersion is applied to command, service, and technical installations. A large insurgent HQ, for example, is divided into several echelons and scattered over the area.

3-177. In the event of a well-conducted, large-scale enemy operation against the insurgent force, the area commander may find it necessary to order the division of units into smaller groups to achieve greater dispersion and facilitate escape from encirclement. This action should be taken only when all other means of evasive action are exhausted because such dispersion renders the force inoperative for a considerable period of time, lowers the morale of insurgents, and weakens the will of the civilians to resist. To assure successful reassembly of dispersed units, emergency plans must include alternate assembly areas.

3-178. **Mobility.** All insurgent installations and forces must have a high degree of mobility. Their evacuation plans must ensure that all traces of insurgent activity are eliminated before abandonment of the area.

3-179. Forces can maintain evacuation mobility by ensuring that equipment that must be moved can be disassembled into one-man loads. The area commander ensures suitable caches are provided for equipment that would reduce mobility, materiel that could provide intelligence for the enemy is destroyed, the area is policed, and signs of the route of withdrawal are eliminated.

Security of Information

3-180. **Safeguarding Plans and Records.** Information concerning insurgent operations is limited to those who need to know it. Only necessary copies are made or maintained. Each person is given only that information that is needed to accomplish his mission. Special efforts are made to restrict the amount of information given to individuals who are exposed to capture.

3-181. Administrative records are kept to a minimum, are cached, and the location made known only to a required few. Whenever possible, references to names and places are coded, and the key to the code is given on a need-to-know basis. Records that are no longer of value to operations or for future reports must be destroyed.

3-182. **Security Discipline.** Strict security discipline is necessary and all security measures must be rigidly enforced. Security instruction of personnel must be extensive. They must be impressed with the importance of not divulging information concerning insurgent activities to persons not requiring it. Individuals seeking such information must be reported to proper authorities.

3-183. Security violations are extremely serious and demand severe punishment. All cases involving a possible breach of security must be reported immediately.

3-184. The key to successful security of information, however, is the individual insurgent himself who must always be security-conscious. One careless individual can destroy the best security system devised.

3-185. **Training.** During the training phase, security consciousness must be stressed. Special emphasis should be placed on safeguarding documents, security of information, and resistance against interrogation.

Security of Movement

3-186. Security of movement can be provided only by an accurate knowledge of the enemy's location and strength. Intelligence regarding enemy disposition and activities is essential. The intelligence section of the area command, informed through its various nets, must provide this vital information for security of movement.

3-187. After the routes have been selected, the units must be briefed on enemy activity, primary and alternate routes, dispersal and reassembly areas along the way, and security measures to be observed en route. If the route leads through areas outside insurgent influence, auxiliary civilian organizations must provide security of movement for the insurgents.

Security of Installations

3-188. Most installations are located in isolated regions known as insurgent base of operations or guerrilla base. They are mobile and are secured by guards and warning systems. Alternate locations are prepared in advance so that any installation threatened by enemy action can be evacuated from the endangered base area to a more secure area. Location of these alternate areas is given to personnel only on a need-to-know basis.

3-189. Physical security of installations will include terrain CI. This may vary from simple deceptive measures, such as camouflage or destruction and reversal of road signs and mileposts, to the creation of physical barriers, such as roadblocks and demolition of roadbeds and bridges. The use of civilian guides to misdirect enemy troops (for example, into ambush) can also be effective.

Tri-Zonal Security System

3-190. A typical means of providing adequate security for the insurgent base area is a tri-zonal security system. This system provides the following series of warning nets:

- *Zone A* is the insurgent base area itself. It is secured by a regular guard system, but it largely depends for its safety upon advance warnings received by clandestine agents in Zone C, or posted observers in Zone B. If enemy action threatens, the insurgents move to another location before the arrival of enemy forces.

- *Zone B*, lying beyond the populated Zone C, is territory not well controlled by the enemy in which the insurgent forces can operate overtly. It is usually open, rugged terrain, and the warning system depends upon stationed observers, watching for enemy movements in the area.

- *Zone C*, the farthest from the insurgent base area, is usually well populated and is located inside enemy-controlled territory. Enemy security forces, police, and military units exercise relatively effective control, and the populace may be predominately hostile to the insurgents. At the same time, there are excellent and rapid LOCs, whereby clandestine agents are able to warn the insurgents quickly of enemy activity. This area is known as the clandestine zone and the functions of the warning system are the responsibility of the underground.

Security of Communications

3-191. Insurgent communications facilities are rigidly regulated by the SOI. These measures include restriction on what may be transmitted; the use of codes and ciphers; and means of concealment, deception, and authentication. Particular emphasis is placed on restricting time and number of radio transmissions to the absolute minimum.

Counterintelligence

3-192. Insurgent security depends not only on security measures taken to safeguard information, installations, and communications, but also on an active CI program to neutralize the enemy's intelligence system and especially to prevent the penetration of insurgent forces by enemy agents.

3-193. The intelligence section of the area command implements the CI program. Specially selected and trained CI personnel carefully screen all members of the insurgent organization and protect the insurgents from enemy infiltration. CI personnel also carry on an active campaign of deception, disseminating false information to mislead the enemy.

3-194. CI personnel must keep a constant check on the civilian population of the area through clandestine sources to ensure against the presence of enemy agents within their midst. Civilians upon whom the insurgents depend heavily for support may compromise the insurgent warfare effort as easily as a disloyal insurgent may.

3-195. False rumors and false information concerning insurgent strength, location, operations, training, and equipment can be disseminated by CI through clandestine nets. Facts may be distorted intentionally to minimize or exaggerate insurgent capabilities at any given time. Although such activities are handled within the intelligence section, they must be coordinated with the security section in order to prevent inadvertent violations of security.

Outlaw Bands

3-196. Outlaw bands, operating as insurgents, also endanger insurgent security by alienating the civilian population through their depredation. The area commander cannot tolerate outlaw bands, which are not willing to join the organized insurgent effort. Every effort must be made to persuade these bands to join forces. If all other methods fail, it may be necessary to conduct operations against these groups.

Reaction to Enemy Operations

3-197. Inexperienced insurgent commanders and troops are often inclined to move too soon and too frequently to escape enemy troops conducting anti-insurgent operations. Unnecessary movement caused by the presence of the enemy may expose insurgents to greater risks than remaining calm and concealed. Such moves disrupt operations and reduce security by dislodging previously established nets and exposing insurgents to enemy agents, informants, and collaborators.

DEFENSIVE OPERATIONS

3-198. Defensive operations are exceptional forms of combat for guerrilla forces. The guerrilla force may engage in defensive operations to—

- Prevent enemy penetration of guerrilla-controlled areas.
- Gain time for their forces to accomplish a specific mission.
- Assemble their main forces for counterattacks.

3-199. Guerrillas normally lack supporting fire: artillery, antitank weapons, and other weapons to face conventional forces. Historically, guerrillas have avoided a prolonged position type of defense. When committed, they modify the principles of defensive operations to best meet their needs and offset the difficulties. They are aware of their limitations. The guerrillas choose the terrain that gives them every possible advantage. They seek terrain that denies or restricts the enemy's use of armor and complicates his logistic support. In the guerrilla-position defense, they raid, ambush, and attack the enemy's LOCs, flanks, reserve units, and supporting arms and installations. The guerrillas provide camouflaged sniper fire on officers, radio operators, and other high-value targets. They mine or booby-trap approach and departure routes.

3-200. Guerrillas may resort to defensive operations to contain enemy forces in a position favorable for attacking their flanks or rear. They often begin or intensify diversionary actions in adjacent areas to distract the enemy. Guerrillas use skillful ruses to lure the attacking forces into dividing their troops or hold objectives pending the arrival of conventional or allied coalition forces.

OFFENSIVE OPERATIONS

3-201. The degree to which the offensive operations of guerrilla forces can be sustained depends, in the long run, on the base camp support available to them. When operating remotely from, or not with, conventional forces, the guerrilla forces establish and hold bases of their own. They locate their bases, if available, with a view to isolation and difficulty of approach by the opposing forces. They also consider strong defensive characteristics and closeness to neighboring supporting states. The bases should be organized for defense and tenaciously defended by trained, motivated forces. FM 7-8, *Infantry Rifle Platoon and Squad*, includes more information.

RAIDS

3-202. A raid is a combat operation to attack a position or installation followed by a planned withdrawal. SF and guerrilla or area sector commanders must consider the nature of the terrain (METT-TC) and the combat efficiency of the raid force. Commanders base target selection on a decision matrix using CARVER. The SFOD assesses the criticality and recuperability of various targets during the area study. Accessibility and vulnerability are situation-dependent and these assessments must be supported by the most current area intelligence. CARVER factors are discussed in the following paragraphs.

3-203. *Criticality* is the importance of a system, subsystem, complex, or component. A target is critical when its destruction or damage has a significant impact on the output of the targeted system, subsystem, or complex, and, at the highest level, on the threat's ability to make or sustain war. Criticality depends on several factors:

- How rapidly will the impact of target destruction affect enemy operations?
- What percentage of output is curtailed by target damage?
- Is there an existence of substitutes for the output product or service?
- What is the number of targets and their position in the system or complex flow diagram?

3-204. *Accessibility* is the ease with which a target can be reached, either physically or by fire. A target is accessible when an action element can physically infiltrate the target, or if the target can be hit by direct or indirect fire. Accessibility varies with the infiltration and exfiltration, the survival and evasion and security situation en route to and at the target, and the need for barrier penetration, climbing, and so on, at the target. The use of standoff weapons should always be considered when evaluating accessibility. Survivability of the attacker is usually most closely correlated to a target's accessibility.

3-205. *Recuperability* is a measure of the time required to replace, repair, or bypass the destruction or damage inflicted on the target. Recuperability varies with the sources and ages of targeted components and with the availability of spare parts. The existence of economic embargoes and the technical resources of the enemy nation will influence recuperability.

3-206. *Vulnerability* is a measure of the ability of the action element to damage the target using available assets (both men and material). A target is vulnerable if the unit has the capability and expertise to successfully attack it. Vulnerability depends on the—

- Nature and construction of the target.
- Amount of damage required.
- Assets available (manpower, transportation, weapons, explosives, and equipment).

3-207. *Effect* is the positive or negative influence on the population as a result of the action taken. Effect considers public reaction in the vicinity of the target, but also considers the domestic and international reaction as well. Effects to consider include the following:

- Will reprisals against friendlies result?
- Will national PSYOP themes be reinforced or contradicted?
- Will exfiltration or evasion be helped or hurt? What will be the allied and domestic reaction?
- Will the enemy population be alienated from its government, or will it become more supportive of the government?

NOTE: Effect is often neutral at the tactical level.

3-208. *Recognizability* is the degree to which a target can be recognized under varying weather, light, and seasonal conditions without confusion with other targets or components. Factors that influence recognizability include the size and complexity of the target, the existence of distinctive target signatures, and the technical sophistication and training of the attackers.

3-209. Target selection factors may be used to construct a CARVER matrix. The matrix is a decision tool for rating the relative desirability of potential targets and for wisely allocating attack resources (Figure 3-11, page 3-51). To construct the matrix, analysts list the potential targets in the left column. For strategic-level analysis, analysts list the enemy's systems or subsystems (electric, power, rail). For tactical-level analysis, analysts list the complexes or components of the subsystems selected for attack by their higher HQ.

3-210. Next, analysts develop concrete criteria for evaluating each CARVER factor. For instance, time may be used to evaluate criticality. If loss of a component results in an immediate halt of output, then that component is very critical. If loss of the component results in a halt of output, but only after several days or weeks, then that component is less critical. Similarly, percentage of output curtailed might be used as the evaluation criterion.

3-211. Once the evaluation criteria have been established, analysts use a numerical rating system (for example, 1-to-5 or 1-to-10) to rank the CARVER factors for each potential target. In a 1-to-10 numbering system, a score of 10 would indicate a very desirable rating (from the attacker's point of view), and a score of 1 would reflect an undesirable rating. The evaluation criteria and numerical rating scheme shown are only included as examples. The analyst must tailor the criteria and rating scheme to suit the particular strategic or tactical situation and the particular targets being analyzed.

3-212. The area commander considers the possible adverse effects target destruction will have on future operations and the civilian population. Targets that will hinder or hurt the civilian population may be attacked only as a last resort. The goal is to diminish the enemy's military potential, not destroy the only footbridge in the area for civilians to go to work. However, an improperly timed operation may provoke enemy counteraction for which resistance units and the civilian population are unprepared. An unsuccessful guerrilla attack often may have disastrous effects on troop morale. Successful operations raise morale and increase prestige in the eyes of the civilians, making them more willing to provide support. PSYOP exploit the impact of successful raids. If a raid is unsuccessful, PSYOP personnel need to diminish the adverse effects on the friendly local indigenous force.

Potential Targets	C	A	R	V	E	R	Higher is Better TOTAL
Fuel Tanks	2	5	3	5	5	5	25
Fuel Pumps	3	4	3	5	5	4	24
Boilers	4	2	5	4	3	3	21
Turbines	4	2	5	4	3	3	21
Generators	2	3	3	4	4	5	21
Condensers	4	2	4	4	3	3	20
Feed Pumps	3	4	3	4	4	3	21
Circular Water Pumps	3	4	4	4	3	3	21

Figure 3-11. Sample CARVER Matrix

3-213. Although detailed, the plan for a raid must be practical and simple. The raid force commander plans activities so that the target is not alerted. He carefully considers time available, allowing enough time for assembly and movement. The best hours for the operation are between midnight and dawn when limited visibility ensures surprise. Personnel favor early dusk when knowledge of the installation is limited or other factors require tight control of the operation. A successful guerrilla withdrawal late in the day or at night makes close, coordinated pursuit by the enemy much more difficult.

3-214. The commander must strictly enforce OPSEC measures during planning. Only those personnel directly involved with the operation must be informed. Civilian sympathizers should never be informed of upcoming operations unless they provide support to the guerrilla forces. Personnel should carefully rehearse all raids and contingencies using real-time and full-size mock-ups. They must also select and rehearse an alternate plan and escape route for use in case of emergencies.

3-215. The raid unit must also plan for medical support. Reactive planning in the medical arena is predictably unsuccessful, resulting unnecessarily in loss of life or limb. Adequate and visible medical planning has considerable positive psychological effects on the raid force's morale. Personnel should plan to handle anticipated casualties with aid and litter teams at the objective, at planned rallying points (RPs), and in the base area. Considerations should include evacuation routes at all levels and priorities for evacuation, nonevacuation, and hospitalization. Personnel should coordinate with treatment facilities before a raid but not divulge the target or timing of the mission.

ORGANIZATION

3-216. The size of the raid force depends on METT-TC. The raid force may vary from a few personnel attacking a checkpoint to a battalion attacking a large supply depot. Regardless of size, the raid force consists of four basic elements: command, assault, security, and support with strategic placement of medical personnel within all elements.

Command Element

3-217. The raid force commander and key personnel normally make up this element. They provide general support to the raid, such as medical aidmen, radio operators and, if a fire support element is part of the raid, a forward observer. The command element is not normally assigned specific duties with any element. Personnel may work with any of the major elements of the raid force. The raid force commander locates himself where he may best control and influence the action.

Assault Element

3-218. Applying METT-TC, the assault element is specifically task organized by what is needed to accomplish the objective. If the raid objective is to attack and render unusable critical elements of a target system, such as a bridge or tunnel, the raid force assaults and demolishes the bridge or tunnel. If the target is enemy personnel, the raid force conducts its attack with a high proportion of automatic assault weapons, covered by mortar fire from the support element. Usually the assault element physically moves on or into the target. This method is the least preferred. A more preferred method is for the assault element to complete its task from a standoff distance. The assault element attacks using lasers, antitank weapons, and other heavy weapons.

Security Element

3-219. The security element supports the raid by securing withdrawal routes, providing early warning of enemy approach, blocking avenues of approach into the objective area, preventing enemy escape from the objective area, and acting as the rear guard for the withdrawing raid force. The size of the security element depends on the enemy's capability to intervene and disrupt the mission. If the threat has armor, then the element needs antiarmor weapons. Where the enemy is known to have aircraft, the security element employs antiaircraft weapons. As the assault element moves into position, the security element keeps the command group informed of all enemy activities, firing only if detected and on order from the command group. Once the assault begins, the security element prevents enemy entry into or escape from the objective area. As the raid force withdraws, the security element, enhanced by sniper teams, conducts a rearguard action to disrupt and ambush any enemy counterattacks and pursuits.

Support Element

3-220. The support element of the raid force conducts diversionary or coordinated attacks at several points on the target to help the assault element gain access to the target. It uses ambushes, roadblocks, and mortar fire on the threat. Support personnel also execute complementary tasks in eliminating guards, breaching and removing obstacles to the objective, and conducting diversionary or holding actions. They assist by providing fire support and acting as demolition teams to set charges and neutralize, destroy, or render parts of the target unusable. Historically, the support element has covered the withdrawal of the assault element from the immediate area of the objective, and then withdrawn on order or prearranged signal.

INTELLIGENCE AND RECONNAISSANCE

3-221. The raid force commander must have maximum intelligence on the target site, enemy reaction forces (including routes, strength, and avenues of approach), and the routine activities and attitudes of the indigenous population in the area. Intelligence and reconnaissance personnel conduct a premission survey of the routes to the target, locations for friendly support weapons, enemy defenses (to include key weapons, minefields, and weak points), critical nodes to be destroyed within the target site, and withdrawal routes. The raid force gains access to the target site itself. Civilian supporters may help in these attempts if they have a good cover for action. If tactically feasible, personnel may conduct surveillance of the target to learn last-minute requirements.

3-222. Intelligence and reconnaissance personnel conduct detailed intelligence gathering and leader reconnaissance before beginning the raid. They construct a basic SALUTE report to include the following:

- Strength and location of the threat and its combat effectiveness.
- The threat's armaments and its location.
- Reaction time, security, and protection.
- Positions of key and automatic weapons.

3-223. Intelligence gathering includes answers to the following questions:

- Are reserve threat troops in the vicinity?
- Are they waiting with armor or aircraft?
- What are their strength, time to reinforce, and communication abilities?
- Is the terrain accessible?
- Can it be blockaded or defended?
- What are the locations and capabilities of local inhabitants?
- What routes to and from the raid site provide cover, concealment, and security and simplify movement?
- Does the threat have armor or air support?
- Where should key support weapons—antitank, antiair, sniper teams, and machine guns—be placed?

3-224. Additionally, intelligence and reconnaissance personnel consult with supporting CA team members to consider the nonmilitary threats to the planned raid. They analyze the civilian component of the target area using CASCOPE. Typical questions are as follows:

- What civilian areas exist between the line of departure and the objective? What activities are employed in these areas?
- What civilian structures (permanent, semipermanent, or temporary) may be encountered along the route? What protection status is assigned to these structures?
- What civilian capabilities exist that could intercede or support the raid as part of a contingency? Is there a credible police capability?
- What organizations (host nation [HN], UN, NGO, multinational corporation, criminal, terrorist) exist in and around the objective area? What activities are they engaged in? What assistance might we obtain from them?
- What types of civilians might we encounter in and around the objective area? What general activities are they engaged in? What might be their reaction to contact with raid forces? What might be their reaction to combat operations?
- Are there any civilian events that may affect the conduct of the military operation, such as call to prayer or church services, festival celebrations, "rush hour" traffic, and planting or harvest season activities?

PARTICIPANT REHEARSALS

3-225. Raid participants conduct realistic, timely rehearsals for the operation using terrain similar to the target area whenever possible. Participants use sand tables, full-size mock-ups, sketches, and photographs, to assist in briefings. They practice immediate action drills (IADs) along with contingency and emergency actions. Guerrillas hold full-scale final rehearsals under conditions and visibility realistically expected in the objective area at the time of attack.

NIGHT RAIDS

3-226. The best time for a raid is during limited visibility. Darkness allows units to maneuver even closer to the enemy. Enemy reinforcements will have difficulty in moving to assist their troops under attack, and air assets will be at a disadvantage. However, maneuvering at night is more difficult to accomplish, and command, control, and communications (C3) are more difficult to maintain.

DAY RAIDS

3-227. Units conduct raids during daylight when the troops at the target location are lacking in security, morale, or discipline. A key question is whether they will get help from adjacent units, especially under adverse weather conditions of sandstorms, rain, or snowstorms.

FINAL INSPECTION

3-228. The raid force commander conducts a final inspection of personnel and equipment before moving to the objective area. He ensures weapons are test-fired, broken equipment is replaced, and the physical condition of each man is checked. He checks personal belongings to ensure that no incriminating documents are carried during the operation. This inspection assures the raid force commander that his unit is equipped and ready for a successful mission.

MOVEMENT

3-229. The raid force commander plans and conducts movement to the objective area so that the raid force's approach to the target is undetected (Figure 3-12). Movement may be by single or multiple routes. The preselected route or routes may end in assembly areas, one or more patrol bases, or MSSs, which enhance mission success. The raid force makes every effort to avoid contact with the enemy during movement. Upon reaching the objective rallying point (ORP), security and leader reconnaissance parties deploy and make final coordination before the assault force moves to the attack position.

Figure 3-12. Movement to and Withdrawal From the Objective Area

ACTIONS IN THE OBJECTIVE AREA

3-230. Support elements move to their positions and eliminate sentries, breach or remove obstacles, and execute other tasks. The assault element quickly follows the select soldiers into the target area. Once the objective of the raid has been accomplished, the assault element and special troops withdraw, covered by fire support on preselected targets. If the attack is unsuccessful, the raid force ends the action to prevent undue loss of personnel, and the support elements withdraw according to plan. The assault and support elements assemble at one or more RPs, while the security elements cover the withdrawal according to plan.

WITHDRAWAL

3-231. The raid force commander designs withdrawal to achieve maximum deception against the enemy and minimum danger to the raid force. The various elements of the raid force withdraw on order, or at a prearranged time, but never the same way twice. The movement uses many doglegs over the previously reconnoitered routes to the base camp through a series of RPs. Should the enemy organize a close pursuit of the assault element, the security element (covering force) assists by fire and movement, harassing the enemy and slowing it down. Other elements of the raid force do not attempt to reach the initial rallying point (IRP) but, on their own initiative, lead the enemy away and attempt to lose them by evasive action in difficult terrain.

3-232. The raid force commander issues specific instructions concerning contingencies. The commander decides which COA to follow based on time and distance to be traveled, firepower or fire support, and the raid force's physical condition. The raid force then attempts to reestablish contact with the main force at other RPs or continues to the base camp as separate groups IAW METT-TC.

BATTALION (LARGE) RAIDS

3-233. When a target is large and well guarded, a much larger raid force conducts the mission to ensure a successful attack. Large raids involve the use of a battalion-sized unit. Conduct is similar to that of smaller raids, but C2 becomes more difficult as the force increases in size.

MOVEMENT TO THE OBJECTIVE AREA

3-234. Surprise is a priority in all raids but is more difficult to achieve during battalion operations. The number of troops to assemble and deploy requires additional MSSs farther from the target to preserve secrecy. Also, the force requires a longer route to the attack position. A large raid force usually moves by small components over multiple routes to an MSS, then to the objective (Figure 3-13, page 3-57).

CONTROL

3-235. Units need extensive radio communications equipment to coordinate C2 operations in an active electronic warfare (EW) environment. Effective coordination is difficult to achieve. Raid planners use pyrotechnics, audible signals, or runners to coordinate action at designated times. Even under optimum conditions, massing of the raid force at the objective is extremely difficult to control. Lights, armbands, or scarves enhance control. During planning, the raid force commander considers the complexity of the plan and the possibility of overall failure if subordinate elements do not arrive on time. He plans for these possible contingencies to ensure mission success.

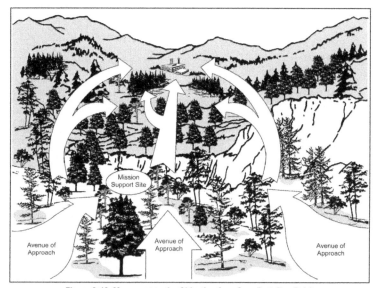

Figure 3-13. Movement to the Objective Area for a Battalion Raid

TRAINING

3-236. Executing a large raid requires a high degree of training and discipline. Extensive rehearsals help prepare the force for the mission. In particular, commanders and staffs learn how to use large numbers of troops as a cohesive and coordinated fighting force.

FIRE SUPPORT

3-237. Raids usually require additional fire support. In the JSOA, such support may mean secretly caching ammunition in MSSs over a long period before the raid. Each member of the raiding force carries an extra mortar round, recoilless rocket round, or a can of machine gun ammunition.

TIMING

3-238. Timing is both crucial and much more difficult for a large raid. The time of the raid takes on increased importance because of the large number of personnel involved. More time is required to coordinate and move units, and the main action element usually needs more time to do its mission. As a result, larger raids require larger security elements to isolate the objective for longer time periods. The element moves to the objective during limited visibility, but due to fire support coordination requirements and the large number of personnel, the mission begins during early daylight hours.

WITHDRAWAL

3-239. Elements usually best withdraw from a large raid in small groups, over multiple routes, to deceive the enemy and discourage enemy pursuit. Dispersed withdrawal also denies a priority target to enemy air and fire support elements. The raid force commander considers the possibility of an alert and aggressive enemy counterattacking the dispersed elements of the force. He carefully weighs all METT-TC factors before deciding how, when, and where he will conduct his withdrawal.

AMBUSHES

3-240. The ambush is a surprise attack from a concealed position upon a moving or temporarily halted target. It is one of the oldest and most effective types of guerrilla tactics. An ambush is executed to reduce the enemy's overall combat effectiveness by destroying or harassing his soldiers and their will to win. An ambush may include an assault to close with and decisively engage the target, or the attack may be by direct or indirect fire to harass the enemy.

NOTE: The following article was originally serialized in *Red Thrust Star*, dated July and October 1995 and October 1996.

Afghanistan is not Europe, yet the Soviet Army that occupied Afghanistan in late December 1979 was trained to fight NATO on the northern European plain. Consequently, the Soviet Army had to reequip, reform and retrain on-site to fight the insurgent *mujahideen* [holy warrior] guerrillas. The Soviets were forced to revise their tactics and tactical methodologies in order to meet the demands of this very different war. One of the tactical areas which the Soviets thoroughly revised was the conduct of ambushes. The Soviets planned to use ambushes in the European theater, but they were primarily ambushes against attacking or withdrawing NATO armored columns. The Soviets constructed most of their ambushes around tanks and tank units. They planned to employ concealed individual tanks, tank platoons and tank companies along high-speed avenues of approach or withdrawal to engage the enemy from the flank and then to depart. Such ambushes were part of security zone defensive planning as well as planning for the deep battle and pursuit. The Soviets also trained their squad and platoon-sized reconnaissance elements to conduct dismounted ambushes to capture prisoners and documents. They employed a command element, a snatch group and a fire support group in these small-scale ambushes.

In Afghanistan, the *mujahideen* seldom used armored vehicles and seldom advanced along high-speed avenues of approach. Instead, they infiltrated light-infantry forces through some of the most inhospitable terrain on the planet to mass for an attack or ambush. The Soviets soon discovered that they had difficulty maintaining control of the limited road network, which constituted the Soviet lines of communication. The guerrillas constantly cut the roads and ambushed convoys carrying material from the Soviet Union to the base camps and cities in Afghanistan. The Soviet ability to maintain its presence in the country depended on its ability to keep the roads open and much of the Soviet combat was a fight for control of the road network. During the war, the guerrillas destroyed over 11,000 Soviet trucks (and reportedly even more Afghan trucks) through ambush. The Soviets learned from *mujahideen* ambushes and used the ambush to interdict the guerrilla supplies coming from Pakistan and Iran. The Soviets conducted ambushes mainly with reconnaissance and other special troops (airborne, air assault, spetsnaz and elements from the two separate motorized rifle brigades which were designed as counter-guerrilla forces). The composition and employment of ambush forces differed with the units involved and the part of Afghanistan in which they were employed.

DESTRUCTION

3-241. Destruction is the primary purpose of an ambush. The number of men killed, wounded, or captured and loss of equipment and supplies critically affect the enemy. Guerrillas benefit from the capture of equipment and supplies through battlefield recovery.

HARASSMENT

3-242. Frequent ambushes harass the enemy and force him to divert men from patrol operations to guard convoys, troop movements, and installations. When enemy patrols fail to accomplish their missions because they are ambushed, the enemy is deprived of the valuable contributions these patrols make to its combat effort. A series of successful guerrilla ambushes cause the enemy to be less aggressive and more defensive-minded. The enemy becomes apprehensive and overly cautious and reluctant to go on patrols, to move in convoys, or to move in small groups. The enemy wants to avoid night operations, is more subject to confusion and panic if ambushed, and is mentally defeated.

ELEMENT OF SURPRISE

3-243. Surprise allows the ambush force to seize control of any situation. The force achieves surprise by carefully planning, preparing, and executing the ambush. Guerrillas attack the targets when, where, and in a manner for which the enemy is least prepared.

COORDINATED FIRES

3-244. The ambush force commander positions and coordinates the use of all weapons, mines, and demolitions. He coordinates all fires, including artillery and mortars when available. Coordinated fire support ensures isolation of the kill zone. This isolation prevents enemy escape or reinforcement due to the large volume of accurate, concentrated fire.

CONTROL MEASURES

3-245. The ambush force commander maintains close control measures during the ambush operation. These control measures include provisions for—

- Early warning signals of target approach.
- Withholding fire until the target has moved into the killing zone.
- Opening, shifting, and halting fire at the proper time.
- Initiating proper actions if the ambush is prematurely detected.
- Timely and orderly withdrawal to a recognized RP.

CATEGORIES OF AMBUSHES

3-246. Ambushes have two general categories: point and area. A point ambush, whether independent or part of an area ambush, positions itself along the target's expected route of approach. It attacks a single kill zone. When there is not sufficient intelligence for a point ambush, the commander establishes an area ambush. An area ambush uses multiple point ambushes around a central kill zone.

3-247. These two variations succeed best in situations where routes of approach by relieving or reinforcing units are limited to those favorable for ambush by the guerrillas. Both variations were used extensively by the North Vietnamese guerrilla forces in Vietnam against U.S. forces in the Republic of Vietnam.

POINT AMBUSH

3-248. A point ambush, whether independent or part of an area ambush, is positioned along the target's expected route of approach. Formation is important because, to a great extent, it determines whether a point ambush can deliver the heavy volume of highly concentrated fire necessary to isolate, trap, and destroy the target.

3-249. The formation to be used is determined by carefully considering possible formations and the advantages and disadvantages of each in relation to terrain, conditions of visibility, forces, weapons and equipment, ease or difficulty of control, target to be attacked, and overall combat situation.

3-250. The following paragraphs discuss a few formations that have been developed for the deployment of point ambushes. Those discussed are named according to the general pattern formed on the ground by the deployment of the attack element.

Line Formation

3-251. The attack element is deployed generally parallel to the target's route of movement (road, trail, stream). This deployment positions the attack element parallel to the long axis of the killing zone and subjects the target to heavy flanking fire. The size of the target, which can be trapped in the killing zone, is limited by the area the attack element can effectively cover with a heavy volume of highly concentrated fire. The target is trapped in the killing zone by natural obstacles, mines (claymore, antivehicular, antipersonnel), demolitions, and direct and indirect fires (Figure 3-14, page 3-61). A disadvantage of the line formation is the chance that lateral dispersion of the target may be too great for effective coverage. Line formation is appropriate in close terrain that restricts target maneuver and in open terrain where one flank is restricted by mines, demolitions, mantraps, or sharpened stakes. Similar obstacles can be placed between the attack element and the killing zone to provide protection from the target's counterambush measures. When a destruction ambush is deployed in this manner, access lanes are left so that the target can be assaulted (Figure 3-15, page 3-62). The line formation can be effectively used by a rise from the ground ambush in terrain seemingly unsuitable for ambush. An advantage of the line formation is its relative ease of control under all conditions of visibility.

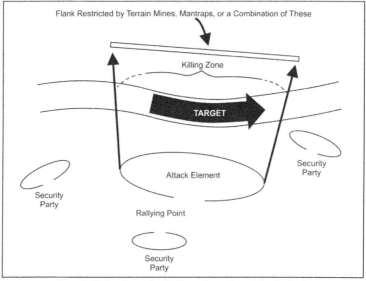

Figure 3-14. Line Formation for Harassing or Destruction Ambush

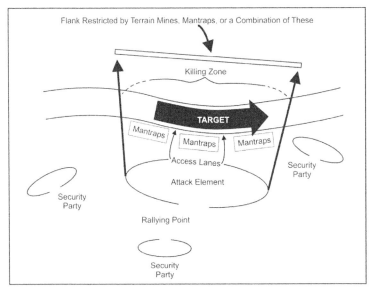

Figure 3-15. Line Formation for Destruction Ambush

L Formation

3-252. The L-shaped formation is a variation of the line formation. The long side of the attack element is parallel to the killing zone and delivers flanking fire. The short side is at the end of and at right angles to the killing zone and delivers enfilading fire that links with fire from the other leg. This formation is very flexible. It can be established on a straight stretch of a trail or stream (Figure 3-16, page 3-63), or a sharp bend in a trail or stream (Figure 3-17, page 3-63). When appropriate, fire from the short leg can be shifted to parallel the long leg if the target tries to assault or escape in the opposite direction. In addition, the short leg prevents escape in the direction of attack element and reinforcement from its direction (Figure 3-18, page 3-64).

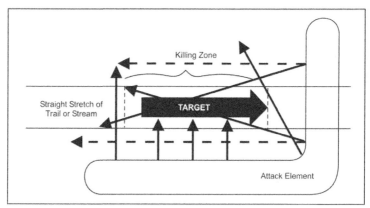

Figure 3-16. L Formation for Destruction Ambush

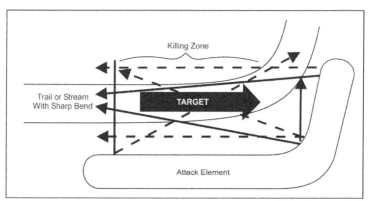

Figure 3-17. L Formation for Destruction Ambush on Bend of Trail or Stream

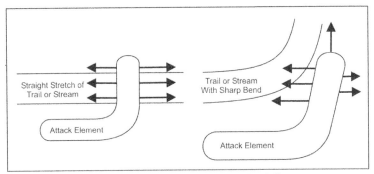

**Figure 3-18. L Formation Where Short Leg of Attack Element
Prevents Escape or Reinforcement**

Z Formation

3-253. The Z-shaped formation is another variation of the line formation. The attack force is deployed as in the L formation, but with an additional side so that the formation resembles the letter Z. The additional side (Figure 3-19, page 3-65) may serve to—

- Engage a force attempting to relieve or reinforce the target.
- Seal the end of the killing zone.
- Restrict a flank.
- Prevent envelopment.

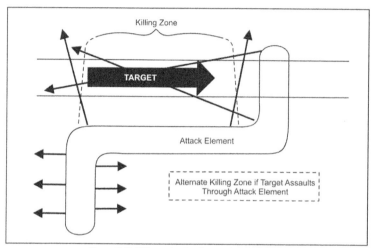

Figure 3-19. Z Formation for Destruction Ambush

T Formation

3-254. In the T-shaped formation, the attack element is deployed across and at right angles to the target's route of movement so that it and the target form the letter T. This formation can be used day or night to establish a purely harassing ambush and at night to establish an ambush to interdict movement through open, hard-to-seal areas (such as rice paddies).

3-255. A small group of persons can use the T formation to harass, slow, and disorganize a larger force. When the lead elements of the target are engaged, they will normally attempt to maneuver right or left to close with the ambush. Mines, mantraps, and other obstacles placed to the flanks of the killing zone slow the enemy's movements and permit the ambush patrol to deliver heavy fire and withdraw without becoming decisively engaged (Figure 3-20, page 3-66).

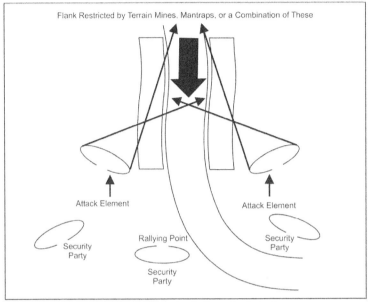

Figure 3-20. T Formation for Harassing Ambush

3-256. The attack element can also use the T formation to interdict small groups attempting night movement across open areas. For example, the attack element is deployed along a rice paddy dike with every second person facing in the opposite direction. The attack of a target approaching from either direction requires only that every second person shift to the opposite side of the dike. Each person fires only to his front and only when the target is at very close range. Attack is by fire only and each person keeps the target under fire as long as it remains on his front. If the target attempts to escape in either direction along the dike, each man takes it under fire as it comes to his vicinity. The T formation is very effective at halting infiltration. But it has one chief disadvantage: while spread out, the ambush may engage a superior force. Use of this formation must, therefore, fit the local enemy situation (Figure 3-21, page 3-67).

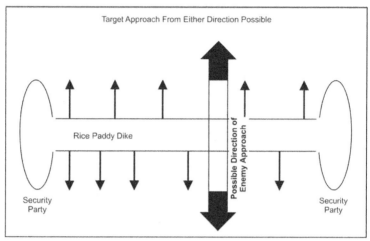

Figure 3-21. T Formation for Harassing Ambush in Rice Paddy

V Formation

3·257. The V·shaped attack element is deployed along both sides of the target's route of movement so that it forms the letter V; care is taken to ensure that neither group (nor leg) fires into the other. This formation subjects the target to both enfilading and interlocking fire. The V formation is best suited for fairly open terrain but can also be used in the jungle. When established in the jungle, the legs of the V close in as the head elements of the target approach the apex of the V; the attack element then opens fire from close range. Here, even more than in open terrain, all movement and fire must be carefully coordinated and controlled to ensure that the fire of one leg does not endanger the other. The wider separation of elements makes this formation difficult to control, and there are fewer sites that favor its use. Its main advantage is that it is difficult for the target to detect the ambush until it has moved well into the killing zone (Figures 3·22, page 3·68, and 3·23, page 3·69).

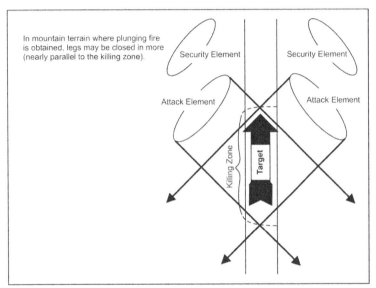

In mountain terrain where plunging fire is obtained, legs may be closed in more (nearly parallel to the killing zone).

Security Element

Security Element

Attack Element

Attack Element

Killing Zone

Target

Figure 3-22. V Formation for Open Mountain Terrain

Triangle Formation

3-258. This formation is a variation of the V and can be used in three different ways. One way is the closed triangle (Figure 3-24, page 3-69). in which the attack element is deployed in three groups or parties, positioned so that they form a triangle (or closed V). An automatic weapon is placed at each point of the triangle and positioned so that it can be shifted quickly to interlock with either of the others. Men are positioned so that their fields of fire overlap. Mortars may be positioned inside the triangle. When deployed in this manner, the triangle ambush becomes a small unit strongpoint. It is used to interdict night movement through rice paddies and other open areas when target approach is likely to be from any direction. The formation provides all-around security, and security parties are deployed only when they can be positioned so that if detected by an approaching target, they will not compromise the ambush. Attack is by fire only, and the target is allowed to approach within close range before fire is opened.

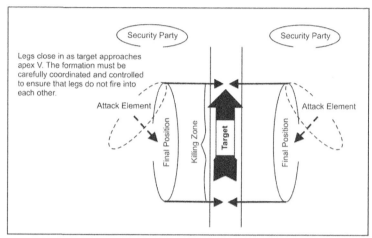

Figure 3-23. V Formation for Jungle Terrain

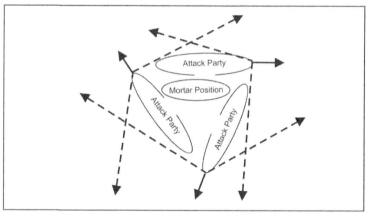

Figure 3-24. Closed Triangle Formation for Night Harassing Ambush

3-259. Advantages of the triangle formation include ease of control and all-around security. In addition, a target approaching from any direction can be brought under fire of at least two automatic weapons.

3-260. There are several disadvantages. For example, an ambush patrol-sized or larger is required to reduce the danger of being overrun by an unexpectedly large target. One or more legs of the triangle may come under enfilade fire. Lack of dispersion, particularly at the points, increases danger from enemy mortar fire.

3-261. The open triangle (during a harassing ambush) is designed to enable a small force to harass, slow, and inflict heavy casualties upon a larger force without itself being decisively engaged. The attack element is deployed in three parties, positioned so that each party becomes a corner of a triangle containing the killing zone. When the target enters the killing zone, the party to the target's front opens fire on the leading element. When the target counterattacks, the group withdraws and an assault party to the flank opens fire. When this party is attacked, the party opposite flank opens fire. This process is repeated until the target is pulled apart. Each party reoccupies its position, if possible, and continues to inflict the maximum damage possible without becoming decisively engaged (Figure 3-25, page 3-71).

3-262. In an open triangle (during a destruction ambush), the attack element is again deployed in three parties, positioned so that each party is a point of the triangle, 200 to 300 meters apart. The killing zone is the area within the triangle. The target is allowed to enter the killing zone; the nearest party attacks by fire. As the target attempts to maneuver or withdraw, the other groups open fire. One or more assault parties, as directed, assault or maneuver to envelop or destroy the target (Figure 3-25, page 3-71). As a destruction ambush, this formation is suitable for platoon-sized or larger forces. A unit smaller than a platoon would be in too great a danger of being overrun.

3-263. The following are more disadvantages of the triangle:

- In assaulting or maneuvering, control is very difficult. Very close coordination and control are necessary to ensure that assaulting or maneuvering assault parties are not fired on by another party.
- The ambush site must be a fairly level, open area that provides (around its border) concealment for the ambush patrol (unless it is a rise from the ground ambush).

Box Formation

3-264. This formation is similar in purpose to the open triangle ambush. The attack element is deployed in four parties, positioned so that each party becomes a corner of a square or rectangle containing the killing zone (Figure 3-26, page 3-72). The box formation can be used as a harassing or destruction ambush in the same manner as the two variations of the open triangle ambush.

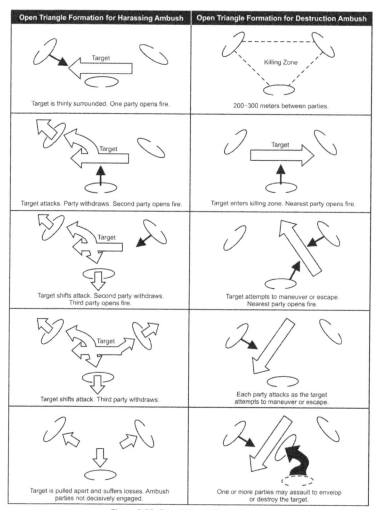

Open Triangle Formation for Harassing Ambush	Open Triangle Formation for Destruction Ambush
Target is thinly surrounded. One party opens fire.	200–300 meters between parties.
Target attacks. Party withdraws. Second party opens fire.	Target enters killing zone. Nearest party opens fire.
Target shifts attack. Second party withdraws. Third party opens fire.	Target attempts to maneuver or escape. Nearest party opens fire.
Target shifts attack. Third party withdraws.	Each party attacks as the target attempts to maneuver or escape.
Target is pulled apart and suffers losses. Ambush parties not decisively engaged.	One or more parties may assault to envelop or destroy the target.

Figure 3-25. Open Triangle Formation

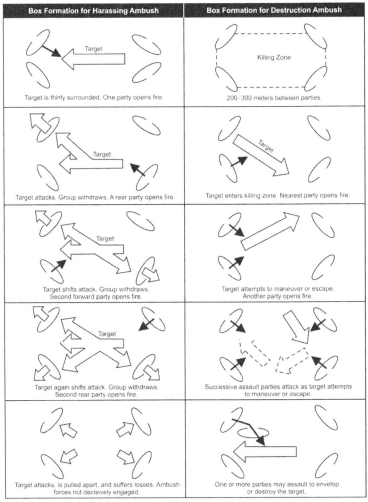

Box Formation for Harassing Ambush	Box Formation for Destruction Ambush
Target is thinly surrounded. One party opens fire.	200–300 meters between parties.
Target attacks. Group withdraws. A rear party opens fire.	Target enters killing zone. Nearest party opens fire.
Target shifts attack. Group withdraws. Second forward party opens fire.	Target attempts to maneuver or escape. Another party opens fire.
Target again shifts attack. Group withdraws. Second rear party opens fire.	Successive assault parties attack as target attempts to maneuver or escape.
Target attacks, is pulled apart, and suffers losses. Ambush forces not decisively engaged.	One or more parties may assault to envelop or destroy the target.

Figure 3-26. Box Formation

AREA AMBUSH

3-265. The origin of the type of ambush now called area ambush is not known. Hannibal used the area ambush against the Romans in the second century B.C. More recently, it was modified and perfected by the British Army in Malaya and, with several variations, used in Vietnam. The British found that point ambushes often failed to produce heavy casualties. When ambushed, the Communist guerrillas would immediately break contact and disperse along escape routes leading away from the killing zone. The British counteracted this tactic by blocking escape routes leading away from the killing zone with point ambushes. They called these multiple-related point ambushes the area ambush.

British Version

3-266. The British Army version of the area ambush involves a point ambush that is established at a site having several trails or other escape routes leading away from it. The site may be a water hole, an enemy campsite, a known rendezvous point, or along a frequently traveled trail. This site is the central killing zone. Point ambushes are established along the trails or other escape routes leading away from the central killing zone.

3-267. The target, whether a single group or several groups approaching from different directions, is permitted to move to the central killing zone. Outlying ambushes do not attack unless discovered. The ambush is initiated when the target moves into the central killing zone. When the target breaks contact and attempts to disperse, escaping portions are intercepted and destroyed by the outlying ambushes. The multiple contacts achieve increased casualties, harassment, and confusion (Figure 3-27, page 3-74).

3-268. The British Army version of the area ambush is best suited to counterguerrilla operations in terrain where movement is largely restricted to trails. It produces the best results when it is established as a deliberate ambush.

3-269. When there is not sufficient intelligence for a deliberate ambush, an area ambush of opportunity may be established. The outlying ambushes are permitted to attack targets approaching the central killing zone, if within their capability. If too large for the particular outlying ambush, the target is allowed to continue and is attacked in the central killing zone.

Baited Trap Version

3-270. A variation of the area ambush is the baited trap version (Figure 3-28, page 3-74), where a central killing zone is established along the target's route of approach. Point ambushes are established along the routes over which relieving or reinforcing units will have to approach. The target in the central killing zone serves as bait to lure relieving or reinforcing units into the killing zones of the outlying ambushes. The outlying point ambushes need not be strong enough to destroy their targets. They may be small, harassing ambushes that delay, disorganize, and eat away the target by successive contacts.

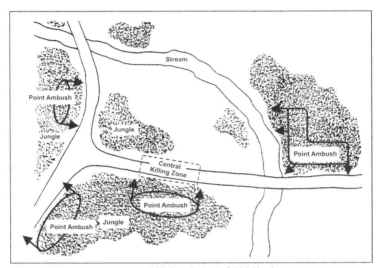

Figure 3-27. Area Ambush, British Version

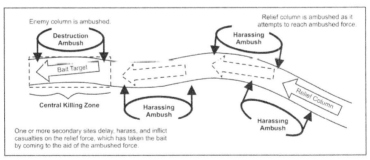

Figure 3-28. Area Ambush, Baited Trap Version

3-271. This version can be varied by using a fixed installation as bait to lure relieving or reinforcing units into the killing zone of one or more of the outlying ambushes. The installation replaces the central killing zone and is attacked. The attack may intend to overcome the installation or may be only a ruse.

3-272. These two variations are best suited for situations where routes of approach for relieving or reinforcing units are limited to those favorable for ambush. They are also best suited for use by guerrilla forces, rather than counterguerrilla forces. Communist guerrilla forces in Vietnam used both variations extensively.

UNUSUAL AMBUSH TECHNIQUES

3-273. The ambush techniques described above are so well known and widely used that they are considered standard. Other, less well known, less frequently used techniques are considered unusual. Two such techniques are described below.

Rise From the Ground Ambush

3-274. The attack element uses this type of ambush (Figure 3-29, page 3-76) in open areas that lack the good cover and concealment and other features normally desirable in a good ambush site. The attack element is deployed in the formation best suited to the overall situation. It is completely concealed in the spider-hole type of covered foxhole. Soil is carefully removed and positions expertly camouflaged.

3-275. When the ambush begins, the attack element throws back the covers and literally rises from the ground to attack. This ambush takes advantage of the tendency of patrols and other units to relax in areas that do not appear to favor ambush. The chief disadvantage is that the ambush patrol is very vulnerable if prematurely detected.

Demolition Ambush

3-276. Electrically detonated mines or demolition charges, or both, are positioned in an area (Figure 3-30, page 3-77) over which a target is expected to pass. This area may be a portion of a road or a trail, an open field, or any location that can be observed from a distance. Activating wires are run to a concealed observation point, which is sufficiently distant to ensure safety of the ambushers.

3-277. As large a force as desired or necessary can be used to mine the area. Two men remain to begin the ambush; others return to the unit. When a target enters the mined area (killing zone), the two men remaining detonate the explosives and withdraw immediately to avoid detection and pursuit.

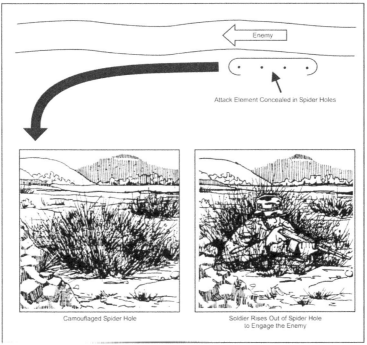

Figure 3-29. Unusual Techniques, Rise From the Ground Ambush

SPECIAL AMBUSH SITUATIONS

3-278. The following techniques are not considered standard ambush scenarios and therefore require special considerations.

Columns Protected by Armor

3-279. Attacks against columns protected by armored vehicles depend on the type and location of armored vehicles in a column and the weapons of the ambush patrol. If possible, armored vehicles are destroyed or disabled by fire of antitank weapons, landmines, Molotov cocktails, or by throwing hand grenades into open hatches. An effort is made to immobilize armored vehicles at a point where they are unable to give protection to the rest of the convoy and where they will block the route of other supporting vehicles.

Figure 3-30. Unusual Techniques, Demolition Ambush

Ambush of Trains

3-280. Moving trains may be subjected to harassing fire, but the most effective ambush is derailment. Train derailment is desirable because the wreckage remains on the tracks and delays traffic for long periods of time. Derailment on a grade, at a sharp curve, or on a high bridge will cause most of the cars to overturn and result in extensive casualties among the passengers. Fire is directed on the exits of overturned coaches, and designated parties, armed with automatic weapons, rush forward to assault coaches or cars still standing. Other parties take supplies from freight yards and then set fire to the train. Rails are removed from the track at some distance from the ambush site in each direction to delay the arrival of reinforcements by train. In planning the ambush of a train, soldiers must remember that the enemy may include armored railroad cars in the train for its protection and that important trains may be preceded by advance guard locomotives or inspection cars to check the track.

Ambush of Waterway Traffic

3-281. Waterway traffic, such as barges or ships, may be ambushed similar to a vehicular column. The ambush patrol may be able to mine the waterway and thus stop traffic. If mining is not feasible, fire delivered by recoilless weapons can damage or sink the craft. Fire should be directed at engine room spaces, the waterline, and the bridge. Recovery of supplies may be possible if the craft is beached on the banks of the waterway or grounded in shallow water.

AMBUSH PATROLS

3-282. An ambush patrol is a combat patrol whose mission is to—

- Harass a target.
- Destroy a target.
- Capture personnel or equipment.
- Execute any combination of these.

3-283. An ambush patrol is planned and prepared in the same general manner as other patrols; that is, by using patrol steps (troop leading procedures). Each step is explained below.

Planning and Preparation

3-284. Planners must first consider whether the ambush is to be a deliberate ambush or an ambush of opportunity. In a deliberate ambush, the greater amount of target intelligence available permits planning for every COA at the target. Plans for an ambush of opportunity must include consideration of the types of targets that may be ambushed, as well as varying situations. In both, plans must be flexible enough to allow modification, as appropriate, at the ambush site. When planning, the principles discussed below apply. All plans must be rehearsed in detail.

3-285. **Simplicity.** Every person must thoroughly understand what he is to do at every stage of the operation. In ambush more so than in other operations, failure of even one person to perform exactly as planned can cause failure.

3-286. **Type of Ambush** (point or area). Many factors affect the types of ambush. They include organization, the number of men required, the equipment and communications required, and all other aspects of the patrol.

3-287. **Deployment.** Each possible formation must be considered for its advantages and disadvantages.

3-288. **Manner of Attack.** An attack may be by fire only (harassing only) or may include an assault of the target (destruction ambush).

3-289. **Size of Ambush Patrol.** The patrol is tailored for its mission. Two men may be adequate for a harassing ambush. A destruction ambush may require the entire unit (squad, platoon, company).

3-290. **Organization.** An ambush patrol is organized in the same manner as other combat patrols to include a patrol HQ, an assault element, a support element, and a security element (Figure 3-31, page 3-79). The assault and support elements are the attack force; the security element is the security force. When appropriate, the attack force is further organized to provide a reserve force. When an ambush site is to be occupied for an extended period, double ambush patrols may be organized. One ambush patrol occupies the site while the other rests, eats, and tends to personal needs at the ORP or other concealed location. They alternate each 8 hours. If the waiting period is more than 24 hours, three ambush patrols are organized (Figure 3-32, page 3-79).

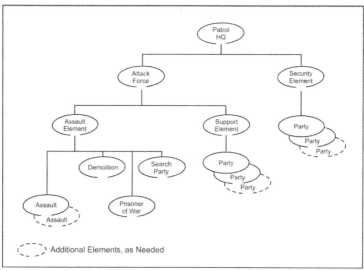

Figure 3-31. Organization of Ambush Patrols, Example 1

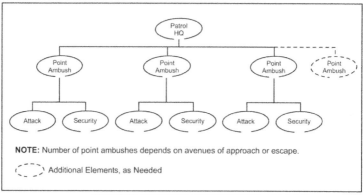

Figure 3-32. Organization of Ambush Patrols, Example 2

3-291. **Equipment.** The selection of accompanying equipment and supplies is based on the—

- Mission.
- Enemy threat.
- Size of the resistance force.
- Means of transportation.
- Distance and terrain.
- Weight and bulk of equipment.

3-292. **Routes.** A primary route is planned that will allow the patrol to enter the ambush site from the rear. The killing zone is not entered if entry can be avoided. If the killing zone must be entered to place mines or explosives, great care must be taken to remove any tracks and signs that might alert the target and compromise the ambush. If mines, mantraps, or explosives are to be placed on the far side, or if the appearance of the site from the target's viewpoint is to be checked, a wide detour around the killing zone is made. Here, too, great care must be taken to remove any traces that might reveal the ambush. An alternate route from the ambush site is planned, as in other patrols.

3-293. **Site.** Maps and aerial photographs are used to analyze the terrain. When possible, the patrol makes an on-the-ground reconnaissance. Against an experienced enemy, so-called ideal ambush sites should be avoided. An alert enemy is suspicious of these areas, avoids them if possible, and increases vigilance and security when they must be entered. Surprise is even more difficult to achieve in these areas. Instead, unlikely sites are chosen that offer—

- Favorable fields of fire.
- Occupation and preparation of concealed positions.
- Channelization of the target into the killing zone.
- Covered routes of withdrawal to enable the ambush patrol to break contact and avoid pursuit by effective fire.

3-294. **Occupation of the Site.** As a general rule, the ambush patrol occupies the ambush site at the latest possible time permitted by the tactical situation and by the amount of time required to perform site preparation required. This not only reduces the risk of discovery but also reduces the time men must remain still and quiet in position.

3-295. **Positions.** The patrol moves into the ambush site from the rear as discussed earlier. Security elements are positioned first to prevent surprise while the ambush is being established. Automatic weapons are then positioned so that each can fire along the entire killing zone. If this is not possible, they are given overlapping sectors of fire so that the entire killing zone is covered. The patrol leader then selects his position, located where he can tell when to begin the ambush. Riflemen and grenadiers are then placed to cover any dead space left by automatic weapons. All weapons are assigned sectors of fire to provide mutual support. The patrol leader sets the position preparation time. The degree of preparation depends on the time allowed. All men work at top speed during the allotted time.

3-296. **Camouflage.** Camouflage is of utmost importance. Each man must be hidden from the target. During preparation for the patrol, each man camouflages himself and his equipment and secures his equipment to prevent noise. At the ambush site, positions are prepared with minimum change in the natural appearance of the site. All debris resulting from preparation of positions is concealed.

Execution

3-297. Effective C2 are essential to mission success. The patrol leader establishes the communications plan and control measures for execution. As the patrol leader makes contact, communications stand a good chance of breaking down. He must plan using the primary, alternate, contingency, and emergency (PACE) method. Rehearsals are conducted to ensure everyone knows and understands the following crucial points.

3-298. **Signals.** Three signals, often four, are needed to execute the ambush. Audible and visual signals, such as whistles and pyrotechnics, must be changed often to avoid establishing patterns. Too frequently, use of the same signals may result in their becoming known to the enemy. A target might recognize a signal and be able to react in time to avoid the full effects of the ambush. For example, if a white star cluster is habitually used to signal withdrawal in a night ambush, an alert enemy may fire one and cause premature withdrawal.

3-299. A signal by the security force to alert the patrol leader to the target's approach may be given by—

- Arm and hand signals.
- Radio (as a quiet voice message), by transmitting a prearranged number of taps, or by signaling with the push-to-talk switch.
- Field telephone, when there is no danger that wire between positions will compromise the ambush.

3-300. A signal to begin the ambush, given by the patrol leader or a designated individual, may be a shot or the detonation of mines or explosives. A signal for lifting or shifting fires, if the target is to be assaulted, may be given by voice command, whistles, or pyrotechnics. All fire must stop immediately so that the assault can be made before the target can react. A signal for withdrawal may also be by voice command, whistles, or pyrotechnics.

3-301. **Fire Discipline.** This is a key part of the ambush. Fire must be withheld until the signal is given, then immediately delivered in the heaviest, most accurate volume possible. Properly timed and delivered fires achieve surprise as well as destruction of the target. When the target is to be assaulted, the lifting or shifting of fires must be equally precise. Otherwise, the assault is delayed and the target has opportunity to recover and react.

3-302. **Withdrawal to the ORP.** The ORP is located far enough from the ambush site that it will not be overrun if the target attacks the ambush.

Routes of withdrawal to the ORP are reconnoitered. Situation permitting, each person walks the route he is to use and picks out checkpoints. When the ambush is executed at night, each person must be able to follow his route in the dark.

3-303. On signal, the patrol quickly but quietly withdraws to the ORP, reorganizes, and begins its return march. If the ambush was not successful and the patrol is pursued, withdrawal may be by bounds. The last group may arm mines, previously placed along the withdrawal route, to further delay pursuit.

3-304. Contingency plans should include removal of the wounded, both friendly and hostile, under pursuit or at a more measured pace. Treatment location and moves from the target site to a rearward position must be flexible. Plans should also include insertion of medical assets within the assault element, as well as within the HQ. Security and support elements should be considered, depending on the mission.

MINES AND BOOBY TRAPS

3-305. Resistance forces may employ both mines and booby traps to enhance their combat operations. In areas occupied and protected by the enemy, the resistance should employ mines to impede, delay, and disrupt traffic using roads and trails. These actions cause the enemy to divert valuable forces to guard and clear those routes. The personnel and equipment patrolling the roads to detect and remove mines are prime targets for guerrilla mines and snipers. In congested areas where the enemy conducts offensive operations or patrol activities, the guerrillas should employ mines and mechanical booby traps. The mines and booby traps will inflict casualties, delay and channelize movement, and damage or destroy equipment. Mines should be deployed to reduce accidental injury of noncombatants. The resistance makes and uses military homemade mines. Most guerrilla mines are handmade, using duds, discarded ammunition, and materials thrown away by the enemy. Materials discarded as trash, such as improperly destroyed rations, ammunition, beer and soda cans, batteries, waterproof packing materials, and ammunition bandoleers, provide the resistance a valuable source of supply for mining and booby trap operations. FMs 5-34 and 20-32 contain more information on mines.

SNIPER OPERATIONS

3-306. Sniping as an interdiction technique has a very demoralizing effect on the enemy. Well-trained and properly used snipers can inflict many casualties. They can hinder or temporarily deny the use of certain routes or areas. Snipers also cause the enemy to use a disproportionate number of troops to clear and secure the area. They must have mission orders outlining priority targets to include key threat personnel. Snipers may cover an area that has been mined to prevent removal or breaching of the minefield. Snipers may be part of a raid or ambush to stop threat personnel from escaping the area under attack. They may also prevent or impede the enemy from reinforcing the objective. Besides their sniping mission, they may collect information for the area command or sector commands. All tactical plans can incorporate sniper missions. Provisions must be made for the sniper's rest and recuperation after continuous operations to prevent fatigue. FM 3-05.222 provides more information on sniper operations.

MAN-PORTABLE AIR DEFENSE SYSTEMS

3-307. The most recent and large-scale UW operation occurred in Afghanistan between the Soviet Union and the Afghanistan freedom fighter (Mujahideen). They were a formidable guerrilla force against Soviet airborne, air assault, Spetsnaz, and ground forces. Initially, the U.S. Army supplied the Mujahideen with Redeye missiles in the early 1980s but soon followed with improved man-portable air defense systems (MANPADS), the Stinger. With the new system the warhead did not have to get a direct hit; hitting close would cause an explosion.

3-308. The premier Soviet helicopter (HIND-D) has a dual-role capability as an air assault vehicle and a gunship platform. This helicopter was quickly rendered out of action with a well-placed hit on the transmission. The Stinger team easily found and exploited this weakness by aiming at and hitting the large red star behind the cockpit. The Soviets had to alter some of their basic tactical doctrine—use of vehicle-equipped ground forces in conjunction with either a helicopter (HELO) assault or gun run on suspected Mujahideen targets.

3-309. Using MANPADS in a UW role can have a significant tactical and operational impact. MANPADS are relatively new U.S. weapons, light and very mobile. They can be concealed easily for movement or cached for future operations. Most are relatively simple to operate. Guerrillas can quickly learn how to use them, as demonstrated very effectively in Afghanistan. They require little maintenance because the missile is self-contained. Personnel can use these systems in various ways, from the traditional defensive coverage to offensive tactics. Included are aerial ambushes, direct action or attacks on specific targets, and harassment attacks meant either to produce a psychological impact or to change enemy tactics. The degradation of the enemy's close air support pays great dividends, both tactically and psychologically, for the guerrilla. FM 44-100, *U.S. Army Air and Missile Defense Operations,* provides additional information on air defense employment.

Considerations

3-310. There are four employment considerations for MANPADS: mass, mix, mobility, and integration. Each of these considerations is discussed in the following paragraphs.

3-311. **Mass.** Units achieve mass employment by allocating enough MANPADS to defend an asset. Soldiers move all the available MANPADS to the key assets or operations that need them.

3-312. **Mix.** Mix results from using different types of weapons; that is, MANPADS and other weapons that may be effective against aircraft. Air defense operations are more effective when the guerrillas use a mix of weapons. This mix of weapons prevents almost any aircraft from countering the weakness of a solitary system with overlapping and concentrated fire. Although a guerrilla force is not likely to use ZSU-23-4s, Vulcans, and Hawks to any large extent, it will more than likely have some of the following or similar weapons systems available:

- ZSU-23s.
- RPG-7s.
- DSHKs.
- M2 HB caliber .50 machine guns.
- Redeyes.
- Stingers.
- Light machine guns and assault rifles.

3-313. **Mobility.** The guerrilla force must be able to move on short notice. Air defense assets must also be able to displace quickly in a UW environment.

3-314. **Integration.** Massing all air defense weapons in a common, coordinated effort provides integration. Units can integrate MANPADS with other weapons for the best effect based on terrain, enemy aerial tactics, and desired effect of the air defense operation, using METT-TC. Air defense personnel may use Stingers to force enemy aircraft to fly at lower altitudes. At lower altitudes, personnel can shoot down the enemy using massed heavy machine guns, rocket-propelled grenades (RPGs), and Stingers.

Employment

3-315. Defensive and offensive uses of MANPADS provide for a balanced defense, overlapping fires, weighted coverage, mutual support, and early engagement. Each use of MANPADS is described below.

3-316. **Balanced Defense.** Critical guerrilla assets may be subject to enemy attack as targets of opportunity. Since the attack can come from any direction, it is desirable to have equal firepower in all directions. The best COA is a balanced defense because the terrain may not favor a most probable avenue of approach by the enemy.

3-317. **Overlapping Fires.** Teams should position MANPADS 2 to 3 kilometers apart, and one team should overlap another. Other types of weapons should be mixed in to complement the MANPADS. This overlapping prevents the MANPADS team from being overwhelmed by multiple aircraft and increases the chances of their successful air defense against any enemy aircraft.

3-318. **Weighted Coverage.** Teams can weight a defense in circumstances where the terrain restricts low-level attacks to only particular avenues of approach. They can also weight a defense when intelligence has established that air attacks will come from a particular direction. Balance may be sacrificed with a weighted defense since most air defense weapons would be positioned to cover the probable direction of approach. The weighted defense then becomes the best COA.

3-319. **Mutual Support.** Support from another MANPADS team allows one to fire into the dead space of the other. If the terrain or situation will not allow covering each other's dead space, teams should make use of similar weapons to cover these areas using Stingers or Redeye missiles.

3-320. **Early Engagement.** Teams should position MANPADS and other similar systems well forward of the guerrilla force's main body or key facilities. This early engagement provides the best opportunity to identify and fix the enemy aircraft before they can attack the guerrillas.

Technical and Tactical Requirements

3-321. In addition to the principles and guidelines previously discussed, there are certain technical and tactical requirements that need to be considered before employing MANPADS. Among the questions are—

- What type of aircraft, ordnance, and electronic countermeasures (ECM) has the threat been using in the area?
- What aerial tactics have the enemy pilots been using in the area?

Terrain and Weather

3-322. Mountains and hills may present terrain-masking problems for MANPADS. Whenever possible, MANPADS teams should position along the commanding heights to detect and engage enemy aircraft effectively. Weather can also adversely affect MANPADS that need an infrared source to lock on. In addition, poor weather conditions, such as snow, fog, or rain, can obscure the gunner's vision.

Routes of Approach

3-323. There are two general categories of routes of approach: probable and forced. A probable route of approach is the one the enemy is most likely to use but to which he is not restricted. A pilot of an aircraft traveling at 500 knots and 150 meters above the ground can see little detail on the ground. He can, however, see large objects (highways, rivers, and buildings) and use them as aids to navigation. If these landmarks lead to key assets, they may be considered a sign of probable approach. A forced route of approach is the one an aircraft will be forced to use and with no options. The forced route will be to the advantage of the guerrilla because he knows the terrain and where he can hide to best engage the aircraft.

Map Analysis and Planning

3-324. Terrain analysis is necessary to find good observation points, fields of fire, routes of approach, and any terrain that may inhibit the full capabilities of MANPADS. The ideal planning range for MANPADS is 3 to 5 kilometers from the target. This positioning greatly enhances their survivability by optimizing the lock-on range to enemy aircraft.

Position Selection

3-325. When selecting positions for MANPADS, personnel should consider observation and fields of fire, communication position, physical security, cover and concealment, alternate positions, and safety considerations.

Offensive Operations

3-326. Aerial ambushes are similar to the ground "baited trap" ambush (Figure 3-33). If the enemy is known to reinforce outposts or ground units with air support, personnel select a target for a ground attack just to draw an aerial response from the enemy. Personnel also select a target that causes a probable or forced avenue of approach for the reinforcing aircraft. The guerrilla MANPADS teams, together with other air defense assets, are positioned at key points along the aircraft's probable approach route. This pattern is very effective in mountainous terrain where valleys are the prime flight routes. An early warning post radios a timely, forewarning alert to prepare an ambush for the aircraft.

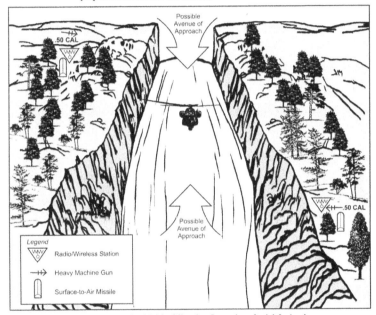

Figure 3-33. MANPADS in Offensive Operation, Aerial Ambush

Direct Action

3-327. Units may use MANPADS in a DA role to take out a specific type of aircraft or aircraft with key personnel. This operation is most effective when employed around airfields. An aircraft is very vulnerable when taking off and, to a lesser extent, when landing. The concept is to use at least two MANPADS against the target. Personnel locate firing positions on a curve, 3 to 5 kilometers from the runway, within range and observation of the probable flight path of the aircraft. Personnel must study carefully the flight patterns to confirm this critical information. If the distance to the airfield is kept to 3 kilometers, a centralized positioning can cover flight routes either approaching or departing the airfield. With longer ranges and longer airfields, the MANPADS team must confirm the aircraft approach and takeoff direction and position the MANPADS toward that end of the airfield. The actual employment will depend heavily on the type of MANPADS available and the terrain around the target. When in doubt, personnel should use METT-TC.

Harassment

3-328. The harassment campaign focuses on disrupting the operational procedures of the airport and aircrews. The intended results are to force the pilots to lower their flight altitudes, making them more vulnerable to guerrilla ground fire. Harassment also forces the enemy to decrease its air reconnaissance and support effort.

Defensive Operations

3-329. In addition to the principles and guidelines of MANPADS employment discussed previously, defense planners must take other considerations into account. Personnel must establish air defense priorities first. Developing a priority list is a matter of assessing each asset to be defended. Air defense priorities include criticality, vulnerability, and recuperability.

3-330. Despite the type of defense used, the same principles, guidelines, and air defense priorities still apply. Among the types are stationary point, moving point, integrated, and pre-positioned defenses.

3-331. **Stationary Point.** The key to a stationary point defense is early engagement so that the enemy force cannot destroy the target. If the target is large, such as a series of facilities or units concentrated in a relatively small area, personnel should use a "star"-type defense. This type of defense makes use of interlocking fields of fire, bunkers, trenches, and concertina and tanglefoot wire along with mines and machine guns. Each leg of the star has central and alternate control capability to defend the base camp.

3-332. **Moving Point.** In the past, units have used this defense to defend march columns. In a UW environment, personnel and supplies may have to move in march columns. These columns consist of vehicles, carts, pack animals, bicycles, and personnel traveling on foot. Personnel use MANPADS to defend the columns by integration or pre-positioning.

3-333. **Integration.** If personnel decide to integrate MANPADS into the march column, they should deploy them evenly along the length of the column. This pattern ensures other weapon systems are tied in to complement the overall air defense plan. When only one MANPADS team of two men is available, both men should only be gunners. A single MANPADS should be placed in the column where it can provide the best air cover.

3-334. **Pre-Positioning.** Personnel pre-position MANPADS to defend a march column as it passes a critical point along the route. This method is preferred for defending a march column. Personnel use it when the distance to be traveled by the march column is relatively short. They also use it when air defense is required at only a few locations along the route. The MANPADS teams may join and integrate with the column after it passes the critical point (Figure 3-34). The MANPADS teams may each receive orders, positioning themselves at a given location. They are then given engagement instructions for a specific window of time. This plan allows both for maintaining OPSEC and receiving air defense coverage. Pre-positioned teams should be used only if the route to be used is relatively secure from enemy patrols (METT-TC) or current guerrilla intelligence reports reflect enemy patrols are minimal.

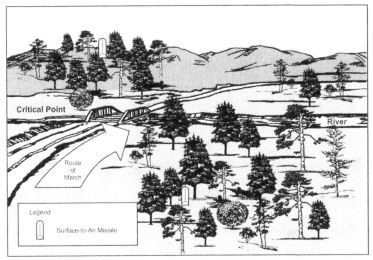

Figure 3-34. MANPADS Pre-Positioning at Critical Point Defending a March Column

SUPPORT AND SUSTAINMENT

3-335. UW missions cannot be accomplished without adequate support and sustainment. All units need food, clothing, water, medical, and personnel services sustainment. The types, quantity, and phasing of supplies influence the guerrillas, their capabilities and limitations, and the type of missions they undertake. Supplies and equipment made available to the guerrillas may influence their morale since each shipment represents encouragement and assurance of support from the outside world. Once a channel of supply is established, the guerrillas will continue to rely on that source for support. Appendix E and Appendix K provide additional information.

INDICATORS OF COUNTERGUERRILLA OPERATIONS

3-336. Tactical counterguerrilla operations are conducted to reduce the guerrilla threat or activity in the area. To effectively combat the enemy's counterguerrilla operations, soldiers must be familiar with the indicators of counterguerrilla operations, effective offensive and defensive tactics, and countertracking methods.

3-337. Security of the UW JSOA requires guerrilla intelligence measures to identify indications of impending counterguerrilla action, population control measures, and guerrilla reaction to enemy counterguerrilla actions. Some activities and conditions that may indicate impending enemy counterguerrilla actions are—

- Suitable weather.
- New enemy commander.
- Changes in battle situation elsewhere.
- Arrival of new enemy units with special training.
- Extension of enemy outposts, increased patrolling, and aerial reconnaissance.
- Increased enemy intelligence effort.
- Civilian pacification or control measures.
- Increased PSYOP against guerrillas.

3-338. Some measures that may be used to control the population of an area are—

- Mass registration.
- Curfews.
- Intensive propaganda.
- Compartmentation with cleared buffer zones.
- Informant nets.
- Party membership drives.
- Land and housing reform.
- Relocation of individuals, groups, and towns.
- Rationing of food and goods.

DEFENSIVE TACTICS

3-339. The existence or indication of counterguerrilla operations requires the SF and guerrilla force commanders to plan and use defensive tactics. Discussed below are some of the defensive tactics applicable against counterguerrilla operations.

Diversion Activities

3-340. A sudden increase in guerrilla activities or a shift of such activities to other areas assists in diverting enemy attention. For example, intensified operations against enemy LOCs and installations require the enemy to divert troops from counterguerrilla operations to security roles. Full use of underground and auxiliary capabilities assists in creating diversions.

Defense of Fixed Positions

3-341. The rules for a guerrilla defense of fixed positions are the same as those for conventional forces, except there are few supporting fires and counterattacks are generally not practicable. In conjunction with their position defense, elements of the guerrilla force conduct raids, ambushes, and attacks against the enemy's LOCs, flanks, reserve units, supporting arms, and installations. Routes of approach are mined and camouflaged snipers engage appropriate enemy targets. Diversionary actions by all elements of the resistance movement are increased in adjacent areas.

Delay and Harassment Activities

3-342. The objective of delay and harassment tactics is to make the attack so costly that the enemy eventually ends its operations. Defensive characteristics of the terrain are used to the maximum, mines and snipers are employed to harass the enemy, and ambushes are positioned to inflict maximum casualties and delay.

3-343. As the enemy overruns various strong points, the guerrilla force withdraws to successive defensive positions to again delay and harass. When the situation permits, the guerrilla force attacks the enemy's flanks, rear, and LOCs. If the enemy continues its offensive, the guerrilla forces should withdraw and leave the area. Under no circumstances should the guerrilla force become so engaged that it loses its freedom of action and permits enemy forces to encircle and destroy it.

Withdrawal

3-344. In preparing to meet enemy offensive action, the SF and guerrilla force commanders may decide to withdraw to another area not likely to be included in the enemy offensive. Key installations within a guerrilla base are moved to alternate bases, and essential records and supplies may be transferred to new locations. Less essential items will be destroyed or cached in dispersed locations. If the commander receives positive intelligence about the enemy's plans for a major counterguerrilla operation, he may decide to withdraw and leave his main base without delay.

3-345. When faced with an enemy offensive of overwhelming strength, the commander may disperse his force in either small units or as individuals to avoid destruction. This COA, however, renders the guerrilla force ineffective for an undetermined period of time and therefore should not be taken unless absolutely necessary.

COUNTERAMBUSH

3-346. The very nature of ambush—a surprise attack from a concealed position—places the ambushed unit at a disadvantage. Obviously, the best defense is to avoid being ambushed, but this is not always possible. A unit must, therefore, reduce its vulnerability to ambush and reduce the damage it will sustain if ambushed. These measures must be supplemented by measures to destroy or escape from an ambush. FM 7-8 contains more detailed information on ambush and counterambush procedures.

Reduction of Vulnerability to Ambush

3-347. No single defensive measure or combination of measures can prevent or effectively counter all ambushes in all situations. The effectiveness of counterambush measures is directly related to the state of training of the unit and the leadership ability of its leader.

3-348. In avoiding ambush, dismounted units have an advantage over mounted units. They are less bound to the more obvious routes of movement, such as roads and trails (as in armored units). However, dismounted units are at a disadvantage when—

- Terrain, such as heavy jungle, restricts or prohibits cross-country movement.
- The need for speed requires movement on roads, trails, or waterways.

Preparation for Movement

3-349. In preparing for movement, the leader must use METT-TC and OAKOC. In doing so, he studies maps of the area and if possible, makes an aerial reconnaissance.

Map Reconnaissance

3-350. In studying maps of the terrain over which the leader will move his unit, the leader first checks the map's marginal data to determine reliability at the time the map was made. If reliability is not good, or if the map is old, he evaluates its reliability in light of all other information he can obtain. For example, a 20-year-old map may not show several nearby roads and trails; more recent building development in the area will not be shown. The leader considers the terrain in relation to all available information of known or suspected enemy positions and previous ambush sites. His map study includes evaluation of the terrain from the enemy's viewpoint: How would the enemy use this terrain? Where could the enemy position troops, installations, and ambushes?

Aerial Reconnaissance

3-351. If possible, the leader makes an aerial reconnaissance. The information gained from the aerial reconnaissance enables him to compare the map and terrain. He also obtains current and more complete information on roads, trails, man-made objects, type and density of vegetation, and seasonal condition of streams. An aerial reconnaissance reveals—

- Movement or lack of movement in an area (friendly, enemy, civilian).

- Indications of enemy activity. Smoke may indicate locations of campsites, patrols, or patrol bases. Freshly dug soil may indicate positions or ambush sites. Shadows may aid in identifying objects. Unusual shapes, sizes, shadows, shades, or colors may indicate faulty camouflage.

3-352. Despite its many advantages, aerial reconnaissance has limitations. Some examples include the following:

- Strength of bridges cannot be determined.
- Terrain surface may be misinterpreted.
- Mines and booby traps cannot be seen.
- Presence of aircraft may warn enemy.

ROUTE SELECTION

3-353. The factors the leader considers are the same whether he is selecting a route or studying a route he has been directed to follow. Each factor is discussed below.

Cover and Concealment

3-354. Cover and concealment are desirable, but a route with these features may obstruct movement. Terrain that provides a moving unit cover and concealment also provides the enemy increased opportunities for ambush. Identification of areas where ambushes may be concealed allows the leader to develop plans for clearing these areas. How the terrain affects *observation* and *fields of fire* available to the unit and to the enemy will influence the selection of and movement over a route, formations, rates of movement, and methods of control.

Key Terrain

3-355. Key terrain is an earth feature that has a controlling effect on the surrounding terrain. It must be identified and actions planned accordingly. If, for example, a hill provides observation and fields of fire on any part of a route, the leader must plan for taking the hill from the enemy or avoiding it altogether.

Obstacles

3-356. Obstacles may impede movement or limit maneuver along a route. They may also limit enemy action.

Current Intelligence

3-357. All available information is considered. This includes but is not limited to—

- Known, suspected, and previous ambush sites.
- Weather and light data.
- Reports of units or patrols that have recently operated in the area.
- Size, location, activity, and capabilities of guerrilla forces in the area.

- Attitude of the civilian population and the extent to which they can be expected to cooperate or interfere.

Counterintelligence

3-358. In counterguerrilla operations, in particular, a key feature of preparing for movement is denying the enemy information. A unit is especially vulnerable to ambush if the enemy knows the unit is to move, what time it is to move, where it is to go, the route it is to follow, and the weapons and equipment it is to carry. The efforts made to deny or delay enemy acquisition of this information comprise the CI plan. As a minimum, the plan restricts dissemination of information.

3-359. The leader gives out mission information only on a need-to-know basis. This procedure is especially important when the native personnel operating with the unit might possibly be planted informers. Once critical information is given, personnel are isolated so that nothing can be passed out. If it is likely that the enemy or enemy informers will observe the departure of a unit, deception plans should be used.

Communications

3-360. The leader plans how he will communicate with elements of his unit; with artillery, air, or other supporting units; and with higher HQ. On an extended move, a radio relay or a field-expedient antenna may be necessary. An aircraft might be used to help communicate with air, artillery support, or other units on the ground.

Fire Support

3-361. The leader plans artillery and mortar fires so they will deceive, harass, or destroy the enemy. They may be planned as scheduled or on-call fires.

3-362. Fires are planned—

- On key terrain features along the route. These can serve as navigational aids or to deceive, harass, or destroy the enemy.
- On known enemy positions.
- On known or suspected ambush sites.
- On the flanks of identified danger areas.
- Wherever a diversion appears desirable. For example, if the unit must pass near an identified enemy position, artillery or mortar fires on the position may distract the enemy and permit the unit to pass undetected.
- At intervals along the route, every 500 to 1000 meters for example. With fires so planned, the unit is never far from a plotted concentration from which a shift can be quickly made.

3-363. Coordination with the supporting unit includes—

- Route to be followed.
- Scheduled and on-call fires.

- Call signs and frequencies.
- Checkpoints, phase lines, and other control measures.
- Times of departure and return.

INTELLIGENCE

3-364. The unit must provide its own intelligence support. Members must be alert to report information and leaders must be able to evaluate the significance of this information in relation to the situation.

3-365. Obvious items from which intelligence may be gained are—

- Signs of passage of groups, such as crushed grass, broken branches, footprints, cigarette butts, or trash. These may reveal identity, size, direction of travel, and time of passage.
- Workers in fields, which may indicate absence of the enemy.
- Apparently normal activities in villages, which may indicate absence of the enemy.

3-366. Less obvious items from which negative information can be gained are the absence of—

- Workers in fields, which may indicate presence of the enemy.
- Children in the village, which may indicate they are being protected from impending action.
- Young men in the village, which may indicate the enemy controls the village.

3-367. Knowledge of enemy signaling devices is very helpful. Those listed below are some that were used by communist guerrillas in Vietnam:

- A farm cart moving at night shows one lantern to indicate that no government troops are on the road or trail behind. Two lanterns mean that government troops are close behind.
- A worker in the field stops to put on or take off his shirt. Either act can signal the approach of government troops. This is relayed to the insurgency.
- A villager, fishing, holds his pole out straight to signal all clear and up at an angle to signal that troops are approaching.

SECURITY

3-368. Security is obtained through organization for movement, manner of movement, and by every man keeping alert at all times. Some examples of these security measures are as follows:

- A two-man patrol can maintain security by organizing into a security team with sectors of responsibility.
- A larger unit can use any standard formation (file, column, V) and establish a reaction force. This reaction force can be positioned to the front, rear, or flanks of the main body so that it does not come under direct contact. Any unit of squad or larger, regardless of the formation used, should have security forces to the front, flanks, and rear.

- A dismounted unit moves by the same methods as a motorized patrol. These methods include continuous movement and traveling, traveling overwatch, and bounding overwatch formations.

COUNTERTRACKING

3-369. To be more effective in combatting counterguerrilla operations, soldiers should be familiar with countertracking techniques. If the person tracking the soldier is not an experienced tracker, some of the following techniques may throw him off.

Moving From a Thick Area to an Open Area

3-370. While moving in any given direction from a thick area to a more open area, soldiers walk past a large (10-inch diameter or larger) tree toward the open vegetation for five paces and then walk backward to the front of the tree and change direction 90 degrees. Soldiers must step carefully and leave as little sign as possible. If this is not the direction the soldiers want to travel, they must change direction again at another large tree in the same manner. The purpose is to draw the trackers into the open area where it is harder to track. This technique may lead the trackers to search in the wrong area before realizing they have lost the track.

3-371. When soldiers are being tracked by trained, persistent enemy trackers (those the soldiers are unable to lose because the trackers keep hearing or seeing them), the soldiers' best COA is to outrun or outdistance the trackers or double back and ambush them, depending on their strength compared to that of the soldiers.

Crossing a Road

3-372. Soldiers approach a trail from an angle and enter the trail in the direction they want to be followed, leaving considerable signs of their presence. After about 30 meters, soldiers walk backward to the point they entered the trail and exit in another direction leaving no sign. Soldiers move off on an angle opposite the one they entered the trail on for about 100 meters and change direction to their desired line of march.

Leaving Footprints

3-373. Soldiers walk backward over soft ground to leave reasonably clear footprints. They try not to leave every footprint clear and do not leave an impression of more than 1/4 inch deep. Soldiers continue this deception until they are on hard ground. They select the ground carefully to ensure that they have at least 20 to 30 meters of this deception. This technique should always be used when exiting a river or stream and can be used in conjunction with all other techniques as well. To add even further confusion to the following party, this tactic can be used several times to lay false trails before actually leaving the stream.

Crossing a Stream

3-374. When approaching a stream, soldiers approach at an angle in the same manner as a road. They move downstream for about 30 meters, backtrack, and move off into the intended direction. To delay the trackers, soldiers set up false tracks leaving footprints as described above.

3-375. Below are some additional tactics that soldiers can use to aid in eluding a following party:

- Stay in the stream for 100 to 200 meters.
- Keep in the center of the stream and in deep water.
- Watch (near the banks) for rocks or roots that are not covered with moss or vegetation, and leave the stream at this point.
- Walk out backward on soft ground.
- Walk up small, vegetation-covered tributaries and replace the vegetation, in its natural position.
- Walk downstream until coming to the main river, and then depart on a log or pre-positioned boat.
- Enter the stream, having first carried out the above tactic, then exit at the point of entry and make a large backward loop, crossing and checking it, and move off in a different direction.

NOTE: Using a stream as a deception technique is one of the best ways to slow down and lose a following party. The deception starts 100 meters from the stream and the successful completion of the tactic is to ensure that the following party does not know where to exit from the stream.

Camouflage Techniques

3-376. Walking backward to leave confusing footprints, brushing out trails, and moving over rocky ground or through streams are examples of camouflage techniques that may be used to confuse the tracker. Moving on hard surfaces or frequently traveled trails may also aid in eluding the tracker. Soldiers should avoid walking on moss-covered rocks as they can be easily displaced.

Techniques Used to Confuse Dogs

3-377. Enemy tracking teams may use dogs to aid in tracking the soldiers. Soldiers may confuse or delay dogs by—

- Scattering black or red pepper or, if authorized, a riot control agent (such as CS powder) along the route.
- Using silence-suppressed weapons against animals.

Chapter 4

Postmission Activities

Upon mission completion, the guerrilla force may withdraw by any method and conduct a linkup with any friendly force or may be exfiltrated to friendly training sites (Appendix L). SFODs should conduct withdrawals immediately unless the objective is key terrain and may influence future operations. After linkup, resistance forces revert to national control. These forces may demobilize or reorganize as conventional combat forces for use in economy-of-force missions.

TRANSITION

4-1. Transition refers to turning over an activity or task to a new indigenous government, allied or coalition force or government, or to private sector agencies. Examples include the—

- Transfer of civil authority from military (guerrilla) forces to civil government.
- Establishment of indigenous police or security forces.
- Privatization or return of facilities, such as public works and utilities, airports, and seaports, to indigenous control.
- Privatization of humanitarian demining operations.

4-2. Transition is as critical to a U.S.-sponsored UW movement as the combat operations that terminated the insurgency in favor of the insurgents. The sustainment of a successfully terminated insurgency depends in large part on how quickly and efficiently the posthostilities government can take control and provide the sustainable stability and functioning infrastructure required to support a population. Transition may begin in areas where conflict has subsided, while combat operations continue elsewhere in the JSOA. Planning and preparation for the transition, therefore, begin during the preparation phase and continue throughout the subsequent phases.

4-3. When planning to transfer an activity or task to indigenous populations or institutions, it is important to—

- Know the capabilities and limitations of the elements of the existing infrastructure. Examples include—
  - Host governments.
  - Bilateral donors.
  - UN agencies.
  - International organizations, especially the International Crisis Group (ICG) and the International Committee for the Red Cross (ICRC).

- NGOs by type; for example, assistance, advocacy, and indigenous organizations.
- Define the desired end state; for example, continuity of current operations or modification of current operations to some other format.
- Identify the organizational structure required to perform the activity or task.
- Identify competent, trustworthy individuals to fill positions within the incoming organizational structure.
- Determine how to conduct demilitarization of indigenous forces and incorporation of former belligerents into the private sector.
- Attempt to fully understand implications of withdrawal as well as tribal or factional breakdown, to include historical boundaries and differences not yet resolved.
- Identify equipment and facilities required to perform the activity or task, and who will provide them. Prepare the appropriate property control paperwork if transferring equipment or facilities to the relieving organization.
- Create timelines that provide sufficient overlap between the outgoing and incoming organizations.
- Determine the criteria that will dictate when the incoming organization will assume control of the activity or task; for example, a target date, task standard, or level of understanding.
- Orient the incoming organization to the activity or task, to include providing procedures, routine and recurring events, and other information critical to the conduct of the activity or task. Demonstrate the activity or task, if possible.
- Supervise the incoming organization in performing the activity or task. The departing organization retains control of the activity or task during this process, providing critiques and guidance as needed.
- Transfer the task according to the transition plan.
- Provide continued support to the incoming organization, as required.
- Bolster the image and prestige of the incoming organization in the eyes of the populace and the international community.

DEMOBILIZATION

4-4. Demobilization is a major activity of transition. It involves demilitarizing the combatants of a resistance movement and reorienting them (or, in some cases, orienting them for the first time) from life as a guerrilla to life as a peaceful, productive member of society. Demobilization planning must be closely coordinated and synchronized with transition planning. As the need for resistance fighters diminishes, the incoming government decides whether to place guerrilla forces in a supporting role or to begin demobilizing them.

4-5. How a guerrilla force is demobilized will affect the postwar attitudes of the civilian population toward the "new" government. To ensure the guerrilla force is aligned with the new government, the combatant commanders, through the SOC, coordinate between SOF, the area commander, and other military organizations. When demobilizing the guerrilla force, the following COAs could be considered:

- Retain the force with weapons and equipment as a new military or police force.
- Integrate personnel, weapons, and equipment into new local, state, or country public services and retrain personnel into new civil sector occupations.
- Turn in all weapons and equipment and return personnel to their former occupations. (The collection of weapons is a time-consuming and sensitive issue. An "arms for cash" reward system may be effective.)
- Combine any of the above methods.

4-6. After the war is over, the guerrilla force's hospitals will be kept operational until patients can be transferred to military or civilian hospitals. Permanently disabled patients should be granted pensions by the new government. Rehabilitation assistance must be available to the guerrillas to assure their place in the civilian community.

CIVIL AFFAIRS SUPPORT

4-7. During combat operations, the SFOD and the guerrilla force conduct postmission activities such as AARs, reconstitution, or preparing for the next mission. CA forces participate by conducting a CA battle damage assessment (BDA). This evaluation assesses the results of the mission on the factors of CASCOPE, validates the CA and CMO CONOPS, and determines whether the established MOEs for the operation have been met. It also helps the SFOD and area commander decide when and how to adjust the plan, when to develop new plans to address unforeseen consequences of operations, and when to terminate or transition an operation.

4-8. In areas where conflict has subsided and conditions indicate a successfully terminated insurgency, transition and demobilization activities may begin. Transition and demobilization require the collaborative efforts of many military and civilian, U.S. and international, and government and nongovernment agencies. CA participation is more prevalent in transition and demobilization than in most other aspects of the UW campaign. CA specialists provide the preponderance of CA support, although CA generalists will still have an important role.

4-9. CA forces support transition by—

- Addressing transition issues early in the planning stages of the UW campaign, including establishment of MOEs and other indicators that determine points at which to transition to different phases of the operation.
- Identifying individuals among the insurgency movement who would provide the experience, knowledge, and leadership required to create and sustain a post-UW infrastructure. Individuals should be identified

who can fill roles in government, economics and commerce, public facilities, and special functions at the national, provincial, and local levels.

- Separating those individuals from the main body of guerrilla forces and, with the assistance of other government and nonmilitary agencies, orienting and training the individuals to their future roles in the post-UW infrastructure. Depending on METT-TC, this may occur inside or outside the JSOA.

- Refining the transition plan based on periodic assessments of the situation within the JSOA, as well as among the international community.

- Observing and validating the MOEs and other indicators that help determine when conditions are right to begin the transition phase.

- Supporting transition operations by providing advisory support to civil administration in a friendly territory.

- Maintaining the CMOC to facilitate collaborative interagency planning, coordination, and synchronization throughout all phases of the UW movement and contracting the CMOC according to the transition plan.

- Providing postredeployment oversight and support mechanisms for the new indigenous government and infrastructure (for example, "reachback" points of contact, periodic visits, combatant commanders' theater engagement programs).

4-10. CA forces support demobilization by—

- Considering demobilization issues in transition plans, to include interpreting the combatant commander's policy on demobilization, demilitarization, and disarming of the former warring factions.

- Supporting SFOD FID missions.

- Identifying civil sector manpower requirements in government, economics and commerce, public facilities, and special functions at the national, provincial, and local levels.

- Establishing programs to screen and identify candidates among the demobilizing guerrilla force to fill required positions in the post-UW infrastructure.

- Establishing and overseeing training programs for former guerrillas to gain new skills and knowledge and to make them peaceful, productive members of the new indigenous society.

PSYCHOLOGICAL OPERATIONS SUPPORT

4-11. The SFOD establishes liaison with the PSYOP element before demobilization. When supporting a UW mission, the supporting PSYOP element trains the indigenous personnel in the conduct of effective PSYOP, assists in gaining converts and recruits for the resistance as they develop the necessary governmental infrastructure, and conducts operations to create popular support for the resistance movement.

4-12. The senior PSYOP commander at the conventional force HQ plans PSYOP to support the linkup and demobilization of the guerrillas. The PSYOP commander prepares and coordinates linkup plans with PSYOP personnel supporting the resistance movement. Because of their extreme sensitivity and importance, demobilization plans must begin in the early phases of operations and have continuous support.

4-13. PSYOP in the JSOA prepare the civilian population to cooperate fully with the conventional tactical forces. PSYOP elements urge the civilian population to remain in place and not hinder operations. PSYOP elements brief the resistance organization's leaders on the importance of cooperating with the tactical force commanders and accepting the conventional force leadership. PSYOP elements psychologically prepare the resistance organization to assume whatever roles the legal government wants it to play. These roles include, but are not limited to, their incorporation into the national army, paramilitary organizations, national police, or demobilization. PSYOP programs explain the demobilization process. They promote the insurgents' orderly transition to peaceful civilian life. PSYOP personnel attempt to prevent the formation of quasi-military or political groups opposing the recognized government. Loyalty to the legitimate government is the major concern.

DANGERS OF DEMOBILIZATION

4-14. The primary concern in any demobilization program is the guerrilla. His personal and political motives vary. The resistance organization can include peasants, laborers, bandits, criminals, merchants, and a few social and intellectual leaders. During the conflict, some guerrillas may have achieved status and leadership positions that they now are reluctant to relinquish. Others may have found adventure in combat that they would not now trade for peace or prosperity. Hostile groups may have clandestinely infiltrated the guerrilla force to continue their own personal or political agenda. They may take advantage of the demobilization program to organize paramilitary or political groups that will be in conflict with the new provisional government or U.S. authorities.

4-15. It is imperative that demobilization programs and procedures be executed quickly and with major political support. The programs and procedures begun are a direct result of decisions made by high-level civilian and military authorities. Their successful implementation requires maximum effort and coordination among SF, CA, and PSYOP.

4-16. Because of their knowledge and history of the guerrilla force, SFODs initially remain in their operational areas to assist in demobilization. The SFOD commanders and their supporting CA and PSYOP elements ensure transfer of U.S. responsibility without loss of control, influence, or property accountability. The key to long-term strategic success in UW is planning and executing postmission responsibilities. Appendix M provides detailed guidance on the SFOD's responsibilities.

Appendix A

Unconventional Warfare in an Urban Environment

In the current international political atmosphere, the emphasis of insurgent activity has shifted from the rural to the urban environment. Therefore, the urban rather than the rural setting will be the battlefield of the future. The phenomenon of urbanization is occurring with increasing acceleration. In virtually every country of the world, urban areas are rapidly expanding, both in area and population. The U.S. northeastern seaboard has become a vast, open megalopolis in only a few short years. In the developing nations, the rate of urbanization is even more pronounced. Their cities' rate of population growth is much greater than the general rate.

BACKGROUND

A-1. If the people support the guerrillas' cause, are neutral, or have been alienated by government actions, the guerrillas will be able to survive. Revolutionaries in Asia and Latin America have turned away from the classic doctrines of rural insurgency as espoused by Mao Tse-tung and Che Guevara, and devoted more attention to the struggle in the cities. Failure in the countryside is one reason. Few of the guerrillas who took to the hills decades ago could boast of much success beyond survival. The dramatic growth of cities in the so-called Third World is another reason.

A-2. The upsurge in urban guerrilla warfare has caused worldwide concern since it has not been confined to developing countries. Terrorist bombings, kidnapping of government officials, street barricades, and open assaults have become commonplace. Even in the United States, the recent terrorist attacks using civilian aircraft and the biological threat within the postal system have proven that we are not immune from this threat.

A-3. The growth of cities everywhere, along with the advent of television and the transmission of news via satellite, provide an instant worldwide audience for almost any act of violence. Like any other form of warfare, urban guerrilla warfare is a form of political struggle. It can be a prelude, a substitute, or an accompaniment to rural guerrilla warfare or to a conventional military contest. Many of Asia's revolutionaries regard the assault on cities as the penultimate stage of takeover. According to their views, the struggle must begin in the countryside.

The countryside, and the countryside alone, can provide the basis from which the revolutionaries can go forward to final victory.

Lin Piao

A-4. Initially, this pattern was followed by the Tupamaros in Uruguay who operated briefly as rural guerrillas, finding their support among the workers on the sugar and rice plantations in the northern part of the country. But they soon realized that Uruguay has too little countryside.

A-5. As stated by one Tupamaro, "We do not have unassailable strongholds in our country where a lasting guerrilla nucleus could be installed. On the other hand, we have a large city with buildings covering more than 300 square kilometers and that allows the development of an urban struggle."

A-6. Carlos Marighella, the posthumously famous Brazilian author of the *Mini-Manual of the Urban Guerrilla*, saw urban guerrilla warfare as a means of diverting government forces while rural guerrillas established themselves in the countryside. In other parts of Latin America, urban guerrilla warfare increased as rural guerrillas were chased into the cities by successful government pacification campaigns in the countryside. Such was the case in Guatemala.

A-7. Cities have always been centers of human activity. The result is a greater centralization and consolidation of a country's entire range of social, political, cultural, and economic activities in the urban centers. In many countries, these activities are centered in only one or two key cities.

A-8. In most cases, the capital city of the nation is the primary area of conflict. The capital city of practically every national political entity is the nerve center of the nation. Even in the democratic nations where decentralization is more common, the capital city occupies the key position in the political control of a country. This is even truer in the case of the developing nations.

A-9. All present-day dissident groups are well aware of this situation and realize they must center the insurgent and terrorist activities on the political center of the country to be successful. The political institutions of a state are centered in its capital, with controls emanating from this hub of sovereign power. Communication media are located in a capital and other urban areas to cover the area of densest population. National police and military forces have their control HQ in the capital with subordinate elements in other urban centers.

A-10. In addition to the political power, most capital cities have symbolic value in terms of custom, culture, traditions, and religion. An insurgent force that can paralyze the capital can effectively paralyze the entire nation, and one that can take over the city with its institutions intact can use these institutions to exercise control over the remainder of the nation.

CHARACTERISTICS OF THE CITY

A-11. Each city is unique. It may be built on hillsides in a mountainous area or lie on a plain. It can be located along a river or the seashore or in the middle of a jungle or desert. Wherever it is located, the site wholly or partially limits or restricts its development and in some respects determines the external form and dimensions of the city. No city is uniform in its internal composition. Rather, just as no two cities are alike, each city varies widely within itself. A city is composed of multiple nuclei—marked, distinct zones, which differ greatly. These zones, quite disparate although the boundaries between them may be blurred, can be residential, ranging from the ghetto neighborhood to the comfortable, affluent suburbs. There are business, service, and industrial areas and sometimes a combination of these. There are often parks and large unbroken expanses of woods. Like activities tend to cluster together while those that are incompatible, such as high-pollutant industries and nurseries, are widely separated.

A-12. The truly rural area is completely self-sustaining. A large urban area never is. The material base on which the city is dependent is largely external to it. The resources cities need and the goods and services it provides determine the functions of the city. Some of the standard functions are: economic, political, religious, educational, residential, or any combination of these.

A-13. Most cities can be characterized as either preindustrial or industrial. In preindustrial cities, the upper class lives at or near the city center and the lower class lives on the outskirts. The reverse is usually true in the industrial city. The preindustrial city tends to be polynuclear, since it is based on a bazaar-type economy, whereas the industrial city is more likely to have a central business district and a distinct industrial zone. Internally, distinctive street patterns place constraints on the type of construction within the city. Preindustrial cities tend to be tightly knit with irregular street patterns and buildings of a fairly uniform height. This height is usually three to six stories, resulting from the limits imposed at the time of construction by lack of technology, building materials available, or weak foundations. A low, nearly uniform skyline characterizes this type of city with buildings very densely concentrated.

A-14. The industrial city presents a quite different form. The business district is usually concentrated near the point of peak accessibility. In this core, buildings are as high as possible to minimize the use of ground space. The result is a cluster of high-rise buildings with the skyline falling away in all directions. In larger cities, smaller versions of the downtown cluster appear at other points throughout the city.

CHARACTERISTICS OF URBAN TACTICAL OPERATIONS

A-15. Despite their differences, urban areas have certain similarities that provide us with some general characteristics of urban tactical operations. These have special significance regardless of the nature or level of conflict.

A-16. Cities are complex and heterogeneous. The nature of the cities presents difficulty to the planner as well as the operator. Planning must be in much greater detail than is normally required. The use of large-scale city plans and street maps is imperative. The texture of the city varies greatly and often changes abruptly. Operators must function in the city core, open suburbs, industrial areas, transportation centers, parks, woods, and waterfronts.

A-17. The nature of the city favors the inhabitant and defender. The city dweller is the man on the ground with an inherent knowledge of his daily surroundings. These surroundings appear to the outsider as a hopelessly tangled web of buildings, streets, and alleyways, but are as familiar to the inhabitant as his own living room. Buildings and street complexes restrict movement and reduce the attacker's mobility, but provide fields of fire to the defender. Obstacles are fairly easy to construct, as is the establishment of population control measures, checkpoints, and traffic control points.

A-18. Small unit engagements will predominate. The normal building and street patterns will reduce any operation to a series of small unit engagements. The advantage of the principle of mass is greatly reduced. Flexibility is decreased for larger units and increased for smaller ones. Cells or teams operating in the city must be limited to no more than five or six members.

A-19. The unique vertical dimension must be considered. The elevation of the buildings provides a vertical dimension not normally encountered in tactical operations. This vertical dimension is not only above the surface but extends to the subterranean level in the form of subways, sewers, tunnels, and basements. Elevated positions offer good observation and fields of fire plus cover and concealment, particularly effective for snipers. Subterranean areas offer protected and concealed areas for storage, as well as effective routes of movement and communication.

A-20. Combat occurs at extremely short ranges, which limits or nullifies the effectiveness of long-range weapons and increases the usefulness of individual weapons. Operators must be proficient in the quick, accurate firing of their personal weapons systems.

A-21. There will be a large number of noncombatants present, which can be expected to restrict the use of firepower, munitions, and explosives on the part of the operator. At the same time, the presence of large numbers of noncombatants can be used to the enemy's advantage, such as the creation of confusion. Large numbers of people also increase the operator's blending-in capability.

A-22. There will be collateral damage constraints. These constraints may affect the selection of targets or the means by which the targets are attacked. The limitations may be imposed by a higher HQ or could take the form of moral constraints, as in the case of critical life-support services. Another form of constraint is where an assigned task would have a significantly adverse effect on the mission; for example, alienating a segment of the population on which the operator's existence depended.

A-23. Intelligence collection is difficult for the outsider. Accurate and timely intelligence is of extreme value. For the inhabitant, day-to-day activities and occurrences are routine and taken in stride, but these same activities could provide a situation for which the operator is totally unprepared. In the final analysis, there is no substitute for on-the-ground experience, training, and conditioning.

NOTE: The following checklist and survey are good tools to develop and assess the urban AO.

URBAN OPERATIONS CHECKLIST

- [ ] Record point of entry, city, and country visited.
- [ ] List documentation required for entry.
- [ ] Document brief description of entry procedures and customs processing, to include drawings of facility, uniforms worn by customs, and weapons.
- [ ] Provide name, address, cost, and phone of housing accommodations.
- [ ] Report public and private transportation used, to include cost, schedule, and routes.
- [ ] Report telephone, telex, and postal services used, to include cost, locations, and restrictions.
- [ ] Report radio and television programs noted, to include language, format, and schedule.
- [ ] Report commercial power sources noted, to include type of plugs, frequency of current, voltage, and stability.
- [ ] Report job opportunities noted in local commercial businesses, to include U.S. businesses. List address, phone number, and name of company.
- [ ] Report exchange rates, both official and black market, to include locations, desired currency, and hours of operation.
- [ ] Report ability to use credit cards and traveler's checks.
- [ ] Report ration control procedures and documentation, if noted.
- [ ] Report any logistics services used, to include medical, mechanical, and food.
- [ ] Report any professional services used, to include secretarial, reproduction, interpreters, and film processing.
- [ ] Report any installations visited, to include churches, libraries, theaters, embassies, restaurants, public buildings, and schools. Include location, address, and phone.
- [ ] Report any recreation used, to include dive shops, golf courses, deep-sea fishing, sailing, camping, shopping, prostitution, beaches, sports facilities, and museums. Include name, address, phone, hours of operation, and personalities.
- [ ] Report any specific ethnic or religious distribution noted within the city or country visited.
- [ ] Report any restricted off-limits areas observed.
- [ ] Report any nonindigenous military or civilian personnel observed, to include nationality, activity, and location.
- [ ] Report exit procedures, to include location, documentation, and processing or customs inspections.

IN-DEPTH OPERATIONS SURVEY

GENERAL

- What is the general political climate?
- What is the official government attitude toward the United States?
- What is the attitude of the general populace?

INTELLIGENCE AND CI SERVICES

- What are the names and subordination of the intelligence and security services?
- What are the names, locations, and descriptions of the—
  - HQ and administration centers?
  - Surveillance observation points and hangouts?
  - Detention facilities?
- What personalities are associated with intelligence and security services?
- What is the description of the following environments?
  - Weapons: Type, caliber, how carried.
  - Vehicles: Makes, models, distinctive markings, and aerials.
  - Communications: Type, frequencies, mobile or fixed.
  - Technical surveillance: Any equipment observed.
  - Uniform and clothing: Similarities and differences from police forces, badges, and epaulets.
- What is the modus operandi?
  - Informants:
    - How are they recruited?
    - How do they report?
  - Surveillance techniques.
  - Wiretaps:
    - How are they used?
    - Who is targeted?
    - How is wiretapping approval gained?
  - Searches:
    - How are they conducted?
    - Must prior approval be obtained?
  - Successful operations:
    - What types have been most successful?
    - What methods were used?
- What is the description of the training and cooperation with foreign services?
  - What type of training is received?

- Which country provides training?
- What facilities are used?

FOREIGN OR HOSTILE INTELLIGENCE SERVICES

- What is the name and subordination of foreign intelligence services operating in the HN?
- Are current operations ongoing against the HN? Against the United States?
- What are the essential elements of information of the services?
  - What cover organizations or positions are being used?
  - What are the locations and phone numbers of the—
    - HQ and administration centers?
    - Surveillance operations and hangouts?
- What personalities are associated with foreign intelligence services?
- What is the description of the following equipment?
  - Weapons: Type, caliber, how carried.
  - Vehicles: Makes, models, special equipment, aerials, special (diplomatic) license plates.
  - Communications: Types, frequencies, with whom.
  - Technical surveillance: Any equipment observed.
  - Uniforms and clothing: Distinctive apparel, uniform markings, badges.
- What is the modus operandi?
  - Informants:
    - How are they recruited?
    - Are they induced or willing?
    - How do they report?
  - Surveillance techniques.
  - Wiretaps:
    - How are they used?
    - Do they have connections with telephone or communications employees?
  - Searches:
    - What methods are used?
    - Are they performed with permission of local authorities?
  - Successful operations:
    - Who was targeted?
    - What methods were used?
- Is there cooperation with insurgent or terrorist groups?
  - What affiliations have been made?
  - What type of support has been provided (training, weapons, logistics, and financing)?

POLICE

- What are the names and identification of HN police forces?
  - Is there a national police force?
  - Are there local or regional forces available? If so, who are these forces subordinate to?
- What are the names, locations, descriptions of the—
  - HQ and administration centers?
  - Operational facilities?
  - Detention facilities (if separate from operations facilities)?
- What personalities are associated with police forces?
- What is the description of the following equipment?
  - Weapons: Type, caliber, common and special situation weapons, how carried.
  - Vehicles: Makes, models, performance modifications, distinctive markings, and communications equipment.
  - Communications: Mobile or fixed, frequencies, codes and cryptograph (crypto) used.
  - Technical surveillance.
  - Uniforms and clothing: Color; distinctive badges, buttons, apparel; rank insignia.
- What is the modus operandi?
  - Arrest procedures:
    - Are police governed by rules regarding apprehension?
    - What procedures do police follow in a routine arrest?
  - Investigative procedures:
    - Are scientific methods involved?
    - Are investigators trained in a HN or foreign facility?
  - Patrol procedures and routes:
    - Are there set patterns to procedures used?
    - Are routes fixed or irregular?
    - What areas receive special emphasis for police patrols?
  - Miscellaneous:
    - Does local populace support police efforts and procedures?
    - Is criminal justice system perceived as fair?

POPULATION CONTROL MEASURES

- What identification or documentation is (or must be) carried?
  - Is photo displayed?
  - If so, is it black and white or color?
- What are curfew hours? How and by whom are they enforced?
- What checkpoints or roadblocks are in place?
  - Who mans them?

- What precipitates temporary checkpoints or roadblocks?
- What is checked at these barriers?
- Are there prohibited and contraband items?
  - What items are normally considered contraband or illegal?
  - What penalties are associated with possession of these items?
- What are travel restrictions and off-limits areas?
  - What areas or roads are normally restricted from general populace?
  - What is the explanation for this designation?

TERRORIST OR INSURGENT GROUPS

- What are the names and acronyms of the terrorist or insurgent groups?
- What are their stated goals and objectives?
- What is the affiliation of these groups with—
  - Countries?
  - External and internal terrorist groups?
  - Political parties?
  - Links with narcotics traffickers?
- What personalities are associated with these groups?
- What is the description of the locations of—
  - Operational areas: Rural, urban, combination?
  - Safe houses and support sites: Active, contingency?
  - HQ: National, regional, local?
  - Training areas?
  - Egress and ingress routes?
  - Facilities available (weapons ranges, hand-to-hand, classrooms, barracks)?
- What is the description of the equipment?
  - What are the sources for terrorist or insurgent equipment?
  - What types of weapons are normally associated with these groups (make, caliber, cycle, quantities)?
  - How are weapons delivered and dispersed?
  - What explosives and incendiary devices do they possess? How are they procured?
  - What vehicles are normally associated with these groups?
    - Are they usually purchased or stolen?
    - How often do they "trade" vehicles?
  - What communications equipment is usually found with these groups?
    - Where is it obtained?
    - How are they trained in the operation of this equipment?
- What is the modus operandi?
  - What are typical U.S. targets for these groups?

- ◆ HN targets?
- ◆ Other (business, corporation, foreign country representatives)?
- ▪ What significant operations (murder, kidnapping, bombing) does this group specialize in or claim responsibility for?
- ▪ How do these groups negotiate?
  - ◆ Do they deal with target face-to-face or through an intermediary?
  - ◆ Are their demands usually reasonable or preposterous?
  - ◆ Do they attempt to solicit media and public support during negotiations?
- ▪ How does the group obtain its intelligence?
  - ◆ Do they operate a formal intelligence network?
  - ◆ Is there evidence of infiltration or HN intelligence services?
  - ◆ U.S. and other diplomatic missions?

COUNTERTERRORISM FORCE

- What is the HN counterterrorism (CT) force's policy for dealing with terrorism?
- Does the HN cooperate with the United States in dealing with terrorist situations?
- What is the organization of the CT force?
  - ▪ How many personnel are assigned?
  - ▪ To whom is the CT force subordinate?
- What is the mission of the CT force?
- What are the locations of HQ, administration centers, and training areas?
- What is the description of the following equipment?
  - ▪ Weapons: Make, caliber, quantity, special situation weapons.
  - ▪ Vehicles: Makes, models, performance modifications, distinctive markings.
  - ▪ Communications: Type, mobile or fixed, with whom.
  - ▪ Specialized equipment: Explosives, SCUBA, airborne or air-mobile.
- What training is received?
  - ▪ Does the HN or foreign services conduct it?
  - ▪ Is the CT force trained in purely military operations?
- Do they possess a PSYOP capability? Are they capable of conducting negotiations?

CRIME/LAW

- What is the description of criminal activity?
  - ▪ What is the general level of criminal activity? Is it normally violent?
  - ▪ Is crime against foreigners more prevalent?
  - ▪ What are high-crime areas and what causes these areas to be crime-prone?
  - ▪ What is normal police response to crime?
    - ◆ What activities cause increased police reaction?
    - ◆ Do police tend to overreact?
- What is the narcotics situation?

- What is official policy and attitude toward local narcotics traffic? International traffic?
- What is local populace reaction toward narcotics?
- What is the narcotics infrastructure in regards to the—
    - Type of drugs?
    - Organizations associated with procurement and distribution?
- What are the locations of high-drug trafficking and use?
- What are the routes of entrance and distribution: Means of transport—air, cars, trucks, "mules"?
- What are the affiliations of traffickers with government agencies and personnel, terrorist or insurgent groups, foreign missions, and other criminal figures?
- What weapons do traffickers use: Type, caliber, quantity, and source?

- What is the description of the HN legal system?
    - Is it perceived to be fair?
    - Is it effective?
    - What legal status do foreigners have? Are there status of forces agreements in effect? With which countries?
    - What are court procedures?
    - Are there legal safeguards in place for defendants?
    - How are punishments determined? Are punishments commensurate with the crimes?
    - Where are prisoners confined?
    - Is there a parole or probation system?
    - What are the laws on espionage and subversion?
    - Do persons accused of these crimes have the same legal protection as those accused of other crimes?
    - What are the punishments for conviction of these crimes?

Communications

Communications requirements are particularly critical in UW missions. The SF team must be able to report near-real-time information directly to the user of the information. Even more important, SF team members must know what specific information the user requires and in what priority.

PLANNING SYSTEM

B-1. Operating in a UW environment poses special problems for the SF communicator. Communications between the SFOD in the JSOA and the SFOB or FOB must be reliable and secure. To meet this demand, communicators should use the PACE communications planning system. The type of communications will be PACE planned along with times and mode of scheduled contacts. Each segment of the communications net should be PACE planned, to include mechanisms used for the communications equipment, antenna systems, power sources, and encryption systems. With this system of planning, communications are made more reliable and secure, despite the tactical situation.

B-2. When a particular part of the communications system (such as a radio) fails, communicators use the alternate radio system. However, they should continue to use the other primary parts of the system as long as they can interface with the alternate equipment. The alternate mechanism may be upgraded to the primary when equipment availability permits. Short-duration missions, such as raids and ambushes, may not need to be PACE planned but should at least contain a primary, alternate, and contingency plan.

B-3. Communications within the JSOA should also be PACE planned. No one system described below will be useful in every situation. However, a combination of the systems in the PACE plan will ensure that communications will continue. Operator training and adherence to communications security (COMSEC) procedures will make communications a success.

PRIMARY

B-4. The primary communications system includes routine communications between the SFOD and the SFOB or FOB. The primary usually consists of radio communications in high frequency (HF) or tactical satellite (TACSAT) modes IAW Standard Audiovisual Service Supplement (SAV SER SUP) 6. The primary communications system can handle the message traffic from the SFODs and the base stations. The base station communicates with the deployed SFODs, transmitting and receiving messages in support of the SFOB or FOB mission requirements.

ALTERNATE

B-5. Communicators plan and use the alternate communications system in case of primary system failure. This system consists of alternate radios, frequencies, and times in open net contacts IAW SAV SER SUP 6. Usually the same type of encryption system will be used. In the event of a primary encryption system compromise, communicators must plan, practice, and use an alternate encryption system.

B-6. The alternate communications system should be able to handle the same amount of traffic as the primary system. When initially used, it alerts the SFOB or FOB to a potential problem. Communicators should use it until the primary system is again operational or until exfiltration. As long as most of the radio equipment used for the primary system is operational, this equipment should be used for the alternate system. However, this system should not remain operational for the duration of the mission. An alternate HF or TACSAT radio must be infiltrated with the SFOD and kept available in case of primary equipment failure. The alternate equipment may or may not be of the same type but must be able to transmit and receive in the required mode of operation (HF or TACSAT). Base station alternate equipment should be installed in case the primary system fails.

CONTINGENCY

B-7. The SFOD plans and uses the contingency communications system in case of primary and alternate systems failure. The contingency system should be able to provide the normal communications between the deployed SFOD and the SFOB or FOB, but only for short durations. An example would be battlefield recovery of equipment able to transmit an HF signal or continuous wave (CW). The guard net frequency, memorized by the SFOD members while in isolation, would be used as a contingency when loss or compromise of the frequency encipher pad occurs. This communication, since it is less secure, would only be used until the primary or alternate communications equipment or system is operational.

B-8. Operating in this mode, the SFOD is in a communications-critical stage, which increases its vulnerability to detection. Therefore, commanders at all levels should take steps to bring the primary and alternate communications systems on line as soon as possible. An emergency resupply of equipment to the SFOD may be necessary. Meanwhile, communicators would use the current "emergency crypto system" as a contingency encryption system. This system could handle the normal amount of message traffic at least for short durations. Communicators would use a primary or alternate encryption system as soon as possible.

EMERGENCY

B-9. The emergency communications system is a last resort medium for the SFOD to inform the SFOB or FOB of its status. If the SFOD is operational, but lacks necessary communications equipment, it uses the emergency communications system to inform the SFOB or FOB of this fact. The SFOD uses the emergency communications system if the emergency resupply is compromised. The SFOD would also use the emergency communications system to inform the SFOB or FOB that all of the SFOD's communications equipment is damaged or compromised and it is in the evasion mode. If the SFOD is evading and has a higher system of communications, such as primary, alternate, or contingency, then it uses those systems.

B-10. The SFOD and the SFOB or FOB prearranges in detail the emergency communications system before infiltration. They also coordinate the communication mechanism and the actions upon receipt. The plan could come in a one- or two-word message exfiltrated by other resistance elements or ground-to-air signals from a particular location. The emergency communications system must be fail-safe, simple, secure, and reliable.

SECURITY

B-11. UW communications techniques and procedures cover the entire spectrum of communications available to the SF communicator. However, as stated above, radio communications dominate communications between the SFOD and the SFOB or FOB. Between elements within the JSOA, communications will be predominantly nontechnical in nature, at least until the EPW threat has been considerably lessened. Security is the communicator's number one concern. Any communications within the JSOA must be totally clandestine until a communications linkup is made with conventional forces. The SFOD's ability to accomplish its mission could be drastically affected if the enemy had knowledge of the—

- Presence of the SFOD in the JSOA.
- Amount of time spent on message traffic being sent and received.
- Areas of concentration and message repetition.
- Extent of the sophistication and size of the communications net.

B-12. Signals security (SIGSEC), which includes physical, transmission, and cryptographic security, allows the SFOD to operate longer without detection. SIGSEC denies the enemy any usable intelligence from traffic analysis or radio direction finder (RDF) data. It also keeps the enemy from using imitative deception against friendly use of the electromagnetic spectrum. For SIGSEC efforts to be successful, all SFOD and guerrilla members must follow COMSEC procedures.

PHYSICAL SECURITY

B-13. Physical security includes all measures taken to safeguard classified materials and equipment from unauthorized persons. These measures have a functional destruction plan for materials and equipment in anticipation of capture of classified materials and equipment by the enemy. The SFOD commander controls the encryption and decryption systems and the encryption and decryption of message traffic. Those personnel transmitting or receiving message traffic should never know the contents of the messages in case of capture and interrogation. Under no circumstance will indigenous personnel be given access to the SFOD's encryption systems or equipment used for communications with the SFOB and FOB. The communicator must sterilize transmission sites after all transmissions.

B-14. Only SFOD members should have access into any area that has classified materials, communications logs equipment, or communications logs and other documentation. Indigenous personnel must be screened before being trained in communications assistance within the JSOA.

TRANSMISSION SECURITY

B-15. Transmission security identifies measures taken to prevent interception, traffic analysis, and imitative deception. It also limits the effect of jamming the friendly use of the electromagnetic spectrum. To reduce chances of detection, communicators use directional antennas and terrain masking from known RDF stations. They also adhere to the transmission procedures IAW ACP-125 (E), *Communications Instructions-Radiotelephone Procedures*, and SAV SER SUP 6 to lessen transmission time and the possibility of threat detection. A safe practice is to assume the threat has intercepted the signal and has located the transmission site. The communicator should keep transmissions short or risk the consequences.

CRYPTOGRAPHIC SECURITY

B-16. Cryptographic security results through technically sound cryptographic systems. It is imperative that communicators use only authorized cryptographic systems for transmissions between the SFOD and the SFOB or FOB. Sufficient quantities and types of cryptographic systems should be infiltrated with the SFOD to ensure all message traffic is encrypted and decrypted using one of these authorized systems. Communicators will not use these systems for encrypting message traffic within the JSOA. The SFOD must infiltrate additional encryption techniques to ensure communications within the JSOA are secure. Under no circumstances will "homemade" cryptographic systems be used for any type of radio transmissions.

METHODS OF COMMUNICATIONS

B-17. Upon infiltration into the JSOA, the SFOD may find communications systems of the guerrilla forces are of low quality, lack reliability, and are unsecured or nonexistent. The SFOD must take immediate steps to develop secure, reliable communications between various guerrilla groups and within the guerrilla elements themselves. Due to the likelihood of a high EPW threat, especially in the initial phases of the resistance movement, nontechnical communications should prevail.

MESSENGERS

B-18. Although slow, messengers are the most secure means of communications. They can carry an encrypted message or signal or memorize traffic to be delivered orally to the intended party. Messengers must be absolutely loyal to the guerrilla organization and thoroughly familiar with the terrain and the indigenous people. This familiarity allows them to operate without suspicion and move about freely to pick up and deliver messages.

B-19. Messenger systems allow the flexibility to send written messages, maps, charts, equipment, or other articles. However, distance, weather, and the tactical situation in the area of the messenger service can decrease the effectiveness of the messenger. The need for speed must be weighed against the need for security since messengers are relatively slow. In addition, information memorized may be forgotten or distorted and then delivered inaccurately. Training for prospective messengers should include memory enhancement, as well as basic movement techniques common to infantry squads. FM 7-8 provides further information.

RADIOS

B-20. Radio communication is fast but the least secure of all types of communication. Radios provide timely and accurate communications from one location to another. If radio communications have already been incorporated, their effectiveness, reliability, and security must be evaluated. Communicators must decide if the current radio nets should be maintained, upgraded, or replaced with other systems. In addition, the EPW threat must be evaluated to decide if using radio communications poses an undue risk to the SFOD or the guerrilla elements. Communicators should use radio communications only when the need for speed and accuracy outweighs the need for security.

TELEPHONES

B-21. Communicators should limit the use of commercial telephone systems in the JSOA during the initial phases of operations. The enemy can trace telephone calls quickly and easily. Even conversations consisting of a few code words are risky and should be avoided in favor of more secure systems of communications. If telephone communications between guerrilla members must be made, they should be kept to an absolute minimum. Wire communications using field telephone and manual switchboards are also risky in the JSOA. Wires are very easy to find and can be followed directly to the points of termination. Even if the points of termination are used sporadically, the enemy can surveil wire for indefinite periods, rendering them compromised and useless.

B-22. Communicators could use wire communications effectively at the OP or LP net in a patrol base or guerrilla base complex. They could use expedient ground return circuits and existing conductors, such as barbed wire fences or railroad rails. When they use the expedient ground return circuit, they must ensure the appropriate parties are hooked to the circuit at the proper time.

VISUAL SIGNALS

B-23. Visual signals can be seen by anyone who happens to be looking in the wrong direction at the right time. Visual communication can relay information using any device such as lights, mirrors, and flags that can be seen from a distance. When communicators use these devices, detailed planning and coordination are needed to ensure security. Visual signals need an encryption system to ensure the meaning is discernible only to the intended party and to secure the information. Signal operators can achieve long-distance communication in a relatively short time when they use binoculars to send and receive messages in relay from hilltop to hilltop.

B-24. Communicators can use any device or object as a signal that can be displayed in a way to produce a specific meaning. A particular color bedsheet hung on a clothesline at a particular time of day at a particular place could mean, for example, that threat patrols were seen in the area within the last 24 hours. The important point is that a visual signal must have a unique way of being identified, a way that is unmistakable, yet not unusual for the area, and have a specific meaning known only to the receiver.

FLASHLIGHTS

B-25. Communicators can use flashlights equipped with lens hoods and expedient lightguns (a form of flashlight equipped with sights and a trigger mechanism to turn the light on and off rapidly) to send manual Morse code. Four trained operators are required: one at each end of the circuit for sending and receiving the message, the other two for recording the message. Experienced operators can use this method to send and receive up to 12 coded groups of characters per minute.

MIRRORS

B-26. Mirror reflections can be seen at great distances but are very susceptible to interception. Communicators should use mirrors to send messages only when bright sunlight is available. They use them in an area where the sun reflecting from shiny surfaces is normal, such as wet brush and leaves in the morning. The distance obtained using mirrors can vary by many miles, depending on current weather conditions.

SINGLE-FLAG METHOD

B-27. Wigwag is a visual communication system that uses one single flag on a staff to send manual Morse code messages. The communicator waves the flag in a figure-eight fashion on the right side of his body to indicate a dot and on the left side to indicate a dash. The communicator then repeats the figure eights on the correct sides of the body to produce a character. For example, one figure eight on the right and one figure eight on the left produces an "A" or dit-dah. The receiver observes the "A" and says "ALPHA" to his buddy who records it. The communicator separates the characters by holding the flag in a vertical position momentarily. The system is slow and has limited usefulness; an experienced crew can only exchange five to seven letters per minute.

DOUBLE-FLAG SYSTEM

B-28. The semaphore visual communications system uses two flags, one for each hand, held in predetermined patterns to send letters of the alphabet. One flag is white with a red square in the center. The other flag is the opposite: red flag with white square in the center. Trained communicators are needed to operate the system, which can "transmit" 12 letters per minute. The Navy used this system during World War II.

AUDIO SIGNALS

B-29. Anyone in the area whether or not they are paying attention can hear unusual sounds. Audio signals should be totally natural to the area but easily recognizable to the receiver, with the meaning clear yet natural and meaningless to others, similar to using visual signals. The communicator should send signals, not text, since Morse code sent from a horn or other audio device would be instantly recognizable to anyone in the area regardless of their training or cultural sophistication.

ANIMALS AND BIRDS

B-30. Communicators can use dogs to carry messages from point to point, but food, weather, and fear can easily distract them. Trainers must actually use the routes to be traveled from the intended locations and acquaint the dogs with personnel on both ends of the route. They make the dogs aware of other personnel, including enemy soldiers and civilians. Dogs should be well cared for and stay with their handlers or trainers. Although some dogs could carry considerable weight, messages should be small and hidden in a collar or similar device so the dog looks less suspicious from a distance.

B-31. Carrier pigeons are more effective and reliable messengers than dogs. They must remain at a central message location for a few days to acquire a sense for the home roost. Pigeons carry messages best when the message container is tied to the leg. The Army used pigeons during World War II in Europe.

Appendix C

Medical Aspects

Before a UW deployment, the SFOD medic should acquire as much medical information as possible at home station to ensure he has current medical intelligence about the JSOA. An SFOD medic prepares a medical area study of the JSOA as part of the overall area study. Some of the sources he will use to prepare this study include CA area studies (available through the CA database), reports by UN agencies, and NGOs operating in the area. Because the study is continuous, he updates it whenever he receives new medical intelligence. A general outline for a medical area study follows.

MEDICAL AREA STUDY

C-1. This format is flexible to allow the medic to tailor it to the needs of the SFOD by using METT-TC (Figure C-1).

General	Provides a brief summary of the nation's health status.
Environmental Health Factors	Discusses the country's topography and climate, to include effects on health, medical evacuation, and logistics.
Demographics	Includes population, ethnic groups, life expectancy, and infant mortality.
Nutrition	Discusses nutrition and facilities for refrigeration and food inspection programs.
Water Supply	Discusses the method of supply, location, treatment, and health hazards as they apply to drinking, bathing, and swimming.
Fauna of Medical Importance	Focuses on disease vectors, hosts, reservoirs, poisonous mammals, reptiles, and spiders.
Flora of Medical Importance	Covers poisonous plants, plants with medical value, and edible plants used for survival.
Epidemiology	Discusses prevalent diseases and their contributing factors. It focuses on diseases of military importance, including communicable diseases and susceptibility to cold and heat injury. It discusses the concerns of indigenous personnel such as physical characteristics, their unique attitudes, dress, religious taboos, and psychological attributes. It also discusses preventive veterinary medicine programs that deal with prevalent animal diseases and their diseases that can be transmitted to man.
Public Health and Military Medical Services	Focuses on public health and military medical services.
Village Organization	Covers such important village concerns as social, physical, and family organization; housing, diet, water and waste disposal, and local medical practices; and rapport with neighboring tribes.
Domestic Animals	Discusses the types and uses of domesticated animals and any possible religious symbolism or taboos associated with these animals.

Figure C-1. Medical Area Study Format

MEDICAL AREA ASSESSMENT

C-2. The initial medical area assessment begins immediately upon infiltration. The medic establishes rapport (using his impressive medical skills) with the local population and guerrillas. He gains a valuable opportunity to receive intelligence and information not available elsewhere. This information may include captured medical order of battle intelligence from medical supplies and documents through battlefield recovery and from indigenous sources. It assesses the actual extent of medical training for the resistance force, availability of medical supplies and facilities, and the state of the sanitation and health within the JSOA. Medics should consider the following when conducting the initial medical area assessment:

- Physical condition and morale of the SFOD.
- Medical status of the guerrilla forces.
- Identification of any immediate threats to the health of the command, to include epidemics and environmental conditions, weather, terrain, lack of sanitation, food, and water problems.

C-3. The medical area assessment is a continuous process based on observations and firsthand factual reports by the deployed SFOD medic. The medical area assessment is a continuation of the initial medical area assessment. It confirms, refutes, or clarifies previously researched information in the medical area study. The medical area assessment provides intelligence to other units, supplements and supports area studies, and forms the basis of the AAR. Results of, and information on, the medical area assessment should not be transmitted out of the JSOA unless significant differences exist between previous intelligence reports and impact on current or planned operations. The following are suggestions and questions to guide SFOD medics in making a medical area assessment.

INDIGENOUS PERSONNEL

C-4. SFOD medics indicate the name of the tribe or native group and describe them in terms of height, build, and color and texture of skin and hair. Medics describe the native group's endurance and ability to carry heavy loads while performing physical labor and determine if they need more physical training.

C-5. SFOD medics describe clothing and adornments. Are shoes or other footgear worn? What symbolism is attached to various articles of clothing and jewelry, if any? Are amulets worn? What do they symbolize? Medics should furnish photographs if possible.

C-6. SFOD medics describe attitudes toward birth, puberty, marriage (monogamy or polygamy), old age, sickness, death, and so on. They consider any rituals associated with these events. They describe principal taboos, especially those about food, animals, and water. They determine what the attitudes are toward doctors and western medicine. Medics describe rites and/or practices by witch doctors during illnesses. What do the practices symbolize? Do the natives respond to events in the same manner as the medics would? Do they show appropriate feelings of sadness, happiness, anger, fear, and love from the medic's point of view?

VILLAGE ORGANIZATION

C-7. SFOD medics determine the status of priests, witch doctors, and chiefs. What is their relationship with the people? How do other community specialists, such as carpenters, weavers, and hunters, fit in socially? Medics describe the physical layout of the community.

FAMILY ORGANIZATION

C-8. SFOD medics determine whether intermarriage occurs outside the clan or between neighboring villages or tribes. Do males or females leave home when they marry? What are the attitudes toward old men and women, children, and deceased ancestors?

RELIGION

C-9. SFOD medics describe their religious beliefs. Are they Buddhist, Hindu, Christian, or animist? Do they worship the sun, moon, or inanimate objects? What role do good and evil spirits play? Are sicknesses, deaths, or births ascribed to evil spirits? Does a priesthood exist, and what influence does it have? Are witch doctors and priests synonymous or different?

HOUSING

C-10. SFOD medics describe construction and materials used. They describe infestations, ectoparasites, and vermin. How many persons inhabit a dwelling? Are there community houses? Are animals housed in the same dwelling? Medics provide photos and diagrams if possible.

FOOD

C-11. SFOD medics describe the native diet. They describe agricultural practices, such as slash-and-burn or permanent farms. Is human excrement used for fertilizer? What domestic crops contribute significantly to the diet? What wild vegetables are consumed? How is food prepared? What foods are cooked, pickled, smoked, or eaten raw? How are foods preserved? At what age are children weaned? What is fed to weaned infants? Which family member is given preference at the table? Are there food taboos and why? Does migration in search of food occur? What food, provided by U.S. personnel, do indigenous personnel prefer or reject?

WATER

C-12. SFOD medics determine the primary sources of potable water (river, spring, and well). Is the water used for bathing, washing, drinking, and cooking? How far is the water source from the village? Is water plentiful or scarce? What is the seasonal relationship to water availability? Is water boiled, filtered, or subjected to other purification process before consumption? What are native attitudes toward standard U.S. purification methods (iodine and bleach)?

WASTE DISPOSAL

C-13. SFOD medics describe the system used for disposal of human excrement, offal, dead animals, and human bodies. Is any excrement collected for fertilizer? What scavengers assist in the process of disposal? What is the relationship of disposal sites to primary watering sites? What are the attitudes of indigenous personnel to standard U.S. methods, such as sit-down latrines?

SOURCE OF INCOME

C-14. SFOD medics determine if there is a monetary system or exchange in the form of barter or if property and service are communal. What items have monetary value or are equivalent to money (food, jewelry, pelts, and drugs)?

LOCAL MEDICAL PRACTICES

C-15. SFOD medics describe the types of local medical practitioners. Are there conventional doctors available, to include missionaries and other nonindigenous personnel? What is their level of formal training and specialization? Do their techniques conform to American practices? Do they have government support or affiliation? Who is the local medical leader? Is he a licensed doctor, witch doctor, or herbalist? What is his status in the community? How do his practices relate to local religious practices or taboos? What drugs or herbs does he use? Does he use surgical techniques? What is the attitude of the local medical leader toward SFOD medics or aidmen? What status does he accord the SFOD medic?

C-16. SFOD medics determine the location of the nearest dispensary, hospital, or laboratory. They describe capabilities, if known, for surgery, radiology, and pharmacy. Do local hospitals accept indigenous personnel from the AO? What pharmaceuticals or biologicals are produced and used locally? What is the overall level of medical supplies, where are they manufactured, what is the quality, who provides them, and how are they delivered?

C-17. SFOD medics describe practices associated with childbirth. Do midwives attend the patient? Is there a period of confinement or banishment before or after delivery? What is the attitude of the father during pregnancy, at delivery, and after birth? How are the placenta and cord treated? What rituals accompany the birth process, and will natives request the assistance of SFOD medics?

LANGUAGE

C-18. SFOD medics describe language, dialect, and speech variants of the basic tongue from village to village. What other tongue does the tribe understand?

RELATIONSHIPS

C-19. SFOD medics describe the relationships with neighboring tribes. Does intermarriage occur? Are the general characteristics of language, dress, and physique the same? What other forms of cooperation occur and for what purpose?

FAUNA

C-20. SFOD medics record species of wild animals, birds, reptiles, and arthropods found on the march, around campsites, and in villages. If their names are unknown, medics describe them. Medics note relationships among these species, including burrows and nesting sites to human habitation, food supplies, and watering sites.

C-21. SFOD medics note the occurrence of dead or dying animals, especially if they involve large numbers of a given species. They note the relationship of any die-off to the occurrence of human diseases.

C-22. SFOD medics report any methods used by indigenous personnel to defend against local ectoparasites (leeches). How effective are these methods compared to standard U.S. protective measures (insect repellent)?

ORGANIZATION OF MEDICAL ELEMENTS WITHIN THE JSOA

C-23. The goals of medical operations in support of UW are to conserve the fighting strength of guerrilla forces and to help secure local population support for U.S. and guerrilla forces operating within the JSOA. Medical requirements within the JSOA differ from those posed by a conventional force doing operations for two reasons: guerrilla forces normally suffer fewer battle casualties and their incidence of diseases and malnutrition is often higher.

C-24. In UW, commanders tailor the organization of medical elements to fit the particular situation. Depending on the skills required, organizers might be able to bring personnel from other medical units into the JSOA. The basic medical organization can expand by using guerrilla force members and recruiting professional medical personnel to establish and operate guerrilla hospitals.

C-25. Clandestine facilities are at first confined to emergency and expedient care with minimum preventive medicine. Once the area command develops sufficiently, the clandestine facilities can expand and become part of the unit's medical organization. A wounded guerrilla allowed to fall into enemy hands can be forced to reveal what he knows and may compromise the mission. Patients with appropriate cover stories can be infiltrated into civilian or enemy military hospitals to receive the care not otherwise available.

MEDICAL REQUIREMENTS

C-26. Guerrilla forces frequently ignore minor injuries and illness due to high motivation and adaptation to frequent hardship and discomfort. Historically, the lack of proper medical attention has led to serious illness and disability causing reduced unit combat effectiveness.

C-27. Health standards in many areas will be below those of the United States. Indigenous personnel may not accept treatment that is desirable for U.S. personnel because of religious beliefs or superstitions. Also, natives may have an acquired immunity to certain diseases of the area.

C-28. A broad range of medical support may be available in the JSOA, although at first, treatment may be limited to rudimentary medical procedures, such as first aid and personal hygiene. Some guerrillas in the past have developed highly organized and effective medical support units and installations. Their organizations paralleled those of conventional forces, to include field hospitals in inaccessible areas.

C-29. Medical elements supporting the resistance forces must be mobile, responsive, and effective in preventing disease and restoring the sick and wounded to duty. There may be no safe rear area where the guerrilla can take casualties for treatment. Wounded and sick personnel become a tactical problem rather than a logistics problem; medical support is a major tactical consideration in all operations. The civilian infrastructure of the guerrillas contributes to medical support by setting up and operating medical facilities. Medical personnel help during combat operations by starting casualty collection points, permitting the remaining members of the guerrillas to keep fighting. Casualties at these points are evacuated to a guerrilla base or civilian care facility.

C-30. In UW, the attitude of the sick and wounded is extremely important. The emotional importance the individual soldier attributes to the medical service goes a long way in his care and treatment. Because the sick and wounded can find themselves in difficult conditions, they have simple wants for shelter, food, and medical treatment. Standards of care are not lowered; these soldiers may just be unaware of any shortcomings in the medical care they receive. Experience has shown that a soldier may have major surgery under extreme hardship conditions and yet demonstrate remarkable recuperative power.

MEDICAL NET

C-31. The medical net in the JSOA is kept as simple as possible, just enough to provide security and fit the estimated needs of future expansion of the JSOA. Medical personnel refine and modify the net after it is functioning and secure. When setting up a medical net, personnel must consider the following:

- Scale of activities already in existence and those planned.
- Potential increase in strength, activities, and operations.
- Physical factors, including topography, climate, and geography, plus transportation and communications.
- The number, availability, and dependability of medically qualified and semiqualified personnel in the JSOA.
- The attitude of the population, government, and guerrilla toward medical problems and the medical standards accepted in the area.
- Existing nonmedical operational facilities of the area command.

C-32. Medical personnel may use the existing intelligence and security nets to start a separate medical net for collecting medical intelligence. They can also use the existing logistics net to transport medical supplies.

AID STATION

C-33. Overall, mission planning includes locating and operating an aid station. Medical personnel provide emergency medical treatment at this location. Evacuation of wounded personnel from the battle area begins here. Because the condition of the wounded may preclude movement to the unit base, they are hidden in secure locations and the auxiliary is notified. The auxiliary will care for and hide the wounded or evacuate them to a treatment facility.

C-34. The evacuation of the dead is important for security reasons. If the enemy identifies the dead, the safety of the guerrilla families may be jeopardized. Personnel evacuate and cache the bodies of those killed in action until they can be properly buried or disposed of IAW the customs of the local population. Removal and burial of the dead will deny the enemy valuable intelligence concerning indigenous casualties.

C-35. As the operational area develops and the situation favors the sponsor, evacuation of the more seriously injured or diseased personnel to friendly areas may become possible. This action will lighten the burden on local facilities and provide a higher standard of medical care for the remaining patients. Air evacuation is the most logical evacuation means but the disadvantage is its inherent threat to security. Landing sites must be located well away from sensitive areas, and guerrilla forces must secure and control the surrounding area until the aircraft leaves.

CONVALESCENT FACILITY

C-36. The area where patients are sent to recuperate is called a convalescent facility. These patients are discharged as soon as possible. A convalescent facility may be a safe house in which one or two convalescents are recuperating with their necessary cover stories, or it could be in any base camp in guerrilla-controlled areas.

GUERRILLA HOSPITAL

C-37. The guerrilla hospital is a medical treatment facility or complex of smaller facilities providing inpatient medical support to the guerrilla force. A guerrilla hospital is established during the organization and buildup phase of a resistance organization, must be ready for operation at the start of combat operations, and must continue to provide medical support until directed otherwise. The hospital is generally in the JSOA it supports but considerations of METT-TC may dictate otherwise. An indigenous medical officer with advice and assistance of the U.S. SF group or battalion surgeon will usually command the guerrilla hospital. However, depending on circumstances within the JSOA, the group or battalion surgeon may be the commander.

C-38. The guerrilla hospital rarely, if ever, outwardly resembles a conventional hospital. The requirement for strict security, flexibility, and rapid mobility precludes visible comparison with conventional military or any civilian medical facilities. As the guerrilla force consolidates its hold on the JSOA, all medical support functions will tend to consolidate. Safe areas allow the establishment of a centralized system of medical care.

Sophisticated hospitals permit care that is more elaborate because they provide a wider selection of trained personnel, specialized equipment, and the capability of more extensive and prolonged treatment. Hospital considerations will depend on the following factors.

Location

C-39. The guerrilla hospital staff conducts a reconnaissance for possible hospital sites and coordinates the training of guerrilla members who will support hospital operations. The hospital should be in a secure area but accessible to casualties. Site planners must consider security, topography, distance, mobility, and enemy counterguerrilla activities. A sanctuary across an international border is ideal for a guerrilla hospital.

Security

C-40. There must be strict security measures to protect the covert nature of the guerrilla hospital operations. Security compromises can lead to the capture of the hospital staff, patients, and supplies, which may compromise members of the auxiliary or underground or jeopardize the entire operation.

Communications

C-41. Rapid communications are essential between the hospital command and the area or sector commander to maintain adequate medical support and ensure survival. Coordinating hospital movement, receiving casualties and supplies, requesting support, and disseminating intelligence all depend on rapid and secure communications.

Medical Supplies

C-42. After infiltration, the SFOD requests adequate medical supplies for initial hospital operations. Plans must provide for automatic and on-call medical resupply, although the staff should make maximum use of locally available supplies. The staff coordinates with the guerrilla force to acquire food and rations for the hospital patients.

Sections

C-43. A guerrilla hospital has several sections. Some sections are collocated; others should be dispersed for security reasons. Staffing a guerrilla hospital depends on the mission and availability of trained medical personnel. Personnel must be attached to the hospital to provide security, communications, and logistic support. There are seven recommended sections of a guerrilla hospital.

C-44. **Command and Control.** The C2 section provides command over hospital personnel and supervision of hospital functions. It maintains communications with the area or sector commander of the hospital. It coordinates security for the hospital.

C-45. **Security.** Security is primarily a function of location, early warning, and movement. The guerrilla hospital should be located in an area where the local populace is friendly or sympathetic to U.S. personnel and the guerrillas.

Security should rely heavily on early warning, diversionary tactics, and movement to alternate locations.

C-46. **Logistics.** This section provides logistic support, to include supply, transportation, and graves registration.

C-47. **Sorting.** Personnel in this section establish and maintain one or more sites that serve as staging areas for limited medical care and movement of patients and supplies to the treatment section. For security reasons, these sites are the only contact the guerrilla force has with the hospital.

C-48. **Treatment.** Medical, surgical, and immediate postoperative care comes from this section. It is the central activity of the hospital, and all other sections support it. Individuals staffing triage sites should not be told the location of the treatment center. Only treatment center staff members will pick up patients at triage sites to take them to the central treatment center.

C-49. **Convalescent.** This section establishes facilities to care for patients no longer requiring the intensive support provided by the treatment section. Such facilities increase the dispersion of patients. Depending on the condition of the patients placed in convalescent facilities, hospital personnel may not be required to continually staff this area.

C-50. **Outstaging.** This section establishes sites where patients may be transported once they have received maximum benefits from hospitalization. These sites are basically unmanned geographic points used as drop-off locations where patients may be returned to their units ready for combat.

MEDICAL TRAINING OF GUERRILLA FORCES

C-51. The SFOD medic begins medical training of guerrilla forces at the earliest possible opportunity. He selects the personnel to be trained and screens them for their abilities. Those with potential are trained as company medics or nurses. He then develops the training program for each of the different functions needed within the guerrilla medical system. He teaches the principles of "self help" and "buddy aid" to the entire guerrilla force. Other training includes preventive medicine procedures, basic sanitation, personal hygiene, and individual protective measures. He also ensures immunizations of the guerrilla force and their families.

C-52. The newly trained medical personnel should make maximum use of all medical facilities. They also help the medic train additional medical personnel. The amount and quality of the training depends on the situation, facilities, and instructors. However, the knowledge and ability of the SFOD medic will ultimately decide the success of the program.

PERIODIC MEDICAL REPORTS

C-53. Depending on the tactical and medical situations in the JSOA, the SFOB or FOB will determine the frequency and contents of periodic medical reports. Before infiltration, the SFOB or FOB briefs the SFOD on the health of the guerrilla forces, casualty rate (wounds or diseases), and overall guerrilla medical condition.

C-54. The training status report will include—

- New training programs since last report.
- Change in number of trainees.
- Change in number of graduates from training programs.
- Adequacy of training aids.

C-55. The medical program report will include—

- Medical supply status, to include the following:
  - Supplies reduced to critical level.
  - Success rate with supply procurement within the AO.
  - General condition of supplies and equipment following air resupply operations.
- New projects and facilities since the last report and any losses due to enemy activity.
- Any serious medical problems that may exist and the level of care patients are receiving in facilities of friendly forces.
- Whether other medical personnel are aiding friendly forces more than expected.
- Number of new guerrilla personnel (both full- and part-time) and their skills and combat effectiveness.
- Any special medical problems unique to the area.
- Any knowledge of enemy medical situation, such as—
  - Standards of medical care.
  - Attitudes or actions toward wounded guerrillas and U.S. personnel.
  - Antiguerrilla activities toward medical facilities.

Legal Principles

Seven basic legal principles forged from the Hague and Geneva Conventions, the International Declaration of Human Rights, and the customary laws of war govern all U.S. military operations. They are as follows:

- Observance of fundamental human rights will recognize the dignity and worth of the individual and the fundamental freedom of all without distinction as to race, sex, language, or religion. Human rights violations will not be tolerated. As with violations of the law of war, U.S. soldiers will report human rights violations when they become aware of them.
- Civilians shall be treated humanely and may not be used to shield military operations.
- EPWs and civilian detainees will be treated humanely and IAW the provisions of the Geneva Conventions.
- U.S. soldiers are entitled to similar humane treatment should they fall into the enemy's hands.
- Orders to commit war crimes **are illegal** and must be disobeyed.
- Soldiers who violate the law of war will be held responsible for their actions. Superiors who order violations of the law of war are criminally and personally responsible for such orders, as are subordinates who carry out the orders.
- Weapons, munitions, and techniques calculated to cause unnecessary pain and suffering are forbidden.

GROUP JUDGE ADVOCATE

D-1. All Army special operations forces (ARSOF) operations will comply with U.S. and international law, national policy, DOD directives, and ARs whether SF operations are conducted during war or stability operations and support operations.

D-2. Department of the Army requires that a judge advocate (JA) be consulted throughout the operational planning process. The JA reviews SO plans to ensure they comply with all applicable laws providing maximum protection to SFOD members in the event they are captured or detained.

RESPONSIBILITIES

D-3. The group JA assigned to the SFOD provides legal advice that an SF group commander requires to perform his assigned mission. SO missions are politically sensitive, particularly in stability operations and support operations, and are fraught with many potential legal pitfalls. During mission planning, the commander considers traditional law of war requirements, domestic U.S. law (such as security assistance and intelligence statutes), and international law in mutual defense treaties and HN support agreements. Failure to comply with such legal and policy demands could cause embarrassment and even criminal investigation and prosecution for the commander and his staff. In consultation with a CA International Law Officer (ILO), the JA also reviews any international agreements, treaties, and other legal documents that may affect or be affected by the UW operation.

QUALIFICATIONS

D-4. The JA provides legal advice to the commander. He knows not only the applicable laws but also the missions of his client. The JA must have a working knowledge of the force structure, missions, doctrine, and tactics of the SFOD he advises. This knowledge should come from prior ARSOF training, experience, and close working relationships with commanders and staffs. In ideal situations, the JA would be at least an SF-qualified major. He would also have at least a Top Secret clearance and access to the information he requires to do his job effectively.

INCIDENTAL ROLES

D-5. The JA serves on the SFOD's targeting panel to review legitimacy of the target, methods used against the target, and the legal implications of civilian and collateral damage. He would participate in traditional staff functions and observe or participate in training. He must demonstrate to the command that he is a soldier as well as an attorney and can carry his own weight as an SFOD member. He must not lose sight of the fact he is an attorney with special obligations and responsibilities, such as dispensing objective and well-reasoned legal advice.

USE OF FORCE

D-6. Force means physical violence, such as terrorist strikes or invasion, not other forms of coercion. International law contains a general prohibition on the use of force; that is, physical violence or the threat of physical violence. This prohibition is memorialized in the UN Charter Article 2(4): "All members shall refrain in their international relations from the threat or use of force against the territorial integrity or political independence of any state."

D-7. The UN Charter also outlaws aggressive war. Aggression is the use of armed force, bombardment, or blockade inconsistent with the UN Charter. The sponsoring of terrorists, mercenaries, or irregular combatants is also considered aggression.

D-8. The International Court of Justice in Nicaragua versus United States has ruled a state is not permitted to resort to "self-defense" against aggression unless it is subjected to an armed attack. The state may be able to take "proportionate countermeasures." It is U.S. policy that once a terrorist or other attack occurs or is expected to occur, the United States can use force to prevent or deter attacks unless reasonable grounds exist to believe that no further attack will be undertaken. The United States is committed to using force in its self-defense only when necessary and only to the extent it is proportionate to the specific threat.

D-9. A recognized exception to the prohibition on the use of force is the law of self-defense. This inherent right of self-defense is also codified in the UN Charter, Article 51. This article states "Nothing in the present charter shall impair the inherent right of individual or collective self-defense if an armed attack occurs against a Member of the United Nations until the Security Council has taken measures necessary to maintain international peace and security." Also recognized by customary international law is the doctrine of "anticipatory self-defense," that is, defensive action taken in response to an imminent armed attack by another State or recognized international state.

ABDUCTIONS

D-10. Abduction is the forcible, nonconsensual removal of a person by one state from the territory of another state. American law enforcement officials refer to such abductions as "arrests." To be acceptable under international law, abduction must satisfy more exacting standards than the availability of an arrest warrant issued by the state responsible for the action. Abduction may be considered criminal conduct in the state from which a person was taken. Additionally, regardless of whether the state from which an individual was taken is hostile to the abducting state, abductions constitute an extremely sensitive operation that can significantly affect international relations. The United States reserves the right to engage in nonconsensual abductions for three specific reasons:

- If a state for internal political reasons may be unwilling to extradite a target or give its public consent to the target's removal. Unofficially, the state may be prepared to have the target removed without granting formal consent and may even offer some cooperation in carrying out the action.

- When the target is an extremely dangerous individual and is accused of grave violations of international law, such as air piracy.

- To prevent terrorists, other dangerous individuals, and their state supporters from assuming they are safe from such unilateral action.

D-11. A 1989 abduction of a Mexican national from Mexico by other Mexican nationals was in response to an offer by the United States to pay his bounty upon delivery to the United States. The U.S. trial court judged this action an illegal acquisition of jurisdiction. The charges that led to the U.S. offer were dismissed for lack of legally acquired custody over the accused. Under U.S. law, custody of the accused cannot be obtained in such a way as to shock the sensitivities of the court.

ATTACKS ON TERRORISTS AND TERRORIST CAMPS

D-12. The United States recognizes and strongly supports the principle that a state, subject to continuing terrorist attacks, may respond with appropriate use of force to actively defend against further attacks. This policy complies with the inherent right of self-defense recognized in the UN Charter.

USE OF OTHER FORCE

D-13. Presidential Executive Order 12333 states, "No person employed by or acting on behalf of the United States Government shall engage in, or conspire to engage in, assassination." Article 23B of the Hague Conventions of 1907 essentially prohibits wartime assassination, outlawing the "treacherous wounding or killing" of the enemy, or offering a reward for an enemy "dead or alive." Neither Executive Order nor the Hague Conventions prohibit attacks on individual soldiers or officers of the enemy whether in the zone of hostilities, occupied territory, or elsewhere. An individual combatant can be targeted lawfully whether he or she is directly involved in combat, providing support, or acting as a staff planner. A harsh but accepted consequence of such military operations is the collateral death of noncombatants following lawful attacks.

ENEMY PRISONERS OF WAR

D-14. The SFOD captures a prisoner and is now at an immediate disadvantage. One or two men must guard the EPWs, which reduces the strength of the SFOD and impacts on its capability to complete the mission. EPWs will hamper the movement of the SFOD and increase the likelihood of the SFOD's compromise.

TREATMENT OF AN EPW

D-15. The SFOD must treat the EPWs humanely and afford them all rights and privileges required under the Geneva Convention for the Treatment of Prisoners of War. EPWs will not be targeted, even if their presence jeopardizes the mission. The SFOD has four options with regard to EPWs:

- Take the individuals into custody and evacuate them later.
- Take the individuals into custody, hold them, and later leave them where they are likely to be found. While in U.S. custody, they must be treated IAW the Geneva Conventions.
- Take the individuals into custody and later turn them in to an allied power. The allied power must be a signatory to the Geneva Conventions and willing to treat the EPWs as required by the Geneva Conventions.
- **DO NOT** take the individuals into custody; just let them walk away.

USE OF THE ENEMY'S UNIFORM

D-16. Article 23F of the Hague Conventions of 1907 prohibits the improper use of the enemy's uniform, that is, wearing its uniform while engaged in combat. The difficult issue is that of finding a proper use of the uniform. Although wearing the uniform while engaged in actual combat is unlawful, U.S. forces may wear it to allow movement into and through the enemy's territory. U.S. policy states that the enemy's uniform may be used for infiltration behind enemy lines. However, Article 39 of Protocol I to the Geneva Conventions prohibits this and other uses of the enemy's uniform. An enemy nation party to Protocol I may consider the use of its uniform by U.S. forces as a war crime and take remedial action.

Appendix E

Logistics Considerations

The types, quantity, and phasing of supplies influence the guerrillas, their capabilities and limitations, and the type of missions they undertake. Supplies and equipment made available to the guerrillas may influence their morale since each shipment represents encouragement and assurance of support from the outside world. Once a channel of supply is established, the guerrillas will continue to rely on that source for support.

RESOURCES

E-1. Historically, guerrillas have lived off the land. The resources of a country and distribution of these resources affect the size and number of guerrillas that may be organized and maintained in a JSOA. The area command provides supplies to the guerrillas within the JSOA. The command must consider resources in food-producing areas when it organizes additional guerrillas. Guerrillas in the JSOA at first depend heavily on these local sources for their support. Logistic plans are based on an equitable system that limits potential hardships to civilians and does not alienate them. This system gives the SFOD strong leverage to guide and mentor the guerrilla leaders.

LOGISTIC SUPPORT TO THE GUERRILLA FORCES

E-2. Logistic support of guerrilla forces includes the same functions as those of conventional forces: labor, maintenance, construction, hospitalization, evacuation, supply, and transportation. Problems of transporting supplies and equipment over or through territory under enemy control complicate this support. It creates a requirement for clandestine delivery, which limits the amount of external logistic support for the JSOA. External sources have not always furnished extensive transportation, maintenance, hospitalization, evacuation, and construction to the JSOA. METT-TC and the delivery means available determine the nature and extent of external logistic support. External support will eventually end, and the guerrillas must be prepared to continue without these supplies.

LOGISTIC SUPPORT TO THE THEATER

E-3. Logistic preparation of the theater (LPT) combines peacetime planning actions to maximize means of providing logistic support to the commander's plan. LPT would reduce the time and resources required to support the UW operation in-theater by maximizing the use of contracting and war reserves strategic lift resources. Three primary considerations that affect support for the guerrilla forces are explained below.

Geographic Location

E-4. Geographic location determines the type and extent of the logistic support needed. In agriculturally productive areas, the guerrilla's need for an external source of food will be less than in those areas unsuitable for agriculture. Location affects the type and amount of personal clothing, equipment, and life expectancy of these items. It also has a bearing on diseases and noncombat injuries. The geography of an area and the enemy situation influence the type of targets to be attacked.

Size of Force

E-5. When local food procurement is only adequate for the existing force, food supply problems will limit the size of forces. Intelligence in the JSOA enables the SFOD and the area commanders to forecast needs and plan appropriate procurement in advance.

Type of Operation

E-6. Available support determines the type of operation that can be conducted. Support for various operations can range from a rifle for one sniper to weapons, communications, food, and medicine for a company raiding an enemy supply depot or troop installation. The expected nonavailability of these logistics in the early phases will dictate doing small, easy combat operations.

PLANNING

E-7. Logistic plans traditionally have provided support to the guerrilla forces on an increasing scale within the limits and capabilities of the sponsoring power. Initial plans are based on forecasts prepared by the staff of the theater SO commander. The ability to meet requirements for any protracted operation depends on the validity of the initial assessment made during isolation.

E-8. The organizations and agencies that execute logistic plans must be able to adjust rapidly to changes. Higher HQ, enemy action, weather, and unforeseen developments within the JSOA may impose changes. The support provided the guerrilla forces should be continuous, and plans to provide that support must be kept flexible to meet changing conditions. Flexibility is achieved by—

- Having primary, alternate, and contingency plans.
- Locating installations throughout the area to reduce to the minimum the travel time of guerrilla forces.
- Providing adequate reserves of supplies, personnel, equipment, communication, and transportation assets from which prompt deliveries can be made.
- Having several principal and alternate points and routes for delivery of equipment and supplies for the guerrilla forces.

E-9. The time between planning and executing and the time involved in executing an operation expose the logistic situation to unforeseen developments. To be successful, the entire logistic scheme must be highly flexible. During joint planning, the SFOB or FOB and the SFOD develop tentative supply plans for each JSOA. The SFOD may alter these plans based on its area assessment.

E-10. The guerrilla force has two sources of logistic support. Those sources are either internal—from within the JSOA—or they are external, from the sponsor.

Internal Support

E-11. The JSOA must first provide the required internal logistic support. The area command must develop an effective internal logistic system tailored to the needs of the operation. It must balance its support requirements against the need to gain and maintain civilian goodwill and cooperation. Imposing excessive demands on the civilian population may adversely affect this cooperation.

E-12. Battlefield recovery is the primary method of resupply in the JSOA using enemy equipment and supplies. Through offensive operations, the guerrilla force can satisfy its logistic requirements and at the same time deny the enemy's use of these supplies. With good intelligence and proper planning, guerrillas can conduct raids and ambushes against small, isolated enemy installations and unescorted convoys to capture the needed items from these targets of opportunity.

E-13. Personnel may use currency to purchase supplies from internal sources. Money may be of the area or be a suitable substitute, such as gold or promissory notes. Procurement through purchase is usually restricted to critical or scarce items not available elsewhere. The guerrilla force must ensure that the infusion of outside currency does not disrupt the local economy, unless economic disruption is also a goal.

E-14. The guerrilla force may organize a levy system based on the ability of each family or group to contribute. This system ensures that the burden of supplying the guerrillas is distributed evenly throughout the civilian population. The local population is told that payment will eventually be made for the supplies taken. The area command supply officer may give receipts to individuals. He also keeps records of the transactions. When establishing the levy system, the commander considers many obstacles that could affect procurement in his operational area. Among them are—

- Chronic food shortages.
- Enemy interference or competition for supplies.
- Impact of combat actions, such as "scorched earth" policies and nuclear, biological, and chemical (NBC) or radioactive contamination.
- Competition from other rival guerrilla units.

E-15. The area command may not want to engage in barter with the civilian population because of possible adverse effects on the levy system. Sometimes it is mutually beneficial to exchange critical items; for example, medical supplies for food, clothing, or services.

E-16. Guerrilla forces cut off from most civilian production facilities and support often find it necessary to improvise their own field expedients. They may have to plant and raise some of their own foodstuff and livestock. Based on the percentage of supplies available from external sources and those available internally, the area commander may consider establishing farms and even factories for the production and repair of hard-to-find items.

E-17. Confiscation is a supply method that the guerrilla force may use to fulfill requirements that cannot be met by other methods of internal supply. It often confiscates items when civilians refuse to cooperate or are actively collaborating with the enemy. Confiscation alienates the civilian population. The guerrilla force uses this method only in emergencies or to punish collaborators. The area command must strictly control confiscation to be sure it does not deteriorate into indiscriminate looting. Confiscation is the least desirable method of gaining internal logistic support.

External Support

E-18. The area command normally limits supplies from an external sponsor to items essential for support of combat operations. These items usually consist of standard arms, ammunition, demolitions, and communications equipment. Under certain conditions, a sponsor may expand its logistic support to include evacuation of the sick and wounded, food, clothing, medicine, and nonstandard items unavailable in the area.

CHARACTERISTICS OF LOGISTICS

E-19. Various services and organizations under theater control render their support to SF through theater directives. The theater supplies requirements peculiar to SF from local sources and agencies within the JSOA. The plans and preparations for combat operations include many difficult logistic problems. Theater command, lower commands under theater, and the JSOA must wrestle with these problems.

E-20. The Army supply system provides logistics support for deployed SFODs with funds allocated to the SF commander for local purchase and contract, or both. The existence and capability of Army support activities in the area, the mission, and duration of the mission determine the level of support. An allocation of funds is required to support deployment for critical or unprogrammed requirements in areas where the Army supply system cannot provide support. The guerrilla force uses these funds for barter, local purchase, local hire, and contractual services in support of the SFODs. Sometimes, funds are required to support indigenous paramilitary or irregular units organized by the SFOD.

E-21. Once the SFOD is assigned or attached to a command for employment, the operational base (SFOD, FOB, or AOB) provides logistics support. The base then contacts the special operations support element (SOSE). A SOSE coordinates external logistics support and sustainment for the operational bases in the rear area. This support follows conventional logistics support procedures, and provisions for it are included in existing unified command UW plans. The theater SOC serves as the agency to prepare UW logistics support estimates, which the SFOB or FOB coordinates and processes. The quantity and types of supplies and equipment carried by SF on their infiltration (accompanying supply) are determined by—

- Physical capabilities.
- Responsiveness to friendly control.
- Contacts existing with guerrilla forces.
- Size and status of training.
- Enemy capabilities.
- Infiltration agency limitations.
- Land and sea infiltration limitations.
- Requirements for survival.
- Available resources in the JSOA.

E-22. Preparation for logistics support of the guerrilla forces requires much time. It is often necessary to move men and equipment to start the buildup of needed facilities and supplies before assigning detailed tasks. In these circumstances, the logistics support activities are based on the broad missions assigned to the SF elements. Time, distance, and enemy action and capabilities affect all logistic activities. The projected JSOA and the enemy's dispositions and capabilities may require special transportation facilities and close coordination with other forces within the theater.

PHASES OF SUPPLY

E-23. Included in phases of supply are accompanying, resupply (automatic and emergency), and on-call or routine. Each of these is discussed in the following paragraphs.

ACCOMPANYING

E-24. The SFOD may take accompanying supplies into the JSOA at the time of infiltration. It receives these supplies in isolation at the SFOB or FOB. While undergoing mission preparation in isolation, the SFOD prepares and rigs its accompanying supply for delivery. The threat in the JSOA dictates the quantity and type of supplies and equipment to be included. Other influences are the—

- Capabilities, size, and responsiveness of the guerrilla force to sponsor assistance.
- Enemy capabilities and situation (METT-TC).
- Method of infiltration (air, land, or sea).
- Requirements for SERE.
- Available resources in the JSOA.
- Size and capability of the reception committee.
- Requirements for sustaining operations pending receipt of an automatic resupply.

- Need for key items of equipment to partially equip a cadre nucleus of the guerrilla force when a reception committee is expected on infiltration.

- Other items of equipment and supplies to help establish rapport with the guerrillas.

RESUPPLY

E-25. The SFOD preselects resupply items in isolation to replenish or supplement consumed supplies. The SFOD receives these items after infiltration. In the past, these items were called follow-up supplies because they followed infiltration. Resupply is delivered automatically on a time schedule or CONPLAN when an event happens or does not happen.

E-26. The SFOB or FOB schedules the delivery of automatic and emergency resupply to the SFODs. Preplanned automatic resupply provides the guerrilla force with immediate supplies and equipment until on-call or routine resupply procedures are established. Supply personnel normally pack equipment and supplies in appropriate aerial delivery containers that have a cargo capacity of 500 pounds or less to ease handling and transportation within the JSOA. Packers mark door bundles for easy ID once they arrive on the DZ. To allow rapid clearance of the DZ, the contents of each container are further packaged in man-portable units of about 50 pounds each. Packers must brief DZ parties on these man-portable containers. If the containers are to be carried long distances, the SFOD must arrange transportation assets with the guerrilla support arm (auxiliary).

Automatic Resupply

E-27. The SFOD plans for automatic resupply before infiltration for delivery time, location, contents, and the ID marking system or authentication. Automatic resupply is delivered after the SFOD successfully infiltrates and establishes radio contact unless the SFOD cancels, modifies, or reschedules the delivery. Automatic resupply augments equipment that could not be carried in on the initial infiltration. Automatic resupply also reinforces U.S. support of the guerrillas. In addition, it fulfills the need for selected items to equip a nucleus of the guerrilla force should the reception committee not appear on infiltration.

Emergency Resupply

E-28. Emergency resupply items include mission-essential equipment and supplies to restore operational capability and survivability of the SFOD. The detachment plans delivery times, methods, and locations and contents of emergency resupply before infiltration.

E-29. As a minimum, resupply should consist of communications equipment and enough mission-essential supplies to establish base contact. Emergency resupply may contain a complete table of organization and equipment (TOE) issue with contents to be determined in isolation.

E-30. Arrangements for emergency resupply delivery begin when radio contact has not been established between the deployed SFOD and the SFOB or FOB within 144 hours. The process is started after 72 hours of no radio contact. It then takes the United States Air Force (USAF) 72 more hours to drop supplies on the DZ. Another triggering event is when a deployed SFOD loses communications with the SFOB or FOB for a predetermined, consecutive number of scheduled call-ups.

ON-CALL OR ROUTINE

E-31. When communications have been established between the SFOD and the SFOB or FOB, external supply begins on-call. Personnel use the abbreviated code in the catalog supply system contained in the SOI to request supplies based on operational need. These supplies consist of major equipment items that are not consumed at a predictable rate. They are held in readiness at theater Army area command (TAACOM) depots or at the SFOB or FOB for immediate delivery on a specific mission-request basis.

E-32. To determine the quantity of supplies to request, the SFOD considers the guerrilla force's rate of expansion; the anticipated tempo of operations; and its ability to receive, transport, store, and secure incoming supplies.

E-33. The SFOD also anticipates its operational needs for supplies and equipment in the JSOA. The MOC at the SFOB or FOB packs and rigs the supplies into man-portable loads and color codes them before infiltration. The MOC color codes the supplies IAW the type of supplies in the load so they will not have to be opened for identification.

E-34. As the guerrilla force expands and logistic requirements increase, internal popular support can no longer provide subsistence without creating hardships or lowering the living standards of the civilians. At this point, the force must obtain logistics support from an external source. This dependence on the external source requires a routine supply system. As the JSOA grows, the need for external supply normally outgrows the on-call method of requesting supplies.

ORGANIZATION OF SUPPLY

E-35. The area command, with advice from the SFOD, plans, develops, operates, and controls the guerrilla force's logistics system. Each element of the area command has a specific role in the logistics system, and each system is developed to meet the specific needs and peculiarities of the JSOA. Supply organization systems may be centralized or decentralized. During the organizational and buildup phase, the command may centralize logistic operations. All supplies are moved into one collection area. The SFOD procures logistics from throughout the JSOA, processes them through a centralized or decentralized collection point, and distributes to all units of the guerrilla force.

E-36. As the JSOA matures, subordinate units take over a sector where they are responsible for establishing a separate and decentralized supply procurement system. They distribute all supplies throughout the JSOA to several distribution centers. This decentralization improves security since the compromise or destruction of the procurement system in one sector will not destroy the entire apparatus. Another advantage of this system is that it permits an equitable distribution of the logistics burden on the civilian population. Movement of supplies between sectors is kept to a minimum, and names, storage sites, and caches are not passed from sector to sector. The area commander delegates supply operations to sector commanders. He retains the responsibility for the overall plans. He also reports supply needs to the sponsoring power and issues directives covering operations. Plans and directives may include—

- Organization of supply and service support units.
- Organization and employment of civilian support units.
- Systems of levy and barter on civilians.
- Receipt of payment for supplies.
- Collection, storage, transportation, and distribution of supplies.
- Quantity and type of supplies to be maintained.
- Allocation of supplies to major lower commands.

E-37. The area commander provides all supply items to the sector commander. The sector commanders supply their units and conduct supply operations according to the plans, directives, and orders of higher HQ. Individual units within their assigned sectors conduct decentralized supply operations. The sector commander makes his needs known to the next-higher HQ for supplies and equipment not available within his area. He distributes all supplies and equipment received from higher HQ. Besides supplying his sector, he may be charged with supplying adjacent sectors as directed by higher HQ.

TYPES OF SUPPLIES

E-38. When compared to a similar-sized conventional force, a guerrilla force has fewer supplies but an even greater need for more basic logistic requirements and equipment for combat operations. These needs consist of food, clothing, shelter, weapons, and ammunition.

E-39. Areas suitable for guerrilla base camps may have some natural foods such as berries, edible plants, and small game. These foods are not sufficient to sustain the energy of active guerrillas. They need high-calorie foods such as rice, sugar, and protein.

E-40. Guerrillas must have seasonal clothing for areas where radical climatic changes occur. Warm and waterproof clothing is a necessity; Gore-Tex is a nice-to-have item for the guerrilla because SFOD members will be wearing their issued Gore-Tex. A guerrilla depends on his feet as the primary mode of transportation. He needs high-quality, well-fitting boots.

E-41. Shelters such as natural caves offer the best protection from the elements and enemy observation. Guerrillas can build sturdy, weatherproof huts from boughs and branches, but they should build them under living foliage for long-term concealment from air observation.

EQUIPMENT AND LOGISTICS

E-42. During mission planning, command personnel identify threat weapons and request and issue similar rifles and ammunition. At first, captured weapons provide the primary source of weapons resupply and replacement parts. In addition, personnel may set up underground facilities to manufacture or repair weapons. They establish accountability by weapon type and quantity to find the rate of ammunition consumption and resupply.

E-43. Usually no replacement of weapons exists except for those captured and provided by the SFOB or FOB. Procedures need to be set up to acquire PLL stock, replace burned out machine gun barrels, and provide armorer repair parts and cleaning kits.

AMMUNITION

E-44. In the early stages of organization and development, ammunition resupply requirements are limited. Once committed to full-scale combat operations, guerrillas will use more ammunition and must determine resupply rates more accurately. Personnel should draw ammunition for combat operations from a cache system. The guerrilla support element normally draws ammunition from the area command or sector command supply caches. Ammunition is distributed on a regular basis. The schedule for distribution is consistent with the tempo of combat operations. Personnel may obtain resupply by setting up caches at preselected RPs or MSSs. They must consider the following when deciding ammunition requirements:

- Each engagement is influenced by the rate of ammunition expenditure—measured in the basic load carried and expenditure per weapon.
- Guerrillas, because they fight on their terms, may use less ammunition than conventional forces. Strict fire discipline should be imposed to conserve the limited amount of ammunition initially available.
- Guerrilla forces are projected to fire one-half to two-thirds of their basic load in any one engagement.
- For planning considerations, guerrilla forces will engage in combat operations once a month.

EXPLOSIVES

E-45. Personnel calculate the amount and type of explosives needed depending on the target. Interdicting complex target systems by multiple attacks at different locations throughout the JSOA requires vast amounts and different kinds of explosives.

INDIVIDUAL EQUIPMENT

E-46. To determine priorities for supplying individual equipment, personnel must study climatic conditions, topography, ethnic groups, and the morale of the guerrillas. Items that are highly ranked include good quality footgear, warm Gore-Tex clothing, ponchos, and first-aid kits. Intermediate priority items may be uniforms, extreme weather clothing, sleeping gear, mission-oriented protective posture (MOPP) gear, load-bearing equipment, PLL, and petroleum, oils, and lubricants (POL) requirements for all weapons and equipment. Normally, 6 months after infiltration, replacement items may be a pair of boots, two or three pairs of woolen socks, and one pair of trousers for each guerrilla. Later, another pair of boots, more pairs of woolen socks, and a uniform for each guerrilla could be expected (METT-TC).

MEDICAL SUPPLIES

E-47. Providing medical supplies and medical treatment is a strong morale factor. Units require basic medicines and supplies to treat sick and wounded guerrillas and the local population. The most important medical supplies are preventive medicines such as antimalaria pills, sulfa, iodine, and various serums for protection against contagious diseases. Also, each platoon-sized element needs at least one first-aid kit. Replacement medical supplies may be made for planning purposes: one third of basic issue after 6 months and one third of total issue after 12 months in the JSOA. Appendix C includes medical aspects.

TRANSPORTATION

E-48. The local auxiliary provides transportation support to the guerrilla forces. In remote or underdeveloped areas, the means of transportation will be on foot or by pack animal. More sophisticated environments will normally have modern forms of transportation available. The guerrilla force may find it advantageous to first acquire and then later operate its own fleet of vehicles. It also requires a supply of PLL and POL.

STORAGE

E-49. The guerrilla force carefully preserves, packs, transports, and stores its equipment as soon as possible to prevent its discovery and loss. It disperses similar equipment throughout cache sites to prevent a complete loss if one cache would be found. Excellent locations are cellars of factories, underground passages, sewers, empty buildings, gardens, and even churches. In Palestine after World War II, small weapons cache sites were concealed within double walls of houses. They also were buried and sealed inside lead pipes. The force usually constructs larger underground caches with special material to withstand the rigors of long-term storage.

CACHES

E-50. The protected storage of supplies and equipment is important to the area command logistics plan. Caches may be used to support current or future operations or be reserved for emergencies. Supplies in excess of current requirements are carefully packaged to prevent damage from exposure. They are then cached in a number of isolated locations known only to the area commander, SFOD members, and key personnel who have access to the cache site map.

E-51. The guerrilla force may establish caches in friendly areas or in enemy-held areas after hostilities have begun. The guerrilla force may locate them in caves, swamps, forests, cemeteries, rivers, or lakes. Dispersed cache systems permit the guerrilla force to operate throughout the JSOA independent of their base areas. Four major considerations for caches are—

- Locations that will help all operations.
- Probability that the particular cache will be needed.

- Maximum storage life of the items involved.

- Problems of providing security to or from the cache.

E-52. SFOD members hide their supplies in remote rural areas to ensure their survival in case of compromise. Possible cache sites are wells, caves, hollow trees, cisterns, unused culverts, and banks below water level of lakes, streams, or rivers. SFOD members must properly prepare the cache site; otherwise, the supplies may be damaged or discovered. They must choose ground that affords adequate drainage of ground water. When caching supplies for more than a few days, the SFOD must be sure the cache is camouflaged, ventilated, and insulated against dampness. It is very important to camouflage the ventilators. SFOD members must also properly preserve the equipment to protect against rust and mildew. Appendix K provides additional guidance on caching.

MISSION SUPPORT SITES

E-53. Guerrillas set up a temporary base or MSS to use when away from their primary base camp during an operation for extended periods. Guerrillas use the MSS for food, shelter, medical support, ammunition, or explosives. Using an MSS eliminates unnecessary movement of supplies and allows the guerrilla force to move rapidly to and from target sites. When selecting an MSS, SFOD members consider cover and concealment, distance to the objective and supply sources, and the presence of enemy security forces in the area.

MAINTENANCE AND REPAIRS

E-54. The SFOD obtains materials from the local civilian economy or through combat operations against the enemy. At first, basic maintenance and minor repair of equipment is limited to operator maintenance. As the movement expands, personnel establish clandestine, makeshift ordnance and repair facilities. The sponsor-provided supply packages contain necessary maintenance and repair items, such as tools, small arms repair kits, replacement parts, and POL cleaning materials. SFOD members must consider the use of special or high-speed equipment that may only complicate the maintenance system by requiring highly trained technicians.

DELIVERY SYSTEMS

E-55. The SFOD in the JSOA delivers all external supplies and equipment to the guerrilla force. It is essential that sensitive items, such as weapons, ammunition, demolitions, radios, drugs, or special equipment, be controlled. An SFOD member must be present at all deliveries of external supplies to ensure positive control and accountability. Usually, sponsor-provided supplies are delivered directly to the individual user. If direct delivery to the user is not desirable or possible, supplies will be delivered to a designated location where they are distributed. Although this system takes much time and effort, it permits centralized control over sponsor-provided supplies and may be the preferred method.

DELIVERY MEANS

E-56. The preferred mission delivery method is by sponsor aircraft, surface ship, or submarine. At first, aerial delivery by parachute may be the best means of supply to a JSOA. Free-drop techniques may be used for certain hardy items. Later, as the JSOA expands and comes under greater friendly control, SFOD members use air-landed supply missions. Supply personnel normally use surface ships or submarines when JSOAs are next to waterways or seas. Resupply operations require secrecy to protect the resupply platform and the reception element. These operations are normally conducted during limited visibility.

PACKAGING

E-57. The SFOB or FOB SPTCEN personnel prepare supplies and equipment for delivery to a JSOA. The size of the package and the number of packages to be transported determines the delivery means. The packaging system is based on man-portable packages weighing about 50 pounds. With this weight limitation, members of the reception committee transportation party can easily move the packages from the supply point to safe sites. Man-portable packages are equipped with carrying straps and are mounted on packboards. The transportation party color codes the packages so personnel can easily identify their contents upon arrival. The SFOB or FOB SPTCEN personnel ensure each package is—

- Waterproofed to permit aboveground and limited underground or underwater cache.
- Packed with instructions (in indigenous language) for all equipment.
- Marked with a prearranged code to identify the contents.
- Packed with an inventory list to aid in identifying lost or damaged material.
- Packed to protect sensitive communications and medical items by using clothing, blankets, or other padding.

E-58. The SFOB or FOB SPTCEN personnel may put combat and morale supply items in the same container. They package ammunition and cleaning equipment with weapons and batteries with flashlights. Additional small arms ammunition, by caliber, may be included as an individual package.

SUPPLY PROCEDURES

E-59. SFOD members use a catalog supply system code to speed up on-call resupply requests and ensure accurate equipment ID and supply items. The system also reduces radio transmission time. To permit maximum user flexibility, the system identifies single major equipment items or several associated items by code words. Personnel catalog these items by class of supplies and group them in individual packaged items or several associated unit items packed together. The catalog supply system is—

- Not secured by itself but reduces message length and transmission time when a variety of supplies are requested.
- Based on mission requirements, CONPLANs, and SOP.
- Prepared under the staff supervision of the group S-4.
- Reproduced in miniature form for operational missions and published in the SOI by the SF group signal officer.

Appendix F

Infiltration

An SF pilot team may infiltrate into the JSOA before the SFOD. The preferred method is for a resistance reception committee to receive the pilot team. Blind infiltrations may be considered, based on METT-TC. The number and type of pilot team personnel will be very dependent on the METT-TC factors. The pilot team may establish contact with the area command element, assess resistance potential, and perform other missions as specified by higher HQ. Based on these factors, an SFOD may be infiltrated later into the JSOA to conduct UW or other SO. The pilot team may exfiltrate on order, according to the OPORD, or at the discretion of the team leader. Pilot team members may exfiltrate anytime before the SFOD's scheduled infiltration, or they may remain in the JSOA as the reception committee for a planned SFOD infiltration. They could also remain and act as an AOB for the infiltration of two or more SFODs.

ARRIVAL SITE

F-1. At the infiltration site, SFOD members must put the sterilization plan into effect and ensure the site is clean and secure. The resistance may execute deception plans if required.

F-2. After infiltration, all personnel must know the assembly and contact plans. The assembly area and the contact point should be close to the DZ (Figure F-1, page F-2). The SFOD's assembly time after infiltration is dependent on the threat reaction time. A minimum number of personnel make contact. The SFOD must employ correct verbal, light, and visual signals. SFOD members must enforce noise, light, and camouflage discipline and keep time spent in the area to a minimum. They must use stealth with proper movement techniques and know their RPs. If enemy contact is made, the SFOD members use IADs, based on METT-TC. A workable alternative CONPLAN, especially on the DZ or LZ, is imperative.

F-3. Movement from the contact site to a "safe area" should be toward the guerrilla base camp. Transportation, if available, would save valuable time; however, movement on foot is always an option.

F-4. During initial assessment, security principles that must be adhered to are—

- Noise and light discipline during transportation or movement.
- Route and halt security (camouflage and IADs are used while maintaining stealth).
- Primary and alternate RPs.

Figure F-1. Assembly Areas and Contact Points

F-5. During movement, SFOD members must anticipate their reaction to orders from the area commander. The SFOD commander conducts observation and security checks during all movement. He also keeps the SFOD oriented to its location and aware of any immediate actions to take in case of enemy confrontation. The SFOD commander must—

- Know the location of key weapons and heavy equipment in the column.
- Begin plans to reestablish contact with the resistance force if the enemy separates the column and the SFOD.
- Check the physical condition of SFOD members during halts.

- Establish initial communications with the SFOB and submit the IER (ANGUS) if possible.

METHODS OF MOVEMENT

F-6. For UW, mission success depends on secrecy. Speed is secondary. Enemy capabilities, disposition, reaction time, and security measures, as well as the CASCOPE factors, affect the selected infiltration method. A heavily guarded border may preclude land infiltration; a strongly defended and patrolled coastline may eliminate infiltration by water; and the enemy's air detection and defense systems may reduce air insertion potential. METT-TC is always an influencing factor.

F-7. SFODs must consider geographic formations when selecting the infiltration method. Terrain affects the selection of an aircraft's altitude, approach and exit routes, landing areas, or parachute operations for any mission aircraft. Mountains could force aircraft to fly higher than desired altitudes, resulting in early aircraft acquisition by enemy radar and increasing its vulnerability.

F-8. Seasonal weather conditions also affect infiltrations. Factors to consider include temperature, precipitation, visibility, clouds, and wind. High altitude or surface winds and their effects on surf conditions or periods of reduced visibility may prohibit the use of parachutes, inflatable boats, or surface and subsurface swimming as entry or recovery techniques. These same conditions generally favor a land infiltration. The adverse weather aerial delivery system (AWADS) reduces the impact of adverse weather as a limiting factor on air infiltrations. Hydrography is the science of describing the sea and marginal land areas and the effect on water operations. The hydrographic conditions on the far-shore and the near-shore sea approach influence water infiltration. These conditions include the offshore water depth, beach gradients, tide, surf, currents, sea bottom, and the location of reefs, sandbars, seaweed, or natural and man-made obstacles.

F-9. Other considerations for UW infiltrations include—

- Light data (periods of twilight, beginning morning nautical twilight [BMNT], early evening nautical twilight [EENT], nautical sunrise, sunset, moon phase, moonrise, and moonset).
- The distance to the contact site, possible base camps, and enemy locations.
- Plans for fire support, deception, E&R, and countermeasures against fratricide. Commanders should use METT-TC as a planning guide.

F-10. The SFOD uses one of three methods to infiltrate into the JSOA—air, land, or water. A combination of the three may also be used. A matrix can be used to determine the type and infiltration method best suited for the mission.

AIR INFILTRATION

F-11. Commanders often consider using air infiltration by Army special operations aviation (ARSOA). Parachute operations are one of the most rapid infiltration methods used by the SFODs. It provides less exposure and risk to the aircraft. Usually standard troop carrier fixed-wing aircraft are well equipped and satisfy airdrop requirements. Some circumstances may require nonstandard aircraft. These situations may require an aircraft capable of parachute delivery of equipment and personnel from high altitudes using MFF parachute techniques. Other techniques include static-line operations on small, unsurveyed DZs or hazardous, tree-covered terrain. Assault aircraft and amphibious or utility aircraft may be available. During infiltration, certain conditions may require that these aircraft conduct air-landing operations on relatively short, unprepared airstrips. Under other circumstances, longer-range tactical aircraft may be used. FM 3-05.210 (currently TC 31-24), *Special Forces Air Operations*, and FM 3-05.211 (currently FM 31-19), *Special Forces Military Free-Fall Operations*, provide detailed planning information on air infiltration.

LAND INFILTRATION

F-12. During land infiltration, the SFOD should move from the launch site clandestinely to an assembly area short of the JSOA border and establish local security. In this scenario, the SFOD will move to the assembly area, conduct a reconnaissance of the crossover point, and conduct the infiltration, preferably during periods of low visibility. The assembly area should provide cover, concealment, and security. The reception committee, through prior coordination, may meet the SFOD at the assembly area to conduct final coordination. It must establish liaison from higher HQ beforehand, in the event friendly forces occupy the border area. The liaison element should remain near the crossover point until the SFOB or FOB has received the initial entry report.

WATER INFILTRATION

F-13. Waterborne operations provide an expanded capability for all SFODs. Through premission analysis, detailed planning, and a unit sustainment training program, the SFOD can deploy for a successful waterborne infiltration. A thorough understanding of all factors affecting successful waterborne-related missions is essential due to the inherently high risk associated with even the most routine waterborne operations. FM 3-05.212 (currently TC 31-25), *Special Forces Waterborne Operations*, provides detailed planning information on waterborne operations.

SFOD EQUIPMENT AND SUPPLIES

F-14. The quantity and type of accompanying equipment and supplies carried by the SFOD on initial infiltration are influenced by the—

- Infiltration and resupply airframes available. The aircraft used to infiltrate the SFOD may be by ARSOA aircraft (MH-60K/L and the MH-47D/E), U.S. Air Force (USAF) aircraft (MC-130, MH-53, or CV-22), or other locally contracted assets.
- Political, psychological, and military threat situation in the JSOA.
- Size and training of the resistance force.
- Infiltration time and site location.
- Contingency operations in the JSOA.

INITIAL ENTRY REPORT

F-15. Infiltration into the JSOA is not complete until the SFOD transmits the IER (ANGUS) by radio to the SFOB or FOB. The SFOB or FOB sends an acknowledgement back to the deployed SFOD. If the SFOD fails to receive the acknowledgment with the primary communication asset (TACSAT radio), SFOD personnel should use HF radio equipment as an alternate means of communicating. Upon receipt of the message, the SFOB will send the SFOD's acknowledgment at the next scheduled call-up, using the alternate HF radio equipment.

F-16. The SFOD should send the IER (ANGUS) within 24 hours after its infiltration time. If the SFOB or FOB does not receive the IER within 72 hours after infiltration, another 72 hours will pass before the emergency resupply is dropped. This procedure gives the SFOD the necessary flexibility to carry out CONPLANs precipitated by enemy action. If possible, it will attempt to contact the SFOB. This flexibility gives the USAF the necessary planning and reaction time. Another option may be to have a preplanned recovery operation on alert for a predesignated recovery site for any survivors. Launch and recovery depend on METT-TC.

EMERGENCY RESUPPLY

F-17. If the deployed SFOD fails to send its IER (ANGUS) to the SFOD or FOB by radio within 72 hours after scheduled deployment, it may, according to the OPORD, start emergency resupply procedures. The SFOD is now assumed to be in an evasion mode. The emergency resupply may be flown by any aircraft and airdropped or airlanded in the JSOA. Any waterborne vessel may transport an emergency resupply to a beach landing site (BLS). The resupply may also be pre-positioned in the evasion corridor by various U.S. agencies.

F-18. When the evasion corridor is long, more than one resupply mission may be needed. SFODs must plan these resupply missions with realistic times and distances traveled. When wounded SFOD members need to be transported, security is difficult but must be maintained. The resupply bundle is dropped primarily to reequip the SFOD for mission accomplishment. The resupply bundle may consist of just enough supplies for the SFOD to establish communications with higher HQ and request further instructions. The resupply bundle might also contain a complete issue of all TOE supplies and weapons for every SFOD member.

Appendix G

Special Forces Area Assessment

This appendix provides an outline format for an area assessment. This format provides a systematic means for compiling and retaining essential information to support SF operations. Although the basic outline is general, it is flexible enough to permit detailed coverage of a given JSOA.

IMMEDIATE—INITIAL ASSESSMENT

G-1. Initial assessment includes those items deemed essential to the operational detachment immediately following infiltration. These requirements must be satisfied as soon as possible after the detachment arrives in the JSOA and should include the—

- Location and orientation.
- Detachment's physical condition.
- Overall security, to include the—
  - Immediate area.
  - Attitude of the local populace.
  - Local enemy situation.
- Status of the local resistance element.

SUBSEQUENT—PRINCIPAL ASSESSMENT

G-2. Principal assessment, a continuous operation, includes those collection efforts that support the continued planning and conduct of operations. It forms the basis for all of the detachment's subsequent activities in the JSOA. The principal assessment should encompass the areas discussed in the following paragraphs.

THE ENEMY

- Disposition.
- Composition, identification, and strength.
- Organization, armament, and equipment.
- Degree of training, morale, and combat effectiveness.
- Operations:
  - Recent and current activities of the unit.
  - Counterguerrilla activities and capabilities with particular attention to reconnaissance units, special troops (airborne, mountain, ranger), rotary-wing or vertical-lift aviation units, CI units, and units having a mass chemical, biological, and radiological (CBR) delivery capability.

G-1

- Unit AORs.
- Daily routine of the units.
- Logistics support to include the following:
  - Installations and facilities.
  - Supply routes.
  - Methods of troop movement.
- Past and current reprisal actions.

SECURITY AND POLICE UNITS

- Dependability and reliability to the existing regime or the occupying power.
- Disposition.
- Composition, identification, and strength.
- Organization, armament, and equipment.
- Degree of training, morale, and efficiency.
- Use and effectiveness of informers.
- Influence on, and relations with, the local populace.
- Security measures over public utilities and government installations.

CIVIL GOVERNMENT

- Control and restrictions, such as—
  - Documentation.
  - Rationing.
  - Travel and movement restrictions.
  - Blackouts and curfews.
- Current value of money, wage scales.
- The extent and effect of the black market.
- Political restrictions.
- Religious restrictions.
- The control and operation of industry, utilities, agriculture, and transportation.

CIVILIAN POPULACE

- Attitudes toward the existing regime or occupying power.
- Attitudes toward the resistance movement.
- Reaction to U.S. support of the resistance.
- Reaction to enemy activities in the country, specifically that portion in the unconventional warfare operating area (UWOA).
- General health and well-being.

POTENTIAL TARGETS

- Railroads.
- Telecommunication.
- POL.
- Electric power.
- Military storage and supply.
- Military HQ and installations.
- Radar and electronic devices.
- Highways.
- Inland waterways and canals.
- Seaports.
- Natural and synthetic gas lines.
- Industrial plants.
- Key personalities.

WEATHER

- Precipitation, cloud cover, temperature, visibility, and seasonal changes.
- Wind speed and direction.
- Light data (BMNT, EENT, sunrise, sunset, moonrise, and moonset).

TERRAIN

- Location of areas suitable for guerrilla bases, units, and other installations.
- Potential LZs, DZs, and other reception sites.
- Routes suitable for—
  - Guerrillas.
  - Enemy forces.
- Barriers to movement.
- The seasonal effect of the weather on terrain and visibility.

RESISTANCE MOVEMENT

- Guerrillas:
  - Disposition, strength, and composition.
  - Organization, armament, and equipment.
  - Status of training, morale, and combat effectiveness.
  - Operations to date.
  - Cooperation and coordination between various existing groups.
  - General attitude toward the United States, the enemy, and various elements of the civilian populace.

- Motivation of the various groups and their receptivity to U.S. presence.
- Caliber of senior and subordinate leadership.
- Health of guerrillas.

- Auxiliaries and the underground:
  - Disposition, strength, and degree of organization.
  - General effectiveness and type of support.
  - Motivation and reliability.
  - Responsiveness to guerrilla or resistance leaders.
  - General attitude toward the United States, the enemy, and various guerrilla groups.

LOGISTICS CAPABILITY OF THE AREA

- Availability of food stocks and water, to include any restrictions for reasons of health.
- Agricultural capability.
- Type and availability of transportation of all categories.
- Types and location of civilian services available for manufacture and repair of equipment and clothing.
- Supplies locally available, to include type and amount.
- Medical facilities, to include personnel, medical supplies, and equipment.
- Enemy supply sources accessible to the resistance.

PREVENTIVE MEDICINE

- Weather:
  - Is the weather cold enough to put emphasis on causes, treatment, and prevention of cold weather injuries?
  - Is the weather hot enough to put emphasis on causes, treatment, and prevention of hot weather injuries?
- Terrain: How does the terrain affect evacuation and medical resupply?
- Indigenous personnel:
  - Physical characteristics. Endurance, ability to carry loads, and performance of other physical feats.
  - Dress. What symbolism is attached to various articles of clothing and jewelry, such as amulets, if any?
  - Attitudes:
    - What taboos and other psychological attributes are present in the society?
    - What rites and practices are used by witch doctors during illness? What do these rites symbolize? Does the practitioner use Western medicines?

- ◆ How do indigenous personnel respond to events such as fear, happiness, anger, and sadness?
- Housing:
  - Analyze physical layout of the community.
  - Determine infestation with ectoparasites and vermin.
- Food:
  - Is food cultivated for consumption? What foods?
  - How do the seasons of the AO influence diet? Does migration in search of food occur?
  - What foods provided by U.S. personnel do the indigenous personnel prefer or reject?
  - What cash crops are raised?
- Water supply, urban. What kind of water treatment plants are used (if any)?
- Water supply, rural:
  - What are the numbers and types of rural water supplies?
  - What treatment is given to water in rural areas? Give attitudes of the indigenous personnel toward standard U.S. purification methods.
- Sewage disposal (when applicable):
  - What are the types and locations of sewage treatment plants?
  - In remote areas, what system is used for disposal of human excrement, offal, and dead animals or humans?
  - What are the attitudes of the indigenous personnel to standard U.S. methods, such as the use of latrines?
- Epidemiology. What specific diseases in each of the three following major categories are present among the guerrillas, their dependents, or their animals?
- Domestic animals:
  - What domestic animals are present?
  - Describe the normal forage.
    - ◆ Do owners supplement the food supply? What food supplements are given, if any?
    - ◆ Are animals penned or allowed to roam?
  - Is any religious symbolism or taboo associated with animals (sacred cows)? Are animals sacrificed for religious purposes?
  - Are local veterinarians available for animal treatment and ante- and post-mortem inspections of meats? What is their training?
- Local fauna. Record species of birds, large and small mammals, reptiles, and arthropods present in the area. If names are unknown, describe (survival purposes).

- Poisonous plants. Record those species that are known to be toxic through contact with the skin, inhalation of smoke from burning vegetation, or through ingestion.

Area Study Outline Format

Copy ___ of ___ Copies

____SFG(A)
Location
Date

AREA STUDY OF JSOA

1. **PURPOSE AND LIMITING FACTORS.**

   a. Purpose. Delineate the area being studied.

   b. Mission. State the mission the area study supports.

   c. Limiting Factors. *Identify factors that limit the completeness or accuracy of the area study.*

2. **GEOGRAPHY, HYDROGRAPHY, AND CLIMATE.** *Divide the operational area into its various definable subdivisions and analyze each subdivision using the subdivisions shown below.*

   a. Areas and Dimensions.

   b. Strategic Locations.

      (1) Neighboring countries and boundaries.

      (2) Natural defenses including frontiers.

      (3) Points of entry and strategic routes.

   c. Climate. *Note variations from the norm and the months in which they occur. Note any extremes in climate that would affect operations.*

      (1) Temperature.

      (2) Rainfall and snow.

      (3) Wind and visibility.

      (4) Light data. *Include BMNT, EENT, sunrise, sunset, moonrise, and moonset.*

      (5) Seasonal effect of the weather on terrain and visibility.

   d. Relief.

      (1) General direction of mountain ranges or ridgelines and whether hills and ridges are dissected.

      (2) General degree of slope.

      (3) Characteristics of valleys and plains.

      (4) Natural routes for and natural obstacles to cross-country movement.

      (5) Location of area suitable for guerrilla bases, units, and other installations.

       (6) Potential LZs, DZs, and other reception sites.

    e. Land Use. *Note any peculiarities especially in the following:*

       (1) Former heavily forested land areas subjected to widespread cutting or dissected bypaths and roads. *Also note the reverse: pastureland or wasteland that has been reforested.*

       (2) Former wasteland or pastureland that has been resettled and cultivated and is now being farmed. *Also note the reverse: former rural countryside that has been depopulated and allowed to return to wasteland.*

       (3) Former swampland or marshland that has been drained, former desert or wasteland now irrigated and cultivated, and lakes created by dams.

    f. Drainage (General Pattern).

       (1) Main rivers, direction of flow.

       (2) Characteristics of rivers and streams. *Include widths, currents, banks, depths, kinds of bottoms, and obstacles.*

       (3) Seasonal variations. *Note dry beds, flash floods.*

       (4) Large lakes or areas with many ponds or swamps. *Include potential LZs for amphibious aircraft.*

    g. Coast. *Examine primarily for infiltration, exfiltration, and resupply points.*

       (1) Tides and waves. *Include winds and current.*

       (2) Beach footing and covered exit routes.

       (3) Quiet coves and shallow inlets or estuaries.

    h. Geological Basics. *Identify types of soil and rock formations. Include areas for potential LZs for light aircraft.*

    i. Forests and Other Vegetation.

       (1) Natural or cultivated.

       (2) Types, characteristics, and significant variations from the norm at different elevations.

       (3) Cover and Concealment. *Include density and seasonal variations.*

    j. Water. *Note ground, surface, seasonal, potability.*

    k. Subsistence.

       (1) Seasonal or year round.

       (2) Cultivated. *Include vegetables, grains, fruits, and nuts.*

       (3) Natural. *Include berries, fruits, nuts, and herbs.*

       (4) Wildlife. *Include animals, fish, and fowl.*

3. **POLITICAL CHARACTERISTICS.** *Identify friendly and hostile political powers and analyze their capabilities, intentions, and activities that influence mission execution.*

a. Hostile Power.

    (1) Number and status of nonnational personnel.

    (2) Influence, organization, and mechanisms of control.

b. National Government (Indigenous).

    (1) Government, international political orientation, and degree of popular support.

    (2) Identifiable segments of the population with varying attitudes and probable behavior toward the United States, its allies, and the hostile power.

    (3) National historical background.

    (4) Foreign dependence or allies.

    (5) National capital and significant political, military, and economic concentrations.

c. Political Parties.

    (1) Leadership and organizational structure.

    (2) Nationalistic origin and foreign ties (if single dominant party exists).

    (3) Major legal parties with their policies and goals.

    (4) Illegal or underground parties and their policies and goals.

    (5) Violent opposition factions within major political organizations.

d. Control and Restrictions.

    (1) Documentation.

    (2) Rationing.

    (3) Travel and movement restrictions.

    (4) Blackouts and curfews.

    (5) Political restrictions.

    (6) Religious restrictions.

4. **ECONOMIC CHARACTERISTICS.** *Identify those economic factors that influence mission execution.*

a. Technological Standards.

b. Natural Resources and Degree of Self-Sufficiency.

c. Financial Structure and Dependence on Foreign Aid.

d. Monetary System.

    (1) Value of money, rate of inflation.

    (2) Wage scales.

    (3) Currency controls.

e. Black Market Activities. *Note the extent and effect of those activities.*

    f.   Agriculture and Domestic Food Supply.

    g.   Industry and Level of Production.

    h.   Manufacture and Demand for Consumer Goods.

    i.   Foreign and Domestic Trade and Facilities.

    j.   Fuels and Power.

    k.   Telecommunications Adequacy by U.S. Standards.

    l.   Transportation Adequacy by U.S. Standards.

        (1) Railroads.

        (2) Highways.

        (3) Waterways.

        (4) Commercial air installations.

    m. Industry, Utilities, Agriculture, and Transportation. *Note the control and operation of each.*

5. **CIVIL POPULACE.** *Pay particular attention to those inhabitants in the AO who have peculiarities and who vary considerably from the normal national way of life.*

    a.   Total and Density.

    b.   Basic Racial Stock and Physical Characteristics.

        (1) Types, features, dress, and habits.

        (2) Significant variations from the norm.

    c.   Ethnic and/or Religious Groups. *Analyze these groups to determine if they are of sufficient size, cohesion, and power to constitute a dissident minority of some consequence.*

        (1) Location or concentration.

        (2) Basis for discontent and motivation for change.

        (3) Opposition to the majority or the political regime.

        (4) Any external or foreign ties of significance.

    d.   Attitudes. *Determine the attitudes of the populace toward the existing regime or hostile power, the resistance movement, and the United States and its allies.*

    e.   Division Between Urban, Rural, or Nomadic Groups.

        (1) Large cities and population centers.

        (2) Rural settlement patterns.

        (3) Area and movement patterns of nomads.

    f.   Standard of Living and Cultural (Educational) Levels.

        (1) Extremes away from the national average.

        (2) Class structure. *Identify degree of established social stratification and percentage of populace in each class.*

g. Health and Medical Standards.

    (1) General health and well-being.

    (2) Common diseases.

    (3) Standard of public health.

    (4) Medical facilities and personnel.

    (5) Potable water supply.

    (6) Sufficiency of medical supplies and equipment.

h. Traditions and Customs (Particularly Taboos). *Note wherever traditions and customs are so strong and established that they may influence an individual's actions or attitude even during a war situation.*

6. **MILITARY AND PARAMILITARY FORCES.** *Identify friendly and hostile conventional military forces (Army, Navy, and Air Force) and internal security forces (including border guards) that can influence mission execution. Analyze nonnational (indigenous) forces using the subdivisions shown below.*

a. Morale, Discipline, and Political Reliability.

b. Personnel Strength.

c. Organization and Basic Deployment.

d. Uniforms and Unit Designations.

e. Ordinary and Special Insignia.

f. Overall Control Mechanism.

g. Chain of Command and Communication.

h. Leadership. *Note officer and noncommissioned officer corps.*

i. Nonnational Surveillance and Control Over Indigenous Security Forces.

j. Training and Doctrine.

k. Tactics. *Note seasonal and terrain variations.*

l. Equipment, Transportation, and Degree of Mobility.

m. Logistics.

n. Effectiveness. *Note any unusual capabilities or weaknesses.*

o. Vulnerabilities in the Internal Security System.

p. Past and Current Reprisal Actions.

q. Use and Effectiveness of Informers.

r. Influence on and Relations With the Local Populace.

s. Psychological Vulnerabilities.

t. Recent and Current Unit Activities.

u. Counterinsurgency Activities and Capabilities. *Pay particular attention to reconnaissance units, special troops (airborne, mountain, ranger), rotary-wing or vertical-lift aviation units, counterintelligence units, and units having a mass NBC delivery capability.*

v. Guard Posts and Wartime Security Coverage. *Note the location of all known guard posts or expected wartime security coverage along the main LOC (railroads, highways, and telecommunications lines) and along electrical power and POL lines.*

w. Forced Labor and/or Detention Camps. *Note exact location and description of the physical arrangement (particularly the security arrangements).*

x. PRC Measures. *Note locations, types, and effectiveness of internal security controls. Include checkpoints, identification cards, passports, and travel permits.*

7. **RESISTANCE ORGANIZATION.** *Identify the organizational elements and key personalities of the resistance organization. Note each group's attitude toward the United States, the hostile power, various elements of the civil populace, and friendly political groups.*

   a. Guerrillas.

      (1) Disposition, strength, and composition.

      (2) Organization, armament, and equipment.

      (3) Status of training, morale, and combat effectiveness.

      (4) Operations to date.

      (5) Cooperation and coordination between various existing groups.

      (6) Motivation of the various groups and their receptivity.

      (7) Quality of senior and subordinate leadership.

      (8) General health.

   b. Auxiliaries and the Underground.

      (1) Disposition, strength, and degree of organization.

      (2) General effectiveness and type of support.

      (3) Responsiveness to guerrilla or resistance leaders.

   c. Logistics Capability.

      (1) Availability of food stocks and water. Include any restrictions for reasons of health.

      (2) Agricultural capability.

      (3) Type and availability of transportation of all categories.

      (4) Types and location of civilian services available for manufacture and repair of equipment and clothing.

      (5) Medical facilities, to include personnel, medical supplies, and equipment.

      (6) Enemy supply sources accessible to the resistance.

8. **TARGETS.** *(The objective in target selection is to inflict maximum damage on the hostile power with minimum expenditures of men and materiel. Initially, a guerrilla force may have limited operational capabilities to interdict or destroy hostile targets.) Study the target areas. Identify and analyze points of attack. List targets in order of priority by system and IAW mission requirements. As appropriate, address both fixed and mobile (generic) targets.*

9. **EFFECTS OF CHARACTERISTICS.** *State conclusions reached through analysis of the facts developed in the previous paragraphs.*

    a.   Effects on Hostile COAs.

    b.   Effects on Friendly COAs.

Appendix I

Administrative Procedures

Based on preinfiltration intelligence, the SFOD makes tentative plans for formalizing administrative machinery to support a resistance force during UW operations in the JSOA. Before the SFOD's infiltration and contact by the Secretary of Defense or DOD agencies with the government-in-exile or area command, the SFOB or FOB can guide the establishment of pay scales, rank structure, codes, and legal systems. This guidance will ensure uniformity in all AOs throughout the country and will preclude inflated rank structures, unrealistic pay scales, and kangaroo courts. Necessary forms to support this administrative machinery may be drafted and printed during the SFOD isolation phase. Final decisions on the administrative organization must be delayed until after infiltration. By then the area commander, in concert with the SFOD, will have resolved the majority of outstanding issues.

PLANNING CONSIDERATIONS

I-1. Administrative systems can be established early in the planning stages of deployment and finalized in the JSOA. They should be simple and effective and, as a minimum, include—

- Accountability of sensitive items, to include weapons, radios, cryptographic material, and drugs.
- Accurate and updated personnel files on the guerrillas. Fingerprints and photos can be used for ID. ID cards can serve as a pay receipt.
- Records of the sick, wounded, and deceased
- Records of awards, decorations, schools, and special skills.
- A daily staff journal. Written OPORDs and reports will be kept to a minimum, coded for security, and issued on a need-to-know basis.

RECORDS

I-2. Each guerrilla base camp must have an administrative section to maintain essential records. As the area complex develops, personnel can centralize administration and duplicate information and records that could compromise the operation. These records should be forwarded to the administrative section of the area command for miniaturization, classification, and disposition.

I-3. Because of its ultimate historical importance, personnel should maintain an operational journal. Reports of combat engagements must include the following information concerning the guerrilla force—the designation and commander, the type of action, approximate strength, and casualties. This data should be made available to PSYOP and CA personnel for their operations.

I-4. The command structure record should reflect the designation of the various units within the guerrilla force (similar to an MTOE) and the auxiliary. It should also include the names and designation of key personnel.

I-5. The personnel dossier should list members of the various organizations within the area command, and it must be kept current. In the initial stages of individual unit development, duplicate copies of their dossier can be sent forward to the next-higher command when feasible.

I-6. Personnel records should be maintained on guerrillas and other key personnel in the resistance movement to prove or refute posthostility claims for wartime service. Opposition may be expected when someone recommends to the area commander that all personnel be photographed and fingerprinted. Such opposition can be overcome, however, with assurances that a viable, secure system can be established and that the records will be exfiltrated from the JSOA and maintained at the SFOB or FOB. Records may be microfilmed and placed in a secure cache in the JSOA as an alternate means to exfiltration. Photographing these documents and subsequently caching or exfiltrating the negatives provides a method of preserving and securing records not obtainable by other means. The SFOD will find its organic photographic equipment useful in making ID photographs for population control. Photographs are also helpful in organizing and controlling resistance forces. Personnel should take photographs at frequent intervals to send forward and avoid having a lot of sensitive material on hand. After processing the negatives and determining their acceptability, personnel may destroy the originals of unit records or send them to higher HQ.

I-7. The information placed on personnel records should include the full name of the individual and—

- His home village or city.
- The date he joined the resistance force.
- Whether an oath of enlistment was taken.
- The date he was discharged.
- Promotions and demotions.
- Acts of bravery.
- Awards and decorations.
- Rank or position attained in the resistance force.
- Any disciplinary action taken against him.

I-8. Posting to the initial records may be by serial number; thus, there is no reference to individuals by name and no incriminating data to associate them with the resistance organization. Code names and simulated records should be maintained to prevent any possibility of compromise if captured.

OATH OF ENLISTMENT

I-9. Resistance leaders must be convinced of the need for a formal oath of loyalty to the resistance movement. This formality will solidify the union of

U.S. and indigenous troops to a common goal: the "freedom" of their country. At an appropriate ceremony, the local indigenous leader may administer an oath of enlistment to each new member of the resistance force. After hostilities, the local government can then recognize the jurisdictional authority commanded by guerrilla leaders over individual guerrillas.

I-10. Personnel must sign the oath. It will become a part of the individual personnel record. It should be secured accordingly. Ideally, the oath refers to the guerrilla code and to punishment for violations.

OTHER DOCUMENTS

I-11. Casualty records include the names of personnel killed, wounded, missing in action, or separated from the guerrilla force because of illness or for other reasons. Grave registration information, at a minimum, should include name, date, cause of death, and location of the remains as accurately plotted as possible.

I-12. Medical records must include data on the type of prevalent diseases, preventive medicine actions taken, types of wounds, and general information on the organization of the medical structure for the area command.

I-13. The administrative section must maintain appropriate payroll records to support any commitment made to members of the resistance force for services rendered. The area command should maintain sufficient records to help settle claims after hostilities.

AWARDS AND DECORATIONS

I-14. Guerrillas should formalize and establish valorous actions and meritorious acts and service within the force. Sometimes, U.S. awards may be recommended; however, the group S-1 is responsible for guidance in this area. He can provide such guidance in the isolation phase. A government-in-exile or the area command may wish to act as the final approving authority and can provide general guidelines for the establishment of an awards and decorations program. Once the S-1 approves an award or decoration, it is awarded at an appropriate ceremony consistent with security regulations.

DISCIPLINE

I-15. Strict discipline is an integral part of C2 procedures instigated over any paramilitary force. Without discipline, the force cannot survive, let alone carry out effective operations against the enemy. Since guerrillas are usually not in similar uniforms and often appear dirty or bedraggled, an impression persists that discipline is loose in guerrilla units. Discipline must be hard but fair in guerrilla units. Orders should be executed without delay or question. Minor infractions of orders, especially during the conduct of operations, may have broad negative consequences for guerrillas and supporting resistance elements.

I-16. More often than not, a guerrilla force will have a code, possibly not in writing, but certainly an understanding of what is expected of all guerrillas. The resistance leader, with assistance from the SFOD, can develop a written code. Each new recruit must know and understand its provisions and the penalties for treason, desertion, and dereliction of duty. Codes for guerrilla forces are usually simple but call for extreme punishment for what would be called minor infractions in conventional forces.

I-17. Any legal code for guerrilla forces should, if possible, be in line with the one that existed for the regular military forces of that country. If this code is impractical, the area commander and his staff may draft a new code.

I-18. Provisions must exist for punishments similar to those imposed under Article 15, Uniform Code of Military Justice, and for more severe punishments. The area commander will be advised to establish a court-martial or tribunal to try cases rather than arbitrarily decide the fate of the alleged perpetrator.

I-19. As soon as possible after infiltration, all parties must reach an understanding concerning the exercise of disciplinary and judicial authority over the SFOD. The SF commander will not give up his disciplinary or judicial authority to the area commander or to any other resistance official, unless directed by U.S. higher HQ.

I-20. With decentralization of command and widely dispersed operations, individuals are habitually given mission orders with little guidance or supervision. They are expected to complete their missions. No excuses are accepted. Therefore, guerrillas must understand that their personal conduct has to be above reproach when interacting with the civilian population. Every act that loses civilian supporters is harmful to the resistance movement. PSYOP forces impress on the resistance organization's leaders that producing favorable reactions among the populace is vital. Such programs must stress proper individual and official conduct toward the populace. They must also point out the need for stringent disciplinary action against offenders.

I-21. The area commander ensures discipline is maintained. The SF commander normally provides advice that will ensure fair and consistent discipline. The ethnic culture of a group may indicate the most effective way to encourage self-discipline.

Appendix J

Example of Training Program
of Instruction for Resistance Forces

Section I. Example of Master Training Program
for a 10-Day Leadership School

The master training program for the 10-day leadership school was developed to provide the indigenous leaders and potential leaders with a general knowledge of the subjects to be taught to all indigenous personnel. Primary emphasis is placed on the role of the leader or commander to prepare these leaders to supervise the activities of their subordinates. It is assumed that most of these personnel have had prior military service and, therefore, should already possess a basic knowledge of the subjects to be covered. Upon completion of the 10-day leadership school, the leaders will return to their units of work and train with their units, thus expanding their own knowledge of the subject covered. Following is an example of a 10-day master training program for a leadership school for selected indigenous personnel.

Subject	Scope	Day	Night	Total	PE
		HOURS			
Map Reading and Compass	Same general scope as in 30-day program. Include how to read scale and coordinates.	4	2	6	(4)
Field Aid, Field Sanitation, and Survival	Same general scope as in 30-day program. Emphasis on field sanitation and responsibility of commanders.	4		4	(1)
Individual Tactical Training (Day and Night)	Same general scope as in 30-day program. Emphasis on security of operational bases, movements, formations, control measures at night, and duties and responsibilities of commanders.	10	9	19	(16)
Patrols, Small-Unit Tactics, Raids, Ambushes (Day and Night)	Same general scope as in 30-day program. Emphasis on planning, organization, preparation, command, control, security, execution of patrols, ambushes and raids.	10	29	39	(25)
Weapons (U.S. and Foreign)	Same general scope as in 30-day program. Familiarization firing. Primary emphasis on employment of weapons.	8	2	10	(7)
Intelligence	Same general scope as in 30-day program. Primary and counterintelligence. Night visions.	6	4	10	(8)

		HOURS			
Subject	Scope	Day	Night	Total	PE
Air Operations	Same general scope as in 30-day program. Primary emphasis on selection and reporting of DZs, organization of reception committee, duties and responsibilities of commanders.	6	8	14	(11)
Demolition	Familiarization with demolition procedures; demonstrating, planning, safety.	5		5	(3)
Communications	Communication means, available systems, communication security, simple cryptographic systems.	4		4	(2)
Leadership Principles and Techniques	Military leadership, traits, principles, indications, actions, and orders. Responsibilities and duties of the commander. Human behavior problem areas and problem-solving process. Selection of junior leaders. Span of control and chain of command. Combat leadership.	6		6	(4)
Tactics and Operations	Characteristics of guerrilla warfare, guerrilla operations, principles, capabilities, and limitations, organization of operational bases, security, civilian support, logistics, counterintelligence, combat employment, missions, tactical control measures, target selection, mission support site, and defensive measures. Responsibilities and duties of indigenous leaders.	7	5	12	(9)
	Total Hours in Master Program	70	59	129	(90)

Notes:

1. Identify those personnel whose leadership ability, knowledge, skill, or desire is below acceptable standards.

2. Upon completion of leadership school, one additional day may be scheduled for coordinating and planning future operations.

3. A suggested arrangement of scheduling is as follows:

29 April - 4 May: Preparation for training and selection of leaders.

5 May - 14 May: Leadership training.

16 May - 14 June: Troop training.

Section II. Example of a 30-Day Master Training Program

Following is an example of a 30-day master training program that may be used as a basis for preparing individual master training programs for each separate indigenous unit.

Subject	Scope	HOURS			
		Day	Night	Total	PE
Map Familiarization and Use of Compass	How to read a map, orientation of map with compass, how to locate oneself, determine azimuth, and day and night use of compass.	14	10	24	(20)
First Aid, Field	Basic treatment of wounds, prevention of infection, simple bandaging, pressure points, prevention of shock, splints, litter construction and use; field sanitation measures regarding water supply, waste disposal, and personal hygiene.	6	4	10	(7)
Individual Tactical Training (Day and Night)	Camouflage, cover, concealment, movement, observation, reporting, discipline, sounds, hand-to-hand combat, combat formations, night movement, night camouflage, preparation of equipment and clothing, night visions, sounds and observation, night security and formations, message writing, immediate action drills, and security of operational bases.	26	9	35	(31)
Patrols, Small-Unit Tactics, Raids, Ambushes (Day and Night)	Planning, organization, preparation, formations, commands, control, security, communications and reporting of patrols; objectives, target selection, organization of raid forces; reconnaissance and intelligence; planning, preparation, movement, deployment, conduct of raids, disengagement, and withdrawal of raiding forces; characteristics, definition, objectives of ambushes, selection of ambush sites, organization of ambush forces, phases of ambush operation, planning, preparation movement, deployment, execution, disengagement, and withdrawal of ambush forces. All subjects covered for both day and night operations.	26	44	70	(60)
Weapons (Foreign and U.S.)	Carbine, M1, submachine gun, automatic rifle; pistol, caliber .45 machine guns; foreign weapons to include care and cleaning, loading, aiming, stoppages, range firing; familiarization firing of all weapons; and day and night firing.	28	10	38	(32)

Subject	Scope	HOURS			
		Day	Night	Total	PE
Intelligence	Security measures, how to obtain and report information, captured documents, and material; interrogation and handling of prisoners; and counterintelligence procedures.	8		8	(5)
Air Operations	Establishment of DZ, marking and identification of DZ, security of DZ, receiving and transporting supplies and equipment.	16	15	31	(25)
Demolitions	Nonelectric and electric firing systems, calculation and placement of charges, rail and bridge destruction, booby traps, and expedient devices.	21	8	29	(24)
Squad Tests	Review and exercise covering all instruction.	23	16	39	(37)
Platoon Tests	Review and exercise covering all instruction.	42	24	66	(63)
	Total Hours in Master Training Program	210	140	350	(304)

Notes:

1. Maximum number of trained, indigenous personnel will be used to assist in training others. Identify those personnel who may qualify as potential cadre or potential leaders.

2. Intelligence, compass, map familiarization, observing and reporting, tactical training of the individual, patrolling, weapons, demolitions, and field sanitation will be integrated whenever possible.

3. Classes to be broken down into platoon-sized groups whenever possible.

4. Practical work exercise, demonstrations, and conferences to be used in lieu of lectures to the maximum extent possible.

5. Stress small-unit training (patrol, squad, and platoon). Develop teamwork and esprit de corps.

Section III. Data Card—Personnel and Training Record

The following is an example of a personnel data card that may also serve as a training record. This simplifies and holds to a minimum the number of records that may be required to be maintained in an AO. The type and amount of information to be recorded will vary with each AO to include the degree of security to be afforded resistance personnel.

1. **Personnel Data:**

   a. JSOA_____ FULL NAME_____ SN_____

   b. RANK_____ DOB_____ POB_____

   c. UNIT_____ DATE OF ENLISTMENT_____

   d. LAST CIVILIAN ADDRESS_____

   e. CIVILIAN OCCUPATION_____

   f. LANGUAGES_____

   g. SPECIAL SKILLS AND APTITUDES (CIVILIAN)_____
   _____

   h. FINANCIAL DATA:

   _____ DATE _____ AMOUNT PAID _____

   _____ DATE _____ AMOUNT PAID _____

   _____ DATE _____ AMOUNT PAID _____

   i. LEFT THUMB PRINT   RIGHT THUMB PRINT

   j. PHOTOGRAPH

   k. DATE OF DISCHARGE OR DEMOBILIZATION _____

2. **Training Record:**   SUBJECTS   DATES

   a. Basic Training:

    _____   _____

   b. Advanced/specialist training:

   c. MOS specialties:

                           AREA OF   DEGREE
                           INTEREST   OF
                                           PROFICIENCY

   d. Weapon qualifications: WEAPON   DEGREE OF SKILL

   e. Combat operations: _____

_____

_____

_____

   f. Awards and decorations: _____

_____

_____

_____

	TYPE	DATE
g. Wounds or injuries:	_____	_____
	_____	_____
	_____	_____
	_____	_____

3. **Disciplinary Actions:**

DATE	OFFENSE	TYPE OF TRIAL	PUNISHMENT
_____	_____	_____	_____
_____	_____	_____	_____
_____	_____	_____	_____
_____	_____	_____	_____

Appendix K

Special Forces Caching

Caching is the process of hiding equipment or materials in a secure
storage place with the view to future recovery for operational use. The
ultimate success of caching may well depend upon attention to detail: that
is, professional competence that may seem of minor importance to the
untrained eye. Security factors, such as cover for the caching party,
sterility of the items cached, and removal of even the slightest trace of the
caching operations are vital. Highly important, too, are the technical
factors that govern the preservation of the items in usable condition and
the recording of data essential for recovery. Successful caching entails
careful adherence to the basic principles of clandestine operations, as well
as familiarity with the technicalities of caching.

CACHING CONSIDERATIONS

K-1. Caching considerations that are vital to the success of the caching
operation may be done in a variety of operational situations (Figure K-1,
page K-2). For example, cached supplies can meet the emergency needs of
personnel who may be barred from their normal supply sources by sudden
developments or who may need travel documents and extra funds for quick
escape. Caching can help solve the supply problems of long-term operations
conducted far from a secure base. Caching can also provide for anticipated
needs of wartime operations in areas likely to be overrun by the enemy.

PLANNING FOR A CACHING OPERATION

K-2. Caching involves selecting items to be cached, procuring those items,
and selecting a cache site. Selection of the items to be cached requires a close
estimate of what will be needed by particular units for particular operations.
Procurement of the items usually presents no special problems. In fact, the
relative ease of procurement before an emergency arises is one of the prime
considerations in favor of caching. When selecting a cache site, planners
should always ensure that the site is accessible not only for emplacement, but
also for recovery. When planning a caching operation, the planner must
consider the following six basic factors.

PURPOSE AND CONTENTS OF THE CACHE

K-3. Planners must determine the purpose and contents of each cache
because these basic factors influence the location of the cache, as well as the
method of hiding. For instance, small barter items can be cached at any
accessible and secure site because they can be concealed easily on the person
once recovered. However, it would be difficult to conceal rifles for a guerrilla
band once recovered. Therefore, this site must be in an isolated area where

the band can establish at least temporary control. Certain items, such as medical stock, have limited shelf life and require rotation periodically or special storage considerations, necessitating easy access to service these items. Sometimes it is impossible to locate a cache in the most convenient place for an intended user. Planners must compromise between logistical objectives and actual possibilities when selecting a cache site. Security is always the overriding consideration.

PURPOSE
• Team E&E
• Underground and guerrilla training
• Equipment and operations

CACHE CONTENTS	
• Money	• Radios
• Weapons	• Food
• Ammunition	• Water
• Explosive ordnance	• Batteries
• Medical supplies	• Clothing
• Tools	• POL

LOGISTICS
1x weapon each man (12) per team + additional gear = 500+ lb x 8 teams = over 4,000 lb + 1x weapon and gear each cell member = ???? lb

CHALLENGE	
• Need for covert movement	• Security
• Large amount of materiel	• Availability of desirable cache placements
• Many caches	• Cache locations over large area
• How to transport	• Placement record maintenance
• Lots of digging	• Additional caches for contingencies

Figure K-1. Logistics Cell

ANTICIPATED ENEMY ACTION

K-4. In planning the caching operation, planners must consider the capabilities of any intelligence or security services not participating in the operation. They should also consider the potential hazards the enemy and its witting or unwitting accomplices present. If caching is done for wartime operational purposes, its ultimate success will depend largely on whether the planners anticipate the various obstacles to recovery, which the enemy and its accomplices will create if the enemy occupies the area. What are the possibilities that the enemy will preempt an ideal site for one reason or another and deny access to it? A vacant field surrounded by brush may seem ideal for a particular cache because it is near several highways. But such a location may also invite the enemy to locate an ordnance depot where the cache is buried.

ACTIVITIES OF THE LOCAL POPULATION

K-5. Probably more dangerous than deliberate enemy action are all of the chance circumstances that may result in the discovery of the cache. Normal activity, such as construction of a new building, may uncover the cache site or impede access to it. Unlucky circumstances cannot be anticipated, but it can probably be avoided by careful and imaginative observation of the prospective cache site and of the people who live near the site. If the cache is intended for wartime use, the planners must project how the residents will react to the pressures of war and conquest. For example, one of the more likely reactions is that many residents may resort to caching to avoid having their personal funds and valuables seized by the enemy. If caching becomes popular, any likely cache site will receive more than normal attention.

INTENDED ACTIONS BY ALLIED FORCES

K-6. Using one cache site for several clandestine operations involves a risk of mutual compromise. Therefore, some planners should rule out otherwise suitable caching sites if they have been selected for other clandestine purposes, such as drops or safe houses. A site should not be located where it may be destroyed or rendered inaccessible by bombing or other allied military action, should the area be occupied by the enemy. For example, installations likely to be objects of special protective efforts by the occupying enemy are certain to be inaccessible to the ordinary citizen. Therefore, if the cache is intended for wartime use, the caching party should avoid areas such as those near key bridges, railroad intersections, power plants, and munitions factories.

PACKAGING AND TRANSPORTATION

K-7. Asset planners should assess the security needs and all of the potential obstacles and hazards that a prospective cache site can present. They should also consider whether the operational assets could be used for packaging and transporting the package to the site. Best results are obtained when experts at a packaging center do the packaging. The first question, therefore, is to decide whether the package can be transported from the HQ or the field packaging center to the cache site securely and soon enough to meet the operational schedules. If not, the packaging must be done locally, perhaps in a safe house located within a few miles of the cache site. If such an arrangement is necessary, the choice of cache sites may be restricted by limited safe house possibilities.

PERSONNEL ASSETS

K-8. All who participate directly in emplacement will know where the cache is located. Therefore, only the fewest possible and the most reliable persons should be used. Planners must consider the distance from the person's residence to the prospective cache site. Consideration must be given to the reason or story of why someone is involved in conducting this activity. Sometimes transportation and cover difficulties require the cache site to be within a limited distance of the person's residence. The above considerations also apply to the recovery personnel.

CACHING METHODS

K-9. Which cache method to use depends on the situation. It is therefore unsound to lay down any general rules, with one exception: Planners should always think in terms of suitability; for example, the method most suitable for each cache, considering its specific purpose; the actual situation in the particular locality; and the changes that may occur if the enemy gains control.

CONCEALMENT

K-10. Concealment requires the use of permanent man-made or natural features to hide or disguise the cache. Concealment has several advantages. Both employment and recovery can usually be done with minimum time and labor, and cached items concealed inside a building or dry cave are protected from the elements. Thus, they require less elaborate packaging. Also, in some cases, a concealed cache can be readily inspected from time to time to ensure that it is still usable. However, there is always the chance of accidental discovery in addition to all the hazards of wartime that may result in discovery or destruction of a concealed cache or denial of access to the site. The concealment method, therefore, is most suitable in cases where an exceptionally secure site is available or where a need for quick access to the cache justifies a calculated sacrifice in security. Concealment may range from securing small gold coins under a tile in the floor to walling up artillery in caves.

BURIAL

K-11. Adequate burial sites can be found almost anywhere (Figures K-2 and K-3, page K-5). Once in place, a properly buried cache is generally the best way of achieving lasting security. In contrast to concealment, however, burial in the ground is a laborious and time-consuming method of caching. The disadvantages of burial are that—

- Burial almost always requires a high-quality container or special wrapping to protect the cache from moisture, chemicals, and bacteria in the soil.
- Emplacement or recovery of a buried cache usually takes so long that the operation must be done after dark unless the site is exceptionally secluded.
- It is especially difficult to identify and locate a buried cache (Figures K-2 and K-3).

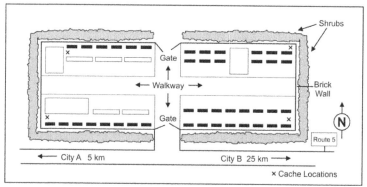

Figure K-2. Cache Locations

Figure K-3. Cache Location (Adjacent to Southwest Corner
of Church on South Side)

SUBMERSION

K-12. Submersion sites that are suitable for secure concealment of a submerged cache are few and far between. Also, the container of a submerged cache must meet such high standards for waterproofing and resistance to external pressure that the use of field expedients is seldom workable. To ensure that a submerged cache remains dry and in place, planners must determine not only the depth of the water, but the type of bottom, the currents, and other facts that are relatively difficult for nonspecialists to obtain (Figures K-4 and K-5).

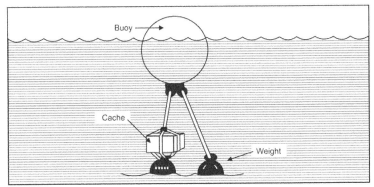

Figure K-4. Submersible Cache, Example 1

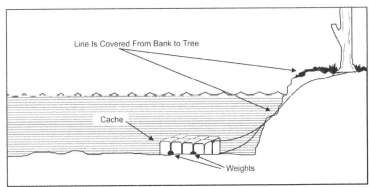

Figure K-5. Submersible Cache, Example 2

EMPLACEMENT

K-13. Emplacement, likewise, requires a high degree of skill. At least two persons are needed for emplacement, and it requires additional equipment. In view of the difficulties—especially the difficulty of recovery—the submersion method is suitable only on rare occasions. The most noteworthy usage is the relatively rare maritime resupply operation where it is impossible to deliver supplies directly to a reception committee. Caching supplies offshore by submersion is often preferable to sending a landing party ashore to bury a cache.

SELECTION OF THE SITE

K-14. The most careful estimates of future operational conditions cannot ensure that a cache will be accessible when it is needed. The following paragraphs address site selection considerations.

CRITERIA FOR SELECTION

K-15. Criteria for a site selection can be met when the following three questions are answered: (1) Can the site be located by simple instructions that are unmistakably clear to someone who has never visited the location? A site may be ideal in every respect, but if it has no distinct, permanent landmarks within a readily measurable distance it must be ruled out. (2) Are there at least two secure routes to and from the site? Both primary and alternate routes should provide natural concealment so that the emplacement party and the recovery party can visit the site without being seen by anyone normally in the vicinity. (3) Can the cache be emplaced and recovered at the chosen site in all seasons of the year? Snow and frozen ground create special problems. Snow on the ground is a hazard because it is impossible to erase a trail in the snow. Planners must consider whether seasonal changes in the foliage will leave the site and the route dangerously exposed.

MAP SURVEY

K-16. Finding a cache site is often difficult. Usually, a thorough systematic survey of the general area designated for the cache is required. The survey is best done with a large-scale map of the area, if available. By scrutinizing the map, the planners can determine whether a particular sector must be ruled out because of its nearness to factories, homes, busy thoroughfares, or probable military targets in wartime. A good military-type map will show the positive features in the topography, proximity to adequate roads or trails, natural concealment (for example, surrounding woods or groves), and adequate drainage. A map will also show the natural and man-made features in the landscape. A map will provide the indispensable reference points for locating a cache site: confluences of streams, dams and waterfalls, road junctures and distance markers, villages, bridges, churches, and cemeteries.

PERSONAL RECONNAISSANCE

K-17. A map survey should normally show the location of several promising sites within the general area designated for the cache. To select and pinpoint the best site, however, a well-qualified observer must examine each site firsthand. If possible, whoever examines the site should carry adequate maps, a compass, a drawing pad or board for making sketch maps or tracings, and a metallic measuring line. (A wire knotted at regular intervals is adequate for measuring. Twine or cloth measuring tapes should not be used because stretching or shrinking will make them inaccurate if they get wet.) The observer should also carry a probe rod for probing prospective burial sites, if the rod can be carried securely.

K-18. Since the observer seldom completes a field survey without being noticed by local residents, his story for his actions is of great importance. The observer's story must offer a natural explanation for his exploratory activity in the area. Ordinarily, this means that an observer who is not a known resident of the area can pose as a tourist or a newcomer with some reason for visiting the area. However, his story must be developed over an extended period before he undertakes the actual reconnaissance. If the observer is a known resident of the area, he cannot suddenly take up hunting, fishing, or wildlife photography without arousing interest and perhaps suspicion. The observer must build up a reputation for being a devotee of his sport or hobby.

REFERENCE POINTS

K-19. When the observer finds a suitable cache site, he prepares simple and unmistakable instructions for locating the reference points (Figure K-6, page K-9). These instructions must identify the general area (the names of general recognizable places, from the country down to the nearest village) and an immediate reference point. Any durable landmark that is identified by its title or simple description can be an immediate reference point (for example, the only Roman Catholic church in a certain village or the only bridge on a named road between two villages). The instructions must also include a final reference point (FRP), which must meet the following four requirements. The FRP—

- Must be identifiable, including at least one feature that can be used as a precise reference point.

- Must be an object that will remain fixed as long as the cache may be used.

- Must be near enough to the cache to pinpoint the exact location of the cache by precise linear measurements from the FRP to the cache.

- Should be related to the immediate reference point by a simple route description, which proceeds from the immediate reference point to the FRP.

K-20. Since the route description should be reduced to the minimum essential, the ideal solution for locating the cache is to combine the immediate reference point and the FRP into one landmark readily identifiable, but sufficiently secluded.

K-21. The following objects, when available, are sometimes ideal reference points:

- Small, unfrequented bridges and dams.

- Boundary markers.

- Kilometer markers and culverts along unfrequented roads.

- A geodetic survey marker.

- Battle monuments and wayside shrines.

K-22. When such reference points are not available at an otherwise suitable cache site, natural or man-made objects may serve as FRPs: distinct rocks, posts for power or telephone lines, intersections in stone fences or hedgerows, and gravestones in isolated cemeteries.

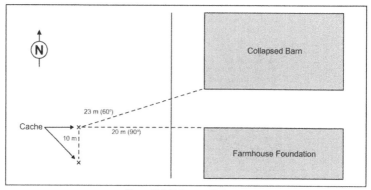

Figure K-6. Reference Points

PINPOINTING TECHNIQUES

K-23. Recovery instructions must identify the exact location of the cache. These instructions must describe the point where the cache is placed in terms that relate it to the FRP. When the concealment method is used, the cache is ordinarily placed inside the FRP, pinpointed by a precise description of the FRP. A submerged cache is usually pinpointed by describing exactly how the moorings are attached to the FRP (Figure K-7, page K-10). With a buried cache, any of the following techniques may be used.

Placing the Cache Directly Beside the FRP

K-24. The simplest method is to place the cache directly beside the FRP. Then pinpointing is reduced to specifying the precise reference point of the FRP.

Sighting the Cache by Projection

K-25. This method may be used if the FRP has one flat side long enough to permit precise sighting by projecting a line along the side of the object. The burial party places the cache a measured distance along the sighted line. This method may also be used if two precise FRPs are available, by projecting a line sighted between the two objects. In either case, the instructions for finding the cache must state the approximate direction of the cache from the FRP. Since small errors in sighting are magnified as the sighted line is extended, the cache should be placed as close to the FRP as other factors permit. Ordinarily this method becomes unreliable if the sighted line is extended beyond 50 meters.

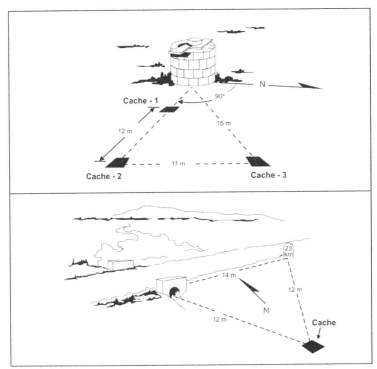

Figure K-7. Pinpointing Techniques

Placing the Cache at the Intersection of Measured Lines

K-26. If two FRPs are available within several paces, the cache can be one line projected from each of the FRPs. If this method is used, the approximate direction of the cache from each FRP must be stated. To ensure accuracy, neither of the projected lines (from the FRPs to the point of emplacement) should be more than twice as long as the base line (between the two FRPs). If this proportion is maintained, the only limitation upon the length of the projected lines is the length of the measuring line that the recovery party is expected to carry. The recovery party should carry two measuring lines when this method is used.

Sighting the Cache by Compass Azimuth

K-27. If the above methods of sighting are not feasible, one measured line may be projected by taking a compass azimuth from the FRP to the point where the cache is placed. To avoid confusion, an azimuth to a cardinal point of the compass (north, east, south, or west) is used. Since compass sightings are likely to be inaccurate, a cache that is pinpointed by this method should not be placed more than 10 meters from the FRP.

MEASURING DISTANCES

K-28. The observer should express all measured distances in a linear system that the recovery party is sure to understand—ordinarily, the standard system for the country where the cache is located. He should use whole numbers (6 meters, not 6.3 or 6.5) to keep his instructions as brief and as simple as possible. To get an exact location for the cache in whole numbers, the observer should take sightings and measurements first.

K-29. If the surface of the ground between the points to be measured is uneven, the linear distance should be measured on a direct line from point to point, rather than by following the contour of the ground. This method requires a measuring line long enough to reach the full distance from point to point and strong enough to be pulled taut without breaking.

MARKING TECHNIQUES

K-30. The emplacement operation can be simplified and critical time saved if the point where the cache is to be buried is marked during the reconnaissance. If a night burial is planned, the point of emplacement may have to be marked during a daylight reconnaissance. This method should be used whenever operational conditions permit. The marker must be an object that is easily recognizable but that is meaningless to an unwitting observer. For example, a small rock or a branch with its butt placed at the point selected for the emplacement may be used.

K-31. Since marking information is also essential to the recovery operation, it must be compiled after emplacement and included in the final cache report. Therefore, the observer should be thoroughly familiar with the Twelve-Point Cache Report before he starts a personal reconnaissance. This report is a checklist for the observer to record as much information as possible. Points 6 through 11 are particularly important. The personal reconnaissance also provides an excellent opportunity for a preliminary estimate of the time required for getting to the site.

ALTERNATE SITE

K-32. As a general rule, planners should select an alternate site in case unforeseen difficulties prevent use of the best site. Unless the primary site is in a completely deserted area, there is always some danger that the emplacement party will find it occupied as they approach, or that the party will be observed as they near the site. The alternate site should be far enough away to be screened from view from the primary site, but near enough so that the party can reach it without making a second trip.

CONCEALMENT SITE

K-33. A site that looks ideal for concealment may be revealed to the enemy for that very reason. Such a site may be equally attractive to a native of an occupied country to hide his valuables. The only real key to the ideal concealment site is careful casing of the area combined with great familiarity with local residents and their customs. The following is a list of likely concealment sites:

- Walls (hidden behind loose bricks or stones or a plastered surface).
- Abandoned buildings.
- Infrequently used structures (stadiums and other recreational facilities, railroad facilities on spur lines).
- Memorial edifices (mausoleums, crypts, monuments).
- Public buildings (museums, churches, libraries).
- Ruins of historical interest.
- Culverts.
- Natural caves and caverns, and abandoned mines and quarries.
- Sewers.
- Cable conduits.

K-34. The concealment site must be equally accessible to the person emplacing and the person recovering. However, visits by both persons to certain interior sites may be incompatible with the story. For instance, a site in a house owned by a relative of the emplacer may be unsuitable because there is no adequate excuse for the recovery person to enter the house if he has no connection with the owner.

K-35. The site must remain accessible as long as the cache is needed. If access to a building depends upon a personal relationship with the owner, the death of the owner or the sale of the property might render it inaccessible.

K-36. Persons involved in the operation should not be compromised if the cache is discovered on the site. Even if a cache is completely sterile, as every cache should be, the mere fact that it has been placed in a particular site may compromise certain persons. If the police discovered the cache, they might suspect the emplacer because it was found in his relative's house.

K-37. The site must not be located where potentially hostile persons frequently visit. For instance, a site in a museum is not secure if police guards or curious visitors frequently enter the museum.

K-38. To preserve the cache material, the emplacer must ensure the site is physically secure for the preservation of the cached material. For example, most buildings involve a risk that the cache may be destroyed or damaged by fire, especially in wartime. The emplacer should consider all risks and weigh them against the advantages of an interior site.

K-39. A custodian may serve to ease access to a building or to guard a cache. However, the use of such a person is inadvisable, as a custodian poses an additional security risk. He may use the contents of the cache for personal profit or reveal its location.

BURIAL SITE

K-40. In selecting a burial site, consider the following factors along with the basic considerations of suitability and accessibility.

DRAINAGE

K-41. Drainage considerations include the elevation of the site and the type of soil. The importance of good drainage makes a site on high ground preferable unless other factors rule it out. Moisture is one of the greatest natural threats to the contents of a cache. Swamp muck is the most difficult soil to work in. If the site is near a stream or river, the emplacer should ensure that the cache is well above the all-year-high-water mark so that the cache will not be uncovered if the soil is washed away.

GROUND COVER

K-42. The types of vegetation at the site will influence the choice. Roots of deciduous trees make digging very difficult. Coniferous trees have less extensive root systems. Also, the presence of coniferous trees usually means that the site is well drained. Does the vegetation show paths or other indications that the site is frequented too much for secure caching? Can the ground cover be easily restored to its normal appearance when burial is completed? Tall grass reveals that it has been trampled, but an overlay of leaves and humus can be replaced easily and will effectively conceal a freshly refilled hole.

NATURAL CONCEALMENT

K-43. The vegetation or the surrounding terrain should offer natural concealment for the burial and recovery parties working at the site. Planners should carefully consider seasonal variations in the foliage.

TYPES OF SOIL

K-44. Sandy loam is ideal because it is easy to dig and drains well. Clay soil should be avoided because it becomes quite sticky in wet weather and in dry weather it may become so hard that it is almost impossible to dig.

SNOWFALL AND FREEZING

K-45. If the cache must be buried or recovered in winter, data on the normal snowfall, the depth to which the ground freezes in winter, and the usual dates of freezing and thawing will influence the choice of the site. Frozen ground impedes digging and requires additional time for burial and recovery. Snow on the ground is especially hazardous for the burial operation. It is practically impossible to restore the snow over the burial site to its normal appearance unless there is more snowfall or a brisk wind. Also, it is very difficult to ensure that no traces of the operation are left after the snow has melted.

ROCKS AND OTHER SUBSURFACE OBSTRUCTIONS

K-46. Large obstructions that might prevent use of a particular site can be located to some extent before digging by probing with a rod or stake at the exact spot selected for the cache.

SUBMERSION SITE

K-47. To be suitable for a submerged cache, a body of water must have certain characteristics. The presence of these characteristics can be determined only by a thorough survey of the site. Their importance will be understood after familiarization with the technicalities of submersion.

EMPLACEMENT

K-48. Submersion usually requires a boat, first for reconnoitering, then for emplacement. Thus, the accessibility problems involved in submersion usually narrow down to the availability of a boat and the story for using it. If there is no fishing or pleasure boating at the site, the story for this peculiar-type boating may be a real problem. In tropical areas, the course of streams or rivers is frequently changed by seasonal rainfall and can cause many problems. Planners should keep this fact in mind when choosing the site and when selecting reference points.

RECOVERY

K-49. Since the method for recovering a cache is generally similar to that for emplacing a cache, it need not be described in full. However, several important considerations should be stressed in training for a recovery operation.

CACHE RECOVERY

K-50. The following paragraphs discuss considerations for recovery operations.

PRACTICAL EXERCISES

K-51. Anyone who is expected to serve as a recovery person should have the experience of actually recovering dummy caches, if field exercises can be arranged securely. It is especially desirable for the recovery person to be able to master the pinpointing techniques. Mastery is best attained by practice in selecting points of emplacement and in drafting, as well as in following instructions.

EQUIPMENT

K-52. Although the equipment used in recovery is generally the same as that used in emplacement, it is important to include any additional items that may be required in recovery in the cache report. A probe rod may not be essential for emplacement, but it is necessary to have some object roughly the same size as the cache container to fill the cavity left in the ground by removal of a buried cache. Some sort of container of wrapping material may be needed to conceal the recovered cache while it is being carried from the cache site to a safe house. Recovery of a submerged cache may require grappling lines and hooks, especially if it is heavy.

SKETCH OF THE SITE

K-53. If possible, the observer should provide the recovery person with sketches of the cache site and the route to the cache site. If the recovery person must rely exclusively on verbal instructions, as in the case when communications are limited to radio-telephone (RT) messages, he should draw a sketch of the site before starting on the recovery operation. He should use all the data in the verbal instructions to make the sketch as realistic as possible. Drawing a sketch will help to clarify any misunderstanding of the instructions. Also, a sketch can be followed more easily than verbal instructions. It may also be helpful for the recovery person to draw a sketch of the route from the immediate reference point to the site. But he should not carry this sketch on him because if he were apprehended the sketch might direct the enemy to the cache.

PRELIMINARY RECONNAISSANCE

K-54. Checking the instructions for locating the cache may be advisable, especially when the recovery operation must be performed under stringent enemy controls or when there is no extra time for searching. Careful analysis of the best available map can minimize reconnoitering activity in the vicinity of the cache and thus reduce the danger of arousing suspicion. If recovery must be done at night, the recovery person should find the cache by daylight and place an unnoticeable marker directly over it.

PROBE ROD

K-55. The recovery person can avoid digging at the wrong spot by using a probe rod before starting to dig. He should push and turn the probe rod into the ground by hand, so that it will not puncture the cache's container. The recovery person should never pound the probe rod with a hammer.

K-56. The recovery procedure is the same as for the burial, except for the following two points:

- First, a pick should never be used for digging the hole because it might puncture the container and damage the cached items.
- Second, it may be necessary to fill the hole with other objects in addition to soil after the cache is removed.

K-57. Sometimes it is possible to fill the hole with rocks, sticks, or other readily available objects at the site. If no such objects are found during the preliminary reconnaissance, the recovery person should carry to the site an object roughly the same size as the cache container.

STERILIZATION OF THE SITE

K-58. As with emplacement, the recovery operation must be preformed in such a way that no traces of the operation are left. Although sterilization is not as important for recovery as for emplacement, it should be done as thoroughly as time permits. Evidence that a cache has been recovered might alert the enemy to clandestine activity in the area and provoke countermeasures.

PACKAGING

K-59. Packaging usually involves packing the items to be cached, as well as the additional processing in protecting these items from adverse storage conditions. Proper packaging is important because inadequate packaging very likely will render the items unusable. Since special equipment and skilled technicians are needed for best results, packaging should be done at HQ or a field packaging center whenever possible. However, to familiarize operational personnel with the fundamentals of packaging so that they can improvise field expedients for emergency use, this section discusses determining factors, steps in packaging, wrapping materials, and criteria for the container.

DETERMINING FACTORS

K-60. The first rule of packaging is that all processing is tailored to fit the specific requirements of each cache. The method of packaging, as well as the size, shape, and weight of the package is determined by the items to be cached, by the method of caching, and especially, by the way the cache is recovered and used. For instance, if circumstances require one man to recover the cache by himself, the container should be no larger than a small suitcase, and the total weight of the container and contents no more than 30 pounds. Of course, these limits must be exceeded with some equipment, but the need for larger packages should be weighed against the difficulties and risks in handling them. Even if more than one person is available for recovery, the material should be divided whenever possible into separate packages of a size and weight readily portable by one man.

K-61. Another very important factor in packaging concerns adverse storage conditions. Any or all of the following conditions may be present: moisture, external pressure, freezing temperatures, and the bacteria and corrosive chemicals found in some soil and water. Animal life may present a hazard; insects and rodents may attack the package. If the cache is concealed in an exterior site, larger animals also may threaten it. Whether the packaging is adequate usually depends upon how carefully the conditions at the site were analyzed in designing the cache. Thus, the method of caching (burial, concealment, or submersion) should be determined before the packaging is done.

K-62. It is equally important to consider how long the cache is to be used. Since one seldom knows when a cache will be needed, a sound rule is to design the packaging to withstand adverse storage conditions for at least as long as the normal shelf life of the contents to be cached.

STEPS IN PACKAGING

K-63. The exact procedure for packaging depends upon the specific requirements for the cache and upon the packaging equipment available. The following eight steps are almost always necessary in packaging.

Inspecting

K-64. The items to be cached must be inspected immediately before packaging to ensure they are complete, in serviceable condition, and free of all corrosive or contaminated substances.

Cleaning

K-65. All corrodible items must be cleaned thoroughly immediately before the final preservative coating is applied. All foreign matter, including any preservative applied before the item was shipped to the field, should be removed completely. Throughout the packaging operation, all contents of the cache should be handled with rubber or freshly cleaned cotton gloves. Special handling is important because even minute particles of human sweat will corrode metallic equipment. Also, any fingerprints on the contents of the cache may enable the enemy to identify those who did the packaging.

Drying

K-66. When cleaning is completed, every trace of moisture must be removed from all corrodible items. Methods of drying include wiping with a highly absorbent cloth, heating, or applying desiccant. Usually, heating is best unless the item can be damaged by heat. To dry by heating, the item to be cached should be placed in an oven for at least 3 hours at a temperature of about 110 degrees Fahrenheit (F). An oven can be improvised from a large metal can or drum. In humid climates, it is especially important to dry the oven thoroughly before using it by preheating it to at least 212 degrees F. Then, the equipment to be cached is inserted as soon as the oven cools down to about 110 degrees F. If a desiccant is used, it should not touch any metallic surface. Silica gel is a satisfactory desiccant and it is commonly available.

Coating With a Preservative

K-67. A light coat of oil may be applied to weapons, tools, and other items with unpainted metallic surfaces. A coat of paint may suffice for other metal items.

Wrapping

K-68. When drying and coating are completed, the items to be cached are wrapped in a suitable material. The wrapping should be as nearly waterproof as possible. Each item should be wrapped separately, so that one perforation in the wrapping will not expose all items in the cache. The wrapping should fit tightly to each item to eliminate air pockets, and all folds should be sealed with a waterproof substance.

K-17

Packing

K-69. The following rules must be observed when packing items in the container:

- All moisture must be removed from the interior of the container by heating or applying desiccant. A long-lasting desiccant should be packed inside the container to absorb any residual moisture. If silica gel is used, the required amount can be calculated by using the ratio of 15 kilograms of silica gel to 1 cubic meter of storage space within the container. (This figure is based on two assumptions: the container is completely moisture proof and the contents are slightly moist when inserted.) Therefore, the ratio allows an ample margin for incomplete drying and can be reduced if the drying process is known to be highly effective.

- Air pockets should be eliminated as much as possible by tight packing. Thoroughly dried padding should be used liberally to fill air pockets and to protect the contents from shock. Clothing and other items, which will be useful to the recovery party, should be used for padding if possible. Items made of different metals should never touch, since continued contact may cause corrosion through electrolytic action.

Enclosing Instructions for Using Cached Equipment

K-70. Written instructions and diagrams should be included if they facilitate assembly or use of the cached items. Instructions must be written in a language that recovery personnel can understand. The wording should be as simple as possible and unmistakably clear. Diagrams should be self-explanatory since the eventual user may not be able to comprehend written instructions because of language barriers.

Sealing and Testing Seals by Submersion

K-71. When packing is completed, the lid of the container must be sealed to make it watertight. Testing can be done by entirely submerging the container in water and watching for escaping air bubbles. Hot water should be used if possible because hot water will bring out leaks that would not be revealed by a cold-water test.

WRAPPING MATERIALS

K-72. The most important requirement for wrapping material is that it be moisture-proof. Also, it should be self-sealing or adhesive to a sealing material; it should be pliable enough to fit closely, with tight folds; and it should be tough enough to resist tearing and puncturing. Pliability and toughness may be combined by using two wrappings: an inner one that is thin and pliable and an outer one of heavier material. A tough outer wrapping is essential unless the container and the padding are adequate to prevent items from scraping together inside the cache. Five wrapping materials are recommended for field expedient use because they often can be obtained locally and used effectively by unskilled personnel.

Aluminum Foil for Use as an Inner Wrapping

K-73. Aluminum foil is the best of the widely available materials. It is moisture-proof as long as it does not become perforated and provided the folds are adequately sealed. The drawbacks to its use for caching are that the thin foils perforate easily, while the heavy ones (over 2 millimeters thick) tend to admit moisture through the folds. The heavy-duty grade of aluminum foil generally sold for kitchen use is adequate when used with an outer wrapping. Scrim-backed foil, which is heat-sealable, is widely used commercially to package articles for shipment or storage. Portable heat sealers that are easy to use are available commercially or sealing can be done with a standard household iron.

Moisture-Resistant Papers

K-74. Several brands of commercial wrapping papers are resistant to water and grease. They do not provide lasting protection against moisture when used alone, but they are effective as an inner wrapping to prevent rubber, wax, and similar substances from sticking to the items in the cache.

Rubber Repair Gum

K-75. This is a self-sealing compound generally used for repairing tires; it makes an excellent outer wrapping. Standard commercial brands come in several thicknesses; 2 millimeters is the most satisfactory for caching. A watertight seal is produced easily by placing two rubber surfaces together and applying pressure manually. The seal should be at least 1/2 inch wide. Since rubber repair gum has a tendency to adhere to items, an inner wrapping of non-adhesive material must be used with it, and the backing should be left on the rubber material to keep it from sticking to other items in the cache.

Grade C Barrier Material

K-76. This is a cloth impregnated with microcrystalline wax that is used extensively when packing for storage of items for overseas shipment. Thus, it is generally available and it has the additional advantage of being self-sealing. Although it is not as effective as rubber repair gum, it may be used as an outer wrapping over aluminum foil to prevent perforation of the foil. Used without an inner wrapping, three layers of grade C barrier material may keep the contents dry for as long as three months, but it is highly vulnerable to insects and rodents. Also, the wax wrapping has a low melting point and will adhere to many items, so it should not be used without an inner wrapping except in emergencies.

Wax Coating

K-77. If no wrapping material is available, an outer coating of microcrystalline wax, paraffin, or a similar waxy substance can be used to protect the contents against moisture. A wax coating will not provide protection against insects and rodents. The package should be hot-dipped in the waxy substance, or the wax can be heated to molten form and applied with a brush.

CONTAINER CRITERIA

K-78. The outer container serves to protect the contents from shock, moisture, and other natural hazards to which the cache may be exposed. The ideal container should be as follows:

- Completely watertight and airtight after sealing.
- Noiseless when handled; its handles should not rattle against the body of the container.
- Resistant to shock and abrasion.
- Able to withstand crushing pressure.
- Lightweight in construction.
- Able to withstand rodents, insects, and bacteria.
- Equipped with a sealing device that can be closed and reopened easily and repeatedly.
- Capable of withstanding highly acidic or alkaline soil or water.

STANDARD STAINLESS STEEL CONTAINER

K-79. The standard stainless steel container comes in several sizes. Since the stainless steel container is more satisfactory than any that could be improvised in the field, it should be used whenever possible. Ideally, it should be packed at HQ or at a field packaging center. If the items to be cached must be obtained locally, it is still advisable to use the stainless steel container because its high resistance to moisture eliminates the need for an outer wrapping. Packers should, however, use a single wrapping even with the stainless steel container to protect the contents from any residual moisture that may be present in the container when it is sealed.

FIELD-EXPEDIENT CONTAINER

K-80. The ideal container cannot be improvised in the field, but the standard military and commercial containers discussed below can meet caching requirements if they are adapted with care and resourcefulness. First, a container must be sufficiently sturdy to remain unpunctured and retain its shape through whatever rough handling or crushing pressure it may encounter. (Even a slight warping may cause a joint around the lid to leak.) Second, if the lid is not already watertight and airtight, packers can make it so by improvising a sealing device. The most common type of sealing device includes a rubber-composition gasket or lining and a sharp, flat metal rim that is pressed against a threaded lid. Applying heavy grease to the threads can increase its effectiveness. (Metallic solder should not be used for sealing because it corrodes metal surfaces when exposed to moisture.) Whenever any nonstainless metal container is used, it is important to apply several coats of high-quality paint to all exterior surfaces.

Instrument Containers

K-81. Ordinarily, aircraft and other precision instruments are shipped in steel containers with a waterproof sealing device. The standard instrument containers range from 1/2-gallon to 10-gallon sizes. If one of suitable size can be found, only minimum modifications may be needed. In the most common type of instrument container, the only weak point is the nut and bolt that tighten the locking band around the lid. These should be replaced with a stainless steel nut and bolt.

Ammunition Boxes

K-82. Several types and sizes of steel ammunition boxes that have a rubber-gasket closing device are satisfactory for buried caches. An advantage of using ammunition boxes as a cache container is that they are usually available at a military depot.

Steel Drums

K-83. A caching container of suitable size may be found among the commercially used steel drums for shipping oil, grease, nails, soap, and other products. The most common types, however, lack an adequate sealing device, so a waterproof material should be used around the lid. Fully removable head drums with lock-ring closures generally give a satisfactory seal.

Glass Jars

K-84. The advantage of using glass is that it is waterproof and does not allow chemicals, bacteria, and insects to pass through it. Although glass is highly vulnerable to shock, glass jars of a sturdy quality can withstand the crushing pressure normally encountered in caching. However, none of the available glass containers have an adequate sealing device for the joint around the lid. The standard commercial canning jar with a spring clamp and a rubber washer is watertight, but the metal clamp is vulnerable to corrosion. Therefore, a glass jar with a spring clamp and a rubber washer is an adequate expedient for short-term caching of small items, but it should not be relied upon to resist moisture for more than a year.

Paint Cans

K-85. Standard cans with reusable lids require a waterproof adhesive around the lids. It is especially important to apply several coats of paint to the exterior of standard commercial cans because the metal in these cans is not as heavy as that in metal drums. Even when the exterior is thoroughly painted, paint cans will not resist moisture for more than a few months.

METHODS OF EMPLACEMENT

K-86. Since burial is the most frequently used method of emplacement, this section describes first the complete procedure for burial, followed by a discussion of emplacement procedures peculiar to submersion and concealment. The last area discussed is the preparation of the cache report— a vital part of a caching operation.

BURIAL

K-87. When planners have designed a cache and selected the items for caching, they must carefully work out every step of the burial operation in advance.

Horizontal and Vertical Caches

K-88. Ordinarily, the hole for a buried cache is vertical (the hole is dug straight down from the surface). Sometimes a horizontal cache, with the hole dug into the side of a steep hill or bank, provides a workable solution when a suitable site on level or slightly sloping ground is not available. A horizontal cache may provide better drainage in areas of heavy rainfall, but is more likely to be exposed by soil erosion and more difficult to refill and restore to normal appearance (Figure K-8).

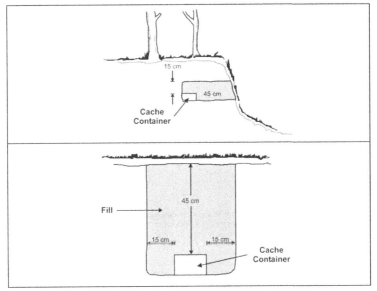

Figure K-8. Burial Procedures for Horizontal and Vertical Caches

Dimensions of the Hole

K-89. The exact dimensions of the hole, either vertical or horizontal, depend on the size and shape of the cache container. As a general rule, the hole should be large enough for the container to be inserted easily. The horizontal dimensions of the hole should be about 30 centimeters longer and wider than the container. Most importantly, it should be deep enough to permit covering the container with soil to about 45 centimeters. This figure is recommended for normal usage because a more shallow burial risks exposure of the cache through soil erosion or inadvertent uncovering by normal indigenous activity.

A deeper hole makes probing for recovery more difficult and unnecessarily prolongs the time required for burial and recovery.

Excavation Shoring

K-90. If there is a risk that the surrounding soil will cave in during excavation, boards or bags filled with subsoil may be used to shore the sides of the hole. Permanent shoring may be needed to protect an improvised container from pressure or shock.

Equipment

K-91. The following items of equipment may be helpful or indispensable in burying a cache, depending upon the conditions at the site:

- Measuring instruments (a wire or metal tape and compass) for pinpointing the site.
- Paper and pencil for recording the measurements.
- A probe rod for locating rocks, large roots, or other obstacles in the subsoil.
- Two ground sheets on which to place sod and loose soil. An article of clothing may be used for small excavation if nothing else is available.
- Sacks (sandbags, flour sacks, trash bags) for holding subsoil.
- A spade or pickax if the ground is too hard for spading.
- A hatchet for cutting roots.
- A crowbar for prying rocks.
- A flashlight or lamp if burial is to be done at night.

BURIAL PARTY

K-92. Aside from locating, digging, and refilling the hole, the most important factor in this part of the emplacement operation may be expressed with one word: personnel. Since it is almost impossible to prevent every member of the burial party from knowing the location of the cache, each member is a prime security problem as long as the cache remains intact. Thus, planners must keep the burial party as small as possible and select each member with utmost care. Once selected, each member must have an adequate story to explain his absence from home or work during the operation, his trip to and from the site, and his possession of whatever equipment cannot be concealed on the way. Transportation for the burial party may be a problem, depending on the number of persons, how far they must go, and what equipment they must take. When planners have worked out all details of the operation, they must brief each member of the burial party on exactly what he is to do from start to finish.

OPERATIONAL SCHEDULE

K-93. The final step in planning the emplacement operation is to make a schedule to set the date, time, and place for every step of the operation that requires advance coordination. The schedule will depend mainly on the circumstances, but to be practical it must include a realistic estimate of how long it will take to complete the burial. Here, generalizations are worthless, and the only sure guide is actual experience under similar conditions. Planners should consider the following with respect to scheduling.

K-94. A careful burial job probably will take longer than most novices will expect. Therefore, if circumstances require a tight schedule, a dry run or test exercise before taking the package to the site may be advisable. Unless the site is exceptionally well concealed or isolated, night burial will be required to avoid detection. Because of the difficulties of working in the dark, a nighttime practice exercise is especially advisable.

K-95. The schedule should permit waiting for advantageous weather conditions. The difficulties of snow have already been mentioned. Rainy weather increases the problems of digging and complicates the story. If the burial is to be done at night, a moonless or a heavy overcast night is desirable.

SITE APPROACH

K-96. Regardless of how effective the individual's story is during the trip to the cache site, the immediate approach must be completely unobserved to avoid detection of the burial. To reduce the risk of the party being observed, planners must carefully select the point where the burial party disappears, perhaps by turning off a road into woods. They should just as carefully select the reappearance point. In addition, the return trip should be by a different route. The burial party should strictly observe the rule for concealed movement. The party should proceed cautiously and silently along a route that makes the best use of natural concealment. Concealed movement requires foresight, with special attention to using natural concealment while reconnoitering the route and to preventing rattles when preparing the package and contents.

Security Measures at the Site

K-97. The burial party must maintain maximum vigilance at the cache site since detection can be disastrous. The time spent at the site is the most critical. At least one lookout should be on guard constantly. If one man must do the burial by himself, he should pause frequently to look and listen. The burial party should use flashlights or lanterns as little as possible, and should take special care to mask the glare. Planning should include emergency actions in case the burial party is interrupted. The party should be so thoroughly briefed that it will respond instantly to any sign of danger. Planners should also consider the various escape routes and whether the party will attempt to retain the package or conceal it along the escape route.

Steps in Digging and Refilling

K-98. Although procedures will vary slightly with the design of the cache, persons involved in caching operations must never overlook certain basic steps. The whole procedure is designed to restore the site to normal as far as possible.

Site Sterilization

K-99. When the hole is refilled, a special effort should be made to ensure that the site is left sterile and restored to normal in every way, with no clues left to indicate burial or the burial party's visit to the vicinity. Since sterilization is most important for the security of the operation, the schedule should allow ample time to complete these final steps in an unhurried, thorough manner. These final steps are to—

- Dispose of any excess soil far enough away from the site to avoid attracting attention to the site. Flushing the excess soil into a stream is the ideal solution.

- Check all tools and equipment against a checklist to ensure that nothing is left behind. This checklist should include all personnel items that may drop from pockets. To keep this risk to a minimum, members of the burial party should carry nothing on their persons except the essentials for doing the job and disguising their actions.

- Make a final inspection of the site for any traces of the burial. Because this step is more difficult on a dark night, use of a carefully prepared checklist is essential. With a night burial, returning to the site in the daytime to inspect it for telltale evidence may be advisable if this can be done safely.

SUBMERSION

K-100. Emplacing a submerged cache always involves two basic steps: weighting the container to keep it from floating to the surface and mooring it to keep it in place.

K-101. Ordinarily, container weights rest on the bottom of the lake or river and function as anchors, and the moorings connect the anchors to the container. The moorings must also serve a second function, which is to provide a handle for pulling the cache to the surface when it is recovered. If the moorings are not accessible for recovery, another line must extend from the cache to a fixed, accessible object in the water or on shore. There are four types of moorings.

Spider Web Mooring

K-102. The container is attached to several mooring cables that radiate to anchors placed around it to form a web. The container must be buoyant so that it lifts the cables far enough off the bottom to be readily secured by grappling. The site must be located exactly at the time of emplacement by visual sightings to fixed landmarks in the water, or along the shore using several FRPs to establish a point where two sighted lines intersect. For recovery, the site is located by taking sightings on the reference points when a mooring cable is engaged by dragging the bottom while diving. This method of mooring is most difficult for recovery. It can be used only where the bottom is smooth and firm enough for dragging, or where the water is not too deep, cold, or murky for diving.

Line-to-Shore Mooring

K-103. A line is run from the weighted container to an immovable object along the shore. The section of the line that extends from the shore to the container must be buried in the ground or otherwise well concealed.

Buoy Mooring

K-104. A line is run from the weighted container to a buoy or other fixed, floating marker, and fastened well below the waterline. This method is secure only as long as the buoy is left in place. Buoys are generally inspected and repainted every six months or so. The inspection schedule should be determined before a buoy is used.

Structural Mooring

K-105. A line for retrieving the weighted container is run to a bridge pier or other solid structure in the water. This line must be fastened well below the low-water mark.

ESSENTIAL DATA FOR SUBMERSION

K-106. Whatever method of mooring is used, planners must carefully consider certain data before designing a submerged cache. The cache very likely will be lost if any of the following critical factors are overlooked.

Buoyancy

K-107. Many containers are buoyant even when filled, so the container must be weighted sufficiently to submerge it and keep it in place. If the contents do not provide enough weight, emplacers must make up the balance by attaching a weight to the container. The approximate weight needed to attain zero buoyancy is shown in Table K-1.

Table K-1. Buoyancy Chart

Container Dimensions (Inches)	Empty Container Weight (Pounds)	Approximate Weight That Must Be Added to Empty Container Weight to Attain Zero Buoyancy (Pounds)
7 x 9 x 8 1/2	5	15
7 x 9 x 16 1/2	8	31
7 x 9 x 40	16	77
7 x 9 x 45	17 1/2	88
7 x 9 x 50	19	97

K-108. This table applies to several sizes of stainless steel containers. The weighting required for any container can be calculated theoretically if the displacement of the container and the gross weight of the container plus its contents are known. This calculation may be useful for designing an anchor, but it should not be relied upon for actual emplacement. To avoid hurried improvisation during emplacement, emplacers should always test the buoyancy in advance by actually submerging the weighted container. This test determines only that a submerged cache will not float to the surface. Additional weighting may be required to keep it from drifting along the bottom. As a general rule, the additional weight should be at least one-tenth of the gross weight required to make the container sink; more weight is advisable if strong currents are present.

Submersion Depth

K-109. Planners must first determine the depth that the container is to be submerged to calculate the water pressure that the container must withstand. The greater the depth, the greater the danger that the container will be crushed by water pressure. For instance, the standard stainless steel burial container will buckle at a depth of approximately 4.3 meters. The difficulty of waterproofing also increases with depth. Thus, the container should not be submerged any deeper than necessary to avoid detection. As a general rule, 2.2 meters is the maximum advisable depth for caching. If seasonal or tidal variations in the water level require deeper submersion, the container should be tested by actual submersion to the maximum depth it must withstand.

Depth of the Water

K-110. Emplacers must measure accurately the depth of the water at the point where the cache is to be placed. This depth will be the submersion depth if the cache is designed so that the container rests on the bottom of the lake or river. The container may be suspended some distance above the bottom, but the depth of the water must be known to determine the length of moorings connecting the containers to the anchors.

High- and Low-Water Marks

K-111. Any tidal or seasonal changes in the depth of the water should be estimated as accurately as possible. Emplacers must consider the low-water mark to ensure that low water will not leave cache exposed. The high-water mark should also be considered to ensure that the increased depth will not crush the container or prevent recovery.

Type of Bottom

K-112. Emplacers should probe as thoroughly as possible the bed of the lake or river in the vicinity of the cache. If the bottom is soft and silty, the cache may sink into the muck, become covered with sediment, or drift out of place. If the bottom is rocky or covered with debris, the moorings may become snagged. Any of these conditions may make recovery very difficult.

Water Motion

K-113. Emplacers should consider tides, currents, and waves because any water motion will put additional strain on the moorings of the cache. Moorings must be strong enough to withstand the greatest possible strain. If the water motion tends to rock the cache, emplacers must take special care to prevent the moorings from rubbing and fraying.

Clearness of the Water

K-114. When deciding how deep to submerge the cache, emplacers must first determine how far the cache can be seen through the water. If the water is clear, the cache may need to be camouflaged by painting the container to match the bottom. (Shiny metallic fixtures should always be painted a dull color.) Very murky water makes recovery by divers more difficult.

Water Temperature

K-115. Planners must consider seasonal changes in the temperature of the water. Recovery may be impossible in the winter if the water freezes. The dates when the lake or river usually freezes and thaws should be determined as accurately as possible.

Salt Water

K-116. Since seawater is much more corrosive than fresh water, tidal estuaries and lagoons should not be used for caching. The only exception is the maritime resupply operation, where equipment may be submerged temporarily along the seacoast until it can be recovered by a shore party.

CONCEALMENT

K-117. There are many different ways to conceal a cache in natural or ready-made hiding places. For instance, if a caching party was hiding weapons and ammunition in a cave and was relying entirely on natural concealment, the emplacement operation would be reduced to simply locating the site. No tools would be needed except paper, a pencil, and a flashlight. On the other hand, if the party was sealing a packet of jewels in a brick wall, a skilled mason would be needed, along with his kit of tools and a supply of mortar expertly mixed to match the original brick wall.

K-118. When planning for concealment, planners must know the local residents and their customs. During the actual emplacement, the caching party must ensure the operation is not observed. The final sterilization of the site is especially important since a concealment site is usually open to frequent observation.

CACHING COMMUNICATIONS EQUIPMENT

K-119. As a general rule, all equipment for a particular purpose (demolitions, survival) should be included in one container. Some equipment, however, is so sensitive from a security standpoint that it should be packed in several containers and cached in different locations to minimize the danger of discovery by the enemy. This is particularly true of communications equipment since, under some circumstances, anyone who acquires a whole RT set with a signal plan and cryptographic material would be able to play back the set. An especially dangerous type of penetration would result. In the face of this danger, the signal plan and the cryptographic material must never be placed in the same container. Ideally, a communications kit should be distributed among three containers and cached in different locations. If three containers are used, the distribution may be as follows:

- Container 1: The RT set, including the crystals.
- Container 2: The signal plan and operational supplies for the RT operator, such as currency, barter, and small arms.
- Container 3: The cryptographic material.

K-120. When several containers are used for one set of equipment, they must be placed far enough apart so that if one is discovered, the others will not be detected in the immediate vicinity. On the other hand, they should be located close enough together so that they can be recovered conveniently in one operation. The distance between containers will depend on the particular situation, but ordinarily they should be at least 10 meters apart. One final reference point ordinarily is used for a multiple cache. The caching party should be careful to avoid placing multiple caches in a repeated pattern. Discovery of one multiple cache would give the opposition a guide for probing others placed in a similar pattern.

CACHING MEDICAL EQUIPMENT

K-121. A feasibility study must be performed to determine the need for the caching of medical supplies. The purpose of caches is to store excess medical supplies to maintain mobility and deny access to the enemy. Also caching large stockpiles of medical supplies allows pre-positioning vital supplies in anticipation of future-planned operations.

TWELVE-POINT CACHE REPORT

K-122. The final step, which is vital in every emplacement operation, is the preparation of a cache report. This report records the essential data for recovery. The cache report must provide all of the information that someone unfamiliar with the locality needs to find his way to the site, recover the cache, and return safely. The report is intended merely to point out the minimum essential data. Whatever format is used, the importance of attention to detail cannot be overemphasized. A careless error or omission in the cache report may prevent recovery of the cache when it is needed.

CONTENT

K-123. The most important parts of the cache report must include instructions for finding and recovering the cache. It should also include any other information that will ease planning the recovery operation. Since the details will depend upon the situation and the particular needs of each organization, the exact format of the report may vary slightly. A format for a cache report and a sample message is included in the SAV SER SUP 6.

PROCEDURES

K-124. The observer should collect as much data as possible during the personal reconnaissance to assist in selecting a site and planning emplacement and recovery operations. Drafting the cache report before emplacement is also advisable. Following these procedures will reveal the omissions. Then the missing data can be obtained at the site. If this procedure is followed, the preparation of the final cache report will be reduced to an after-action check. This check ensures that the cache actually was placed precisely where planned and that all other descriptive details are accurate. Although this ideal may seldom be realized, two procedures always should be followed:

- The caching party should complete the final cache report as soon as possible after emplacement, as details are fresh in mind.

- Someone who has not visited the site should check the instructions by using them to lead the party to the site. When no such person is available, someone should visit the site shortly after emplacement, provided he can do so securely. If the cache has been emplaced at night, a visit to the site in daylight may also provide an opportunity to check on the sterilization of the site.

Linkup Operations

The JSOA commander plans and coordinates linkup operations if the JSOA is coming under the operational control (OPCON) of a conventional force. A physical juncture is necessary between the conventional and guerrilla forces. The mission of the conventional force may require SF and guerrilla force personnel to support conventional combat operations. All elements involved must conduct detailed centralized planning. The conventional force commander, in coordination with the SFOB, prepares an OPLAN and coordinates a PSYOP program to simplify the linkup of forces within the JSOA. Linkup planning involves the JSOA command, the conventional force or SOF commands, and any adjacent JSOA commands.

LIAISON

L-1. The SFOD and guerrilla leaders coordinate the plans for linkup. If linkup is with SOF, guerrilla liaison personnel coordinate with the senior SOF commander, his staff, and leaders of the linkup element. When the linkup is with a guerrilla force in an adjacent JSOA, both area commands provide liaison coordination.

L-2. The conventional and guerrilla forces coordinate communications between them. An obvious requirement is for all communications equipment to be compatible. The SFOD will ensure that the radios and SOI used for linkup remain under its control.

L-3. A liaison party consisting of SFOD members and area commanders may exfiltrate from the JSOA and assist in linkup planning. Conventional forces do not infiltrate into the JSOA to conduct their own liaison planning. SOF or designated U.S. agencies infiltrate the JSOA to conduct linkup planning and coordination. The SFOB or FOB monitors the linkup and provides administrative and logistic support to the guerrilla force until physical linkup is complete. After linkup, the OPCON element assumes a support responsibility.

PHYSICAL AND NONPHYSICAL LINKUPS

L-4. Normally, a joint or allied force uses a physical linkup when operating in the JSOA. A physical linkup is difficult to plan, conduct, and control. It requires detailed, centralized coordination and a planning conference between those involved. Commanders conduct physical linkups for the following reasons:

- Joint tactical operations.
- Resupply and logistic operations.

- Intelligence operations.
- Exfiltration of sick and wounded U.S. and indigenous personnel.
- Exfiltration of very important persons and EPWs.
- Infiltration of U.S. and indigenous personnel.
- Transfer of guides and liaison personnel to the conventional forces.

L-5. Forces must establish a nonphysical linkup when operations are conducted in a JSOA and a physical linkup is not required or desirable. The conventional force is the attacking force and the guerrillas are in support. A nonphysical linkup also requires coordination between the linkup forces. Commanders must state procedures before operations begin and when joint communications are established. Compatible communications equipment and current SOI must be available to the participants. Commanders use nonphysical linkups when the conventional force conducts a deep raid and guerrillas conduct security missions. Commanders also use these linkups when the conventional force attacks and guerrillas—

- Serve as a blocking force.
- Screen flanks and block threats.
- Conduct deception operations.
- Conduct reconnaissance or surveillance.

LINKUP WITH AIRBORNE OR AIR ASSAULT FORCES

L-6. Command linkup plans for airborne or air assault forces depend on the ground tactical plan. (FM 7-20, *The Infantry Battalion*, provides detailed linkup planning.) The airborne or air assault task force commander, the area command liaison personnel, and the SOCCE conduct a planning conference. Either an SFOD or a SOCCE remains with the guerrilla force in the JSOA as an advisor for all postlinkup operations.

L-7. Precise timing of the airborne operation with the supporting guerrilla operation is desirable. Premature commitment of the guerrilla force may stop the surprise effect of the conventional force mission and lead to its defeat. If committed late, the desired effects from the guerrilla force may not occur. Guerrilla forces may have to secure DZs or LZs, seize objectives within the airhead, occupy reconnaissance and security positions, or delay or harass enemy movements toward the objective area.

L-8. The guerrilla force may act as a reception committee and mark the DZ and LZ. The reception committee links up with airborne or air assault force personnel at one of the designated LZ or DZ markers and guides them to the area commander. Linkup is complete when the airborne or air assault force commander establishes contact with the area commander.

L-9. Concurrent with the landing of the airborne or air assault elements, the guerrilla force furnishes current intelligence data, provides guides, and conducts reconnaissance and security missions. The guerrilla force interdicts approaches, controls areas between separate airheads, and attacks enemy reserve units and installations. It also helps control the civilian population within the objective area.

LINKUP WITH AMPHIBIOUS FORCES

L-10. Timing is critical when the guerrilla force supports an amphibious operation. Premature commitment may alert the enemy and lead to the possible defeat of the guerrilla force. Late employment may not produce the desired effects. A SOCCE deploys early for the amphibious task force to ensure joint planning is complete and attempts to participate in the beach landing. The element establishes command relationships and support during the planning conference. During an amphibious assault or linkup, the task force commander assumes OPCON of the guerrilla forces. When the amphibious force commander links with the area commander, the linkup operation is complete.

MULTIPLE LINKUPS

L-11. Linkups can occur at several points and at separate times. Planning and conducting multiple linkups simultaneously is difficult. All guerrilla forces should not be involved in the linkup because deception and interdictions should continue during the linkup. A physical linkup with a large guerrilla force may not even be required or desired. A small reception committee can conduct the linkup and act as guides or liaisons with the linkup force. Conventional forces may conduct a relief in place after the guerrillas have conducted a raid or seized key terrain. (FM 7-20 provides detailed relief planning.) The SOCCE may remain with SOF forces in the JSOA or region.

CONDUCT OF LINKUP

L-12. When a linkup appears imminent, the SOCCE deploys to the conventional force HQ and begins detailed, centralized planning to involve all parties. The involvement of the SOCCE in the linkup planning process is especially critical as it coordinates the actions between external forces and the area command in the JSOA. The SOCCE plans and coordinates at all levels, especially with the units conducting the linkup. Units develop linkup planning and contingencies during premission training. The initial planning conference establishes command relationships. Planners consider the following linkup factors:

- The guerrilla force may continue to conduct UW operations under the umbrella of the unified commander.

- The guerrilla force may be under control of the joint task force (JTF) unified commander or national command of the guerrilla force (shadow government or area commander).

- The conventional force commander will be advised of the capabilities and limitations of the guerrilla force, which may conduct combat operations and rear area security.

- The guerrilla force may be under tactical control (TACON) to SOF in support of SO.

- An adjacent JSOA guerrilla force may link with the internal guerrilla force and conduct joint UW operations. The guerrilla force is under the control of the unified commander, or both forces may be under TACON to a conventional force or SOF.

- The guerrilla force may be under TACON to SOF temporarily, and then revert to the relationships described above.

L-13. The SFOD coordinates operations, control measures, and the scheme of maneuver with the conventional and guerrilla forces. The SFOD coordinates TACON measures with the guerrilla force commanders to assist linkup. In addition, it establishes fire control measures to provide support for the linkup. Both forces must understand the plans for securing objectives and have access to dedicated assets to ensure mission success. Before physical linkup occurs, the guerrilla force first confirms the location of the linkup contact point and secures it. The SFOD ensures security is emplaced and maintained at this location until the linkup is complete.

CONTACT PROCEDURES

L-14. The participating forces establish simple primary and alternate contact procedures and mutual control measures for physical and nonphysical linkups. At the initial planning conference, participating forces can modify the primary, alternate, and contingency plans developed during premission training, based on METT-TC.

L-15. At a coordinated date and time, the conventional and guerrilla forces move toward the contact point on a specific azimuth. The contact point is near a well-defined, easy-to-locate terrain feature. Both forces stop about 500 meters short of the contact point and send a small element forward. The elements display distinct, mutual, and simple recognition signals. They provide security for the person making the contact. The smallest possible contact element makes contact to preclude unnecessary personnel losses. The SFOD and the guerrilla force begin the linkup by displaying prearranged recognition signals to identify themselves to the conventional force. The conventional force responds with its own prearranged signal. Radio contact before this action is highly advisable to decrease the chances for any mistaken identity and fratricide. These additional principles apply:

- SF may be included in both contact elements.
- Guerrillas dispatched during the planning conference may guide the conventional force to the contact point.
- Both forces will establish and maintain communications not later than (NLT) 24 hours before linkup.
- Deception and feints may be used to cover linkup operations.

POSTLINKUP OPERATIONS

L-16. After linkup, guerrilla forces convert to national control and reorganize into conventional forces or demobilize. The unified commander, in coordination with U.S. and allied officials, determines the further use of guerrilla forces following linkup. With this guidance, the tactical commander may employ these guerrilla forces. The SFOD stays with and helps them become an effective combat unit operating under the JTF or higher commanders.

POSTLINKUP EMPLOYMENT CONSIDERATIONS

L-17. Conventional force commanders should be aware of several important factors when they employ guerrilla forces following linkup. Some of those factors are as follows:

- Know the guerrillas, their organization, concepts of operation, capabilities, and limitations.
- Make sure the subordinate leaders understand the value of guerrilla forces and know how to use them.
- Anticipate the problems of providing administrative, logistic, and operational support to attached guerrilla forces.
- Anticipate possible language and political problems in establishing liaison.
- Know that the high value of guerrilla forces is limited to those operations conducted in areas familiar to them.
- Maintain guerrilla force integrity as much as possible.
- Work through existing channels of the guerrilla command. (Imposing a new organizational structure may hamper their effectiveness.)
- Respect guerrilla leaders. (Give them the same consideration as officers of the conventional forces.)
- Maintain guerrilla morale by awarding decorations and letters of commendation. (Express appreciation whenever such action is justified and warranted.)
- Do not make political commitments or promises to guerrilla forces unless authorized by higher HQ.
- Recognize when the value of the guerrilla forces has ended and promptly return them to the control of the unified commander.

POSTLINKUP MISSIONS AND OPERATIONS

L-18. If the guerrilla force is to be employed as light infantry, it must undergo a period of retraining and reequipping before its commitment in the new combat role. Also, commanders may reorganize, retrain, and reequip SF-advised guerrilla forces to conduct reconnaissance, airmobile, or other similar light infantry operations. Guerrilla, paramilitary, or irregular forces supporting conventional forces may conduct the following missions.

RECONNAISSANCE

L-19. Familiarity with the terrain and people qualifies guerrilla forces for reconnaissance missions. Guerrilla forces provide the principal sources of intelligence on the enemy. They can patrol difficult terrain and gaps between units, establish roadblocks and OPs, screen flanks, and provide guides.

DEFENSIVE **OPERATIONS**

L-20. Control of terrain is rarely critical for the guerrilla. These guerrilla forces, with relatively light weapons and equipment, are normally inferior to the organized enemy forces in manpower, firepower, mobility, and communications. Guerrilla forces do not undertake defensive operations unless forced to prevent enemy penetration of guerrilla-controlled areas or gain time for their forces to accomplish a specific mission. Guerrilla forces may defend key terrain or installations for a limited time in support of conventional forces. When the guerrilla does defend an area, he modifies the principles of conventional defensive combat to maximize his specific assets and minimize any deficiencies. He demonstrates his best-planned efforts using METT-TC.

COUNTERGUERRILLA OPERATIONS

L-21. The experience and training of guerrilla forces make them very useful for counterguerrilla operations. They detect enemy sympathizers in villages and towns and implement control measures in unfriendly areas. Tactical commanders should exploit their knowledge of, and experience with, guerrilla techniques, language, terrain, and population. When properly supported, the guerrilla forces may be given complete responsibility for counterguerrilla operations in selected areas.

REAR AREA SECURITY

L-22. Guerrilla forces may act as security forces within the TAACOM. Tactical commanders assign these forces to a rear area security role based on their knowledge and experience. Whenever possible, guerrilla forces should be assigned on an area basis to guard lines of communications, supply depots, airfields, pipelines, railroad yards, or port facilities. They also patrol terrain that contains bypassed enemy units or stragglers, aid in recovering prisoners, help control civilians and refugees, and police towns and cities. When provided with appropriate transportation, guerrilla forces may act as a mobile security force in their JSOA.

CIVIL SUPPORT

L-23. Because of their area knowledge and experience, guerrilla forces help restore an area to its "normal state." They perform DC collection and control duties. They assist in PSYOP campaigns in rear areas, apprehend collaborators and spies, recruit labor, and guard key installations and public buildings.

CONVENTIONAL FORCE OPERATIONS

L-24. Guerrilla forces conduct combat operations and augment, relieve, or replace conventional forces in the rear area. However, guerrilla forces usually cannot complete the same size mission a conventional force can. The operations or tactical commander considers the guerrillas' capabilities and takes advantage of their special expertise and area knowledge.

L-25. Shortages of adequate voice communications and transportation may severely limit the use of guerrilla forces for conventional force combat operations. The strength, organization, leadership, training, equipment, and extent of civilian support for guerrilla forces affect their combat capability.

L-26. After linkup with guerrilla forces, the SFOD may have to retrain HN forces. The SFOD can retrain and reconstitute HN forces that have suffered reversals in combat actions. The goal is to rapidly train the units' cadres in leadership, operations, and combat tactics, techniques, and procedures.

Demobilization of Guerrilla Forces

This appendix provides guidance to operational detachments engaged in UW during the demobilization phase. During the demobilization phase of UW, all members of the SFOD perform duties and assume responsibilities as outlined in subsequent paragraphs. In addition, detachment members not mentioned perform duties as directed by their immediate supervisor, the operations sergeant, or the detachment commander. Users may deviate from the guidance provided in this appendix as required by special mission considerations or peculiarities of a UW JSOA.

DETACHMENT COMMANDER

M-1. The SFOD commander commands and controls detachment members and directs, advises, and gives guidance to all staff and special staff sections and resistance force leaders in accomplishing the following:

- Conducting inventory, inspection, and check of—
  - Weapons and other serial-numbered items.
  - Rosters of tactical and logistical units.
  - Rosters of auxiliary units and all other supporters.
  - Rosters of leaders, staff, and special staff sections.
  - Administrative records; for example, war records for decorations and awards pay, and personnel records.
  - All equipment, ammunition, supplies, and material in storage, cache sites, or in the possession of resistance force units and personnel.
  - Minefield, obstacle, and hazardous material data and records.
- Compiling, posting, correcting, and making available—
  - The principal area assessment.
  - Supply records and inventory documents.
  - Personnel and pay records.
  - Intelligence and security files.
  - E&R files.
  - Operation plans, orders, and estimates.
  - Communication records and cryptographic material.
  - Medical records.
  - Rosters of potential political assistance personnel.

M-2. In addition, the detachment commander directs and coordinates detailed briefings for resistance force personnel to ensure that everyone understands—

- The need for demobilization.
- Demobilization requirements on the part of commanders and individuals.
- The importance of remaining in preselected assembly areas.
- Police and sanitation functions.
- Collection of arms, ammunition, and equipment.
- Immediate care for and processing of sick and wounded.
- The CA team's requirements, to include—
  - Necessary records and rosters:
    - Roster of legal survivors of killed in action (KIA) or missing in action (MIA) soldiers as a direct result of hostile action.
    - Roster of resistance force personnel.
    - Other supporters who are auxiliary, bartering assets, doctors, and persons holding levy receipts.
  - Combat records for preparation of decorations and awards.
  - Pay records.
  - Medical records.
  - Personnel records for preparation of and discharge.
  - Preparation and conduction of ceremonies.
  - Implementation of rehabilitation procedures as planned within stipulations by higher HQ.
  - Preparation for exfiltration of SFOD members.

ASSISTANT DETACHMENT COMMANDER

M-3. The ADC supervises and assists in the preparation of the following:

- Rosters of all resistance force personnel, guerrillas, and auxiliary.
- Rosters of other known supporters, such as bartering and levy assets or doctors.
- Rosters of persons who possess potential assistance qualifications, to include—
  - Outstanding political attitudes.
  - Leadership ability (political).
  - Administrators.
  - Police and security qualifications.
- Inventory documents and records of the following supplies and equipment reflecting serial number, amount, and location:
  - Weapons.
  - Other serial-numbered items and sensitive items.

- Ammunition and munitions.
- Clothing.
- Field equipment.
- Rations.

M-4. The ADC also makes available to CA personnel all records and rosters necessary to accomplish their mission. He assists the CA team in the administration of resistance force personnel. The ADC prepares SFOD members for briefing and debriefing by CA officers. He provides guidance for and assists in the—

- Preparation and completion of principal area assessment.
- Preparation of intelligence and security files.
- Collection and accountability of cryptographic and other sensitive communication material.

M-5. The ADC assists CA personnel in execution of demobilization plans. He provides guidance and assistance to SFOD members in preparation for exfiltration.

INTELLIGENCE SERGEANT

M-6. The intelligence sergeant prepares all classified documents and material for destruction or exfiltration as directed by the detachment commander. The intelligence sergeant compiles and prepares intelligence and security files for the ADC or for use in briefing the CA team and subsequent exfiltration. The intelligence sergeant should be prepared to present the—

- Intelligence and security briefing to the CA team.
- Security briefing to SFOD members.

M-7. The intelligence sergeant also prepares and presents to the SFOD ADC files on and rosters of potential political assistance personnel as follows:

- Persons with outstanding political attitudes and qualifications.
- Political leadership ability and experience.
- Potential administrators.
- Police and security assets.
- Other favorable assets.

M-8. The intelligence sergeant also assists SFOD members in—

- Police and sanitation functions.
- Demobilization procedures.
- Collecting arms, ammunition, munitions, supplies, and equipment.
- Preparing for exfiltration.

OPERATIONS SERGEANT

M-9. The operations sergeant selects assembly areas for resistance force CPs or units. He assists the SFOD commander in directing, supervising, and coordinating the collection of—

- Personnel.
- Resistance force units.
- Weapons.
- Ammunition and munitions.
- Clothing and equipment.
- Records and rosters.
- Equipment and supplies.
- Classified material.

M-10. The operations sergeant directs and advises conduct of assembly, briefings, and control of resistance force personnel. He completes and compiles the—

- Principal area assessment.
- Operation orders and plans.
- Estimates.
- Damage assessments.

M-11. The operations sergeant plans and conducts briefings of the CA team. He assists CA personnel in the conduct of demobilization procedures and advises on a rehabilitation program. The operations sergeant also plans SFOD exfiltration as follows:

- Selects and secures landing site.
- Reports and confirms landing site.
- Directs and supervises preparation of detachment members, documents, and supplies for exfiltration.
- Organizes brief and rehearses reception committee.
- Plans and conducts demobilization ceremony.

MEDICAL SUPERVISOR

M-12. The medical supervisor prepares, posts, and makes the following information available to the ADC:

- All medical records.
- Immunization records.
- Plans for continued treatment of patients.
- Medical rehabilitation programs.
- Recommendations for awards and decorations for both detachment and guerrilla medical personnel.

M-13. The medical supervisor prepares, posts, and makes the following information available to the S-4 sergeant:

- Plans for collection, use, storage, issue, exfiltration, or destruction of medical supplies and equipment.
- Inventory documents and records reflecting serial number, location, type, and amount of—
  - Medical equipment.
  - Instruments.
  - Installations and facilities.
  - Medicine.
  - Other equipment.

M-14. The medical supervisor executes plans for medical treatment, hospitalization, and evacuation during demobilization. Guerrilla hospitals are kept in operation until the patients can be taken over by military hospitals or civilian institutions. He briefs and assists CA personnel. The medical supervisor executes plans for the disposition of medical supplies, equipment, facilities, instruments, and installations. He also assists SFOD members in preparation of personnel and equipment for exfiltration. The medical supervisor coordinates the—

- Final contribution of medical intelligence to S-2.
- Latest contribution to the medical portion of the principal area assessment (S-3).
- Assistance in sanitation, police, and sterilization functions.

The medical supervisor also supervises the final discharge physical examinations.

SENIOR WEAPONS LEADER

M-15. The senior weapons leader assists the SFOD ADC in the preparation of administrative matters. The senior weapons leader advises the detachment commander on the future disposition of weapons, ammunition, and explosives, to include—

- Use.
- Issue.
- Storage.
- Exfiltration.
- Destruction.
- Methods of collecting and accounting.

M-16. The senior weapons leader advises and assists the operations sergeant in the—

- Selection, reconnaissance, and occupation of unit assembly areas.
- Selection and reconnaissance of exfiltration landing sites.
- Organization and rehearsals of exfiltration committee.

M-17. The senior weapons leader plans, organizes, and conducts briefings of the CA team as directed by the operations sergeant. The senior weapons leader assists the CA team in the conduct of demobilization procedures. He also assists SFOD members in plans and preparation of equipment for—

- Use.
- Issue.
- Storage.
- Infiltration.
- Exfiltration.
- Destruction.

M-18. The senior weapons leader makes final contribution to the principal area assessment. He also continues to assist in, direct, and supervise—

- Police functions.
- Sanitation measures.
- Sterilization requirements.

COMMUNICATIONS SUPERVISOR

M-19. The communications supervisor provides necessary communications for—

- Administrative contact with the following:
  - SFOB.
  - Conventional linkup command.
  - Resistance and auxiliary force units during demobilization.
  - Supporting naval and air units.
  - Exfiltration activities.
- Population control by the following:
  - Police units.
  - Other security elements.
  - CA team use.

M-20. The communications supervisor advises the detachment commander on amount and type of equipment necessary to accomplish demobilization mission, number of personnel required for operation of equipment, and number and location of sites to be occupied.

M-21. The communications supervisor collects, inventories, and accounts for all classified documents and material and makes them available to the intelligence sergeant (S-2) for future—

- Use.
- Exfiltration.
- Destruction.

M-22. The communications supervisor plans for collection and disposition of communication equipment and supplies. He inventories, documents, and records up-to-date information reflecting serial number, amount, and location of all communication equipment and supplies. He also executes plans for—

- Collection.
- Issue.
- Use.
- Storage.
- Exfiltration.
- Destruction.

ENGINEER SERGEANT

M-23. The engineer sergeant collects all demolitions and engineer equipment and prepares it for turn-in. He inventories mine, obstacle, and hazardous material data and makes sure it is properly recorded. He assists the ADC in preparing inventories and supply documents and in readying equipment and weapons for exfiltration or turnover to civil authorities. The engineer sergeant presents engineer portions of briefings as directed. He also assists the operations sergeant in preparing assigned portions of the area assessment.

It's more than a game.
JMEA

Glossary

AAR	after-action report
ADC	assistant detachment commander
AO	area of operations
AOB	advanced operational base
AOR	area of responsibility
AR	Army regulation
area assessment	The collection of specific information about the general situation encountered by the SFOD immediately after infiltration. The area assessment is expanded throughout the deployment, concluding in the debriefing after exfiltration. The area assessment confirms, corrects, refutes, or adds to previous intelligence acquired from area studies and other sources prior to infiltration.
area command	In unconventional warfare, the organizational structure established within a joint special operations area to command and control resistance forces. An area command consists of the area commander, his staff, and representatives of the resistance element, to include Special Forces after infiltration.
area complex	A clandestine, dispersed network of facilities to support resistance activities. It is a "liberated zone" designed to achieve security, control, dispersion, and flexibility.
ARSOA	Army special operations aviation
ARSOF	Army special operations forces
ARTEP	Army Training and Evaluation Program
ASO	advanced special operations
asset (intelligence)	Any resource—person, group, relationship, instrument, installation, or supply—at the disposition of an intelligence organization for use in an operational or support role. Often used with a qualifying term such as agent asset or propaganda asset. (JP 1-02)
auxiliary	In unconventional warfare, that element of the resistance force established to provide the organized civilian support of the resistance movement. (AR 310-25)
AWADS	adverse weather aerial delivery system
BDA	battle damage assessment
BFA	battle focus analysis
BG	brigadier general

BLS	beach landing site
BMNT	beginning morning nautical twilight
BOS	battlefield operating systems
C2	command and control
C3	command, control, and communications
C3I	command, control, communications, and intelligence
C4I	command, control, communications, computers, and intelligence
CA	Civil Affairs
CA activities	A group of planned activities in support of military operations that enhance the relationship between military forces and civilian authorities and population and which promote the development of favorable emotions, attitudes, or behavior in neutral, friendly, or hostile groups.
cal	caliber
CARVER	criticality, accessibility, recuperability, vulnerability, effect, and recognizability
CAS	close air support
CASCOPE	civil areas, structures, capabilities, organizations, people, and events
CBR	chemical, biological, and radiological
CCIR	**commander's critical information requirements**—The CCIR is a prioritized list incorporating all information requirements identified by the commander as being critical in developing his timely information management, tactical decision process, and his actions and reactions, which affect successful mission accomplishment.
CDQC	Combat Diver Qualification Course
CF	communications facility
CI	**counterintelligence**—Information gathered and activities conducted to protect against espionage, other intelligence activities, sabotage, or assassinations conducted by or on behalf of foreign governments or elements thereof, foreign organizations, or foreign persons, or international terrorist activities. (JP 2-0)
clandestine operation	An activity to accomplish intelligence, counterintelligence, and other similar activities sponsored or conducted by governmental departments or agencies, in such a way as to assure secrecy or concealment.
cm	centimeter(s)
CMO	**civil-military operations**—The activities of a commander that establish, maintain, influence, or exploit relations between military forces and the civilian population in a friendly, neutral,

or hostile area of operations in order to facilitate military operations and consolidate operational objectives. CA may include performance by military forces of activities and functions normally the responsibility of the local government. These activities may occur, if directed, in absence of other military operations. (JP 3-57)

CMOC **civil-military operations center**—The joint force commander's nerve center for CMO and coordination with other non-DOD agencies. CMOC members are primarily CA personnel augmented by other DOD and non-DOD (for example, Department of State, United States Agency for International Development, Federal Emergency Management Agency) liaison personnel.

COA course of action

compartmentation 1) Establishment and management of an organization so that information about the personnel, internal organization, or activities of one component is made available to any other component only to the extent required for the performance of assigned duties. (JP 1-02) 2) In unconventional warfare, the division of an organization or activity into functional segments or cells to restrict communication between them and prevent knowledge of the identity or activities of other segments except on a need-to-know basis. (AR 310-25)

COMSEC communications security

CONOPS concept of operations

CONPLAN contingency plan

CONUS continental United States

conventional force A non-SOF force supported by SOF. It is normally a conventional military organization; however, it may or may not be military, and it may not be U.S. forces.

CP command post

crypto cryptograph

CS combat support

CSM command sergeant major

CSS combat service support

CT counterterrorism

CW continuous wave

DA direct action

DAR designated area of recovery

DC dislocated civilian

denied area	A primary area for SOF. An area that is operationally unsuitable to the conventional force for political, tactical, environmental, or geographical reasons.
DOD	Department of Defense
DZ	drop zone
E&R	evasion and recovery
ECM	**electronic countermeasures**—That division of electronic warfare involving actions taken to prevent or reduce an enemy's effective use of the electromagnetic spectrum.
EENT	early evening nautical twilight
electronic counter-countermeasures	That division of electronic warfare involving actions taken to ensure friendly effective use of the electromagnetic spectrum despite the enemy's use of electronic warfare.
EPW	enemy prisoner of war
EW	electronic warfare
exfiltration	The removal of personnel or units from areas under enemy control by stealth, deception, surprise, or clandestine means. (JP 1-02)
F	Fahrenheit
FA	feasibility assessment
FID	foreign internal defense
FM	field manual
FOB	forward operational base
foreign power	Any foreign government (regardless of whether recognized by the United States), foreign-based political party (or faction thereof), foreign military force, foreign-based terrorist group, or any organization composed, in major part, of any such entity or entities. (AR 381-10) Foreign powers may be classified as friendly, neutral, or hostile.
FRP	final reference point
GTA	graphic training aid
GW	**guerrilla warfare**—Military and paramilitary operations conducted in enemy-held or hostile territory by irregular, predominantly indigenous forces. (JP 1-02)
HALO	high altitude low opening
HELO	helicopter
HF	high frequency
HN	**host nation**—A nation in which representatives or organizations of another state are present because of government invitation or

international agreement. The term particularly refers to a nation receiving assistance relevant to its national security.

HQ headquarters

HRO humanitarian relief organization

human intelligence A category of intelligence derived from information collected and provided by human sources. (JP 1-02)

IAD **immediate action drill**—A collective action rapidly executed without applying a deliberate decision-making process. Drills provide swift and positive small unit reaction to enemy visual or physical contact. They are simple COAs in which all men are so well trained that minimum signals or commands are required to initiate action.

IAW in accordance with

ICG International Crisis Group

ICRC International Committee for the Red Cross

ID identification

IER initial entry report

IEW intelligence and electronic warfare

ILO International Law Officer

indigenous Native, originating in, or intrinsic to an area or region. (FM 3-05.20)

infiltration 1) The movement through or into an area or territory occupied by either friendly or enemy troops or organizations. The movement is made either by small groups or by individuals at extended or irregular intervals. When used in connection with the enemy, it infers that contact is avoided. 2) In intelligence usage, placing an agent or other person in a target area in hostile territory. Usually involves crossing a frontier or other guarded line. (JP 1-02)

insurgency An organized movement aimed at the overthrow of a constituted government through use of subversion and armed conflict. (JP 1-02)

insurgent Member of a political party who rebels against established leadership. (JP 1-02)

internal security 1) The state of law and order prevailing within a nation. (JP 1-02) 2) The prevention of action against United States resources, industries, and institutions; and the protection of life and property in the event of a domestic emergency by the employment of all measures, in peace or war, other than military defense. 3) Condition resulting from the measures taken within a command to safeguard defense information coming under its cognizance, including physical security of documents and materials. (AR 310-25)

INTSUM	intelligence summary
IPB	intelligence preparation of the battlespace
IR	information requirement
IRP	initial rallying point
ISOFAC	isolation facility
IW	information warfare
JA	judge advocate
joint operations	Operations carried on by two or more of the Armed Forces of the United States (Army, Navy, Air Force). (AR 310-25)
JP	joint publication
JSCP	Joint Strategic Capabilities Plan
JSOA	**joint special operations area**—A restricted area of land, sea, and airspace assigned by a joint force commander to the commander of a joint special operations force to conduct SO activities.
JSOTF	joint special operations task force
JTF	joint task force
KIA	killed in action
km	kilometer(s)
lb	pound(s)
LOC	line of communications
LP	listening post
LPT	logistic preparation of the theater
LZ	landing zone
M	medic; motor(s)
MANPADS	man-portable air defense system
MCA	military civic action
MDMP	military decision-making process
METL	mission-essential task list
METT-TC	mission, enemy, terrain and weather, troops and support available—time available and civil considerations
MFF	military free-fall
MI	military intelligence
MIA	missing in action
MICON	mission concept
MOC	**mission operations cell**—(Formerly known as area specialist team.) The MOC is made up of a pool of SF-qualified soldiers that

support high-priority mission planning. The MOC officers and NCOs operate on the three principles of compartmentation, replaceability, and deconfliction.

MOE measure of effectiveness

MOPP mission-oriented protective posture

MOS military occupational specialty

MPA mission planning agent

MSP mission support package

MSS **mission support site**—A preselected area used as a temporary base or stopover point. The MSS is used to increase the operational range within the JSOA. The MSS can be used before and after an operation for resupply, resting, and coordination, based on METT-TC. The site is occupied for short periods of time, seldom longer than a 24-hour period. The MSS should be reconnoitered and outposted.

MTOE modified table of organization and equipment

MTP mission tasking package

NAR **nonconventional assisted recovery**—All forms of personnel recovery conducted by an entity, group of entities, or organizations that are trained and directed to contact, authenticate, support, move, and exfiltrate U.S. military and other designated personnel from enemy-held or hostile areas to friendly control through established infrastructure or procedures. NAR includes unconventional assisted recovery conducted by special operations forces. (DOD Directive 2310.2)

national strategy The art and science of developing and using the political, economic, and informational powers of a nation, together with its armed forces, during peace and war to secure national objectives. (JP 1-02)

NATO North Atlantic Treaty Organization

NBC nuclear, biological, and chemical

NCO noncommissioned officer

NEO noncombatant evacuation operation

NFA no-fire area

NGO nongovernmental organization

NLT not later than

O&I operations and intelligence

OAKOC observation and fields of fire, avenues of approach, key terrain, obstacles, and cover and concealment

OAS Organization of American States

OGA	other government agency
OP	observation post
OPCON	operational control
OPLAN	operation plan
OPORD	operation order
OPSEC	operations security
ORP	objective rallying point
overt operation	An operation conducted openly, without concealment. (JP 1-02)
PACE	primary, alternate, contingency, emergency (plan)
paramilitary forces	Forces or groups distinct from the regular armed forces of any country, but resembling them in organization, equipment, training, or mission. (JP 1-02)
PCP	peacetime campaign plan
PE	practical exercise
PIR	priority intelligence requirements
PLL	prescribed load list
POE	plan of execution
POI	program of instruction
POL	petroleum, oils, and lubricants
PRC	populace and resources control
PSS	personnel service support
psychological warfare	The planned use of propaganda and other psychological actions having the primary purpose of influencing the opinions, emotions, attitudes, and behavior of hostile foreign groups in such a way as to support the achievement of national objectives. (JP 1-02)
PSYOP	**psychological operations**—Planned operations to convey selected information and indicators to foreign audiences to influence their emotions, motives, objective reasoning, and ultimately the behavior of foreign governments, organizations, groups, and individuals. The purpose of psychological operations is to induce or reinforce foreign attitudes and behavior favorable to the originator's objectives. (JP 1-02)
RDF	radio direction finder
resistance movement	An organized effort by some portion of the civil population of a country to resist the legally established government or an occupying power and to disrupt civil order and stability. (JP 1-02)
RFA	restricted fire area
RFI	request for information

RII	request for intelligence information
ROE	rules of engagement
RP	rallying point
RPG	rocket-propelled grenade
RT	radio-telephone
S-1	battalion or brigade personnel staff officer
S-2	battalion or brigade intelligence staff officer
S-3	battalion or brigade operations staff officer
S-4	battalion or brigade logistics staff officer
S-5	civil-military operations officer
sabotage	An act or acts with intent to injure, interfere with, or obstruct the national defense of a country by willfully injuring or destroying, or attempting to injure or destroy, any national defense or war materiel, premises, or utilities, to include human and natural resources. (JP 1-02)
SAFE	selected area for evasion
safe area	A designated area in hostile territory that offers the evader or escapee a reasonable chance of avoiding capture and of surviving until he can be evacuated. (JP 1-02)
SALUTE	size, activity, location, unit, time, and equipment
SAV SER SUP	Standard Audiovisual Services Supplement
sector	That portion of a JSOA assigned by a joint SO commander to a subordinate SO commander for the conduct of a specific SO mission.
SERE	survival, evasion, resistance, and escape
SF	**Special Forces**—Military personnel with cross training in basic skills, organized into small, multiple-purpose detachments with the mission to train, organize, supply, direct, and control indigenous forces in guerrilla warfare and counterinsurgency operations, and to conduct unconventional warfare operations.
SFERP	Special Forces evasion and recovery plan
SFG(A)	Special Forces group (airborne)
SFOB	Special Forces operational base
SFOD	Special Forces operational detachment
SFODA	Special Forces operational detachment A
SFODB	Special Forces operational detachment B
SGM	sergeant major
SIGSEC	signal security

SME	subject-matter expert
SO	**special operations**—Operations conducted by specially organized, trained, and equipped military and paramilitary forces to achieve military, political, economic, or informational objectives by unconventional military means in hostile, denied, or politically sensitive areas. These operations are conducted across the full range of military operations, independently or in coordination with operations of conventional non-SO forces. Political-military considerations frequently shape special operations, requiring clandestine, covert, or low visibility techniques, and oversight at the national level. Special operations differ from conventional operations in degree of physical and political risk, operational techniques, mode of employment, independence from friendly support, and dependence on detailed operational intelligence and indigenous assets. (JP 3-05)
SOC	special operations command
SOCCE	special operations command and control element
SOCRATES	Special Operations Command, Research, Analysis, and Threat Evaluation System
SOF	special operations forces
SOI	signal operating instructions
SOMPF	special operations mission planning folder
SOP	standing operating procedure
SOSE	special operations support element
SOT-A	special operations team A
SPTCEN	support center
SR	special reconnaissance
SRP	soldier readiness processing
surrogate	Someone who takes the place of or acts for another. (FM 3-05.20)
TAACOM	theater Army area command
TACON	tactical control
TACSAT	tactical satellite
TASKORD	tasking order
TIP	target intelligence packet
TOE	table of organization and equipment
UAR	unconventional assisted recovery
UARM	unconventional assisted recovery mechanism
UART	unconventional assisted recovery team
UCMJ	Uniform Code of Military Justice

UN	United Nations
underground	A covert unconventional warfare organization established to operate in areas denied to the guerrilla forces or conduct operations not suitable for guerrilla forces. (AR 310-25)
U.S.	United States
USAF	United States Air Force
USAJFKSWCS	United States Army John F. Kennedy Special Warfare Center and School
USAR	United States Army Reserve
USASFC(A)	United States Army Special Forces Command (Airborne)
USG	United States Government
UW	**unconventional warfare**—A broad spectrum of military and paramilitary operations, normally of long duration, predominantly conducted by indigenous or surrogate forces who are organized, trained, equipped, supported, and directed in varying degrees by an external source. It includes guerrilla warfare and other direct offensive, low visibility, covert or clandestine operations, as well as the indirect activities of subversion, sabotage, intelligence activities, and evasion and escape. (JP 3-05.5)
UWOA	unconventional warfare operating area
WO	warrant officer (senior and master)
XO	executive officer

Bibliography

ACP 125 (E). *Communications Instructions—Radiotelephone Procedures.* 1 August 1987.

AR 40-562. *Immunizations and Chemoprophylaxis.* 1 November 1995.

AR 220-10. *Preparation for Oversea Movement of Units (POM).* 15 June 1973.

AR 310-25. *Dictionary of United States Army Terms (Short Title: AD).* 21 May 1986.

AR 600-8-101. *Personnel Processing (In-and-Out and Mobilization Processing).* 1 March 1997.

Article 39 of Protocol I to the Geneva Conventions.

DOD Directive 2310.2. *Personnel Recovery.* 22 December 2000.

Executive Order 12333. *U.S. Intelligence Activities.*

FM 3-0. *Operations.* 14 June 2001.

FM 3-05.20. *Special Forces Operations.* 26 June 2001.

FM 3-05.30. *Psychological Operations.* 19 June 2000.

FM 3-05.220. *(S/NF) Special Forces Advanced Special Operations (U).* 13 February 2003.

FM 5-34. *Engineer Field Data.* 30 August 1999 (Change 2, 1 October 2002).

FM 7-0. *Training the Force.* 22 October 2002.

FM 7-8. *Infantry Rifle Platoon and Squad.* 22 April 1992 (Change 1, 1 March 2001).

FM 7-10. *The Infantry Rifle Company.* 14 December 1990 (Change 1, 31 October 2000).

FM 7-20. *The Infantry Battalion.* 6 April 1992 (Change 1, 29 December 2000).

FM 20-32. *Mine/Countermine Operations.* 29 May 1998 (Change 3, 1 October 2002).

FM 22-100. *Army Leadership.* 31 August 1999.

FM 25-101. *Battle Focused Training.* 30 September 1990.

FM 31-19. *Military Free-Fall Parachuting Tactics, Techniques, and Procedures.* 1 October 1999.

FM 31-23. *Special Forces Mounted Operations Tactics, Techniques, and Procedures.* 5 May 1999.

FM 41-10. *Civil Affairs Operations.* 14 February 2000.

FM 44-100. *U.S. Army Air and Missile Defense Operations.* 15 June 2000.

FM 100-25. *Doctrine for Army Special Operations Forces.* 1 August 1999.

FM 101-5. *Staff Organization and Operations.* 31 May 1997.

GTA 31-1-3. *Detachment Mission Planning Guide.* 29 May 1997.

Hague Conventions of 1907.

JP 1-02. *Department of Defense Dictionary of Military and Associated Terms.* 12 April 2001.

JP 3-05. *Doctrine for Joint Special Operations.* 17 April 1998.

JP 3-05.1. *Joint Tactics, Techniques, and Procedures for Joint Special Operations Task Force Operations.* 19 December 2001.

JP 3-05.5. *Joint Special Operations Targeting and Mission Planning Procedures.* 10 August 1993.

JP 3-09. *Doctrine for Joint Fire Support.* 12 May 1998.

JP 3-13. *Joint Doctrine for Information Operations.* 9 October 1998.

JP 3-57. *Joint Doctrine for Civil-Military Operations.* 8 February 2001.

Selected Works of Mao Tse-tung, Vol. IV. Foreign Languages Press, Peking, 1969.

Special Operations Targeting Handbook. Edition 8.

Standard Audiovisual Services Supplement (SAV SER SUP) 6.

TC 31-24. *Special Forces Air Operations.* 9 September 1988.

TC 31-25. *Special Forces Waterborne Operations.* 3 October 1988.

TC 31-32. *Special Operations Sniper Training and Employment.* 29 September 1997.

Tse-tung, Mao. *On Guerrilla Warfare.* Garden City, NY: Anchor Press, 1978.

United Nations Charter.

USASFC(A) Reg 350-1. *Component Training*, 28 June 2001 (Change 1, 22 October 2001).

USASOC Reg 350-1. *Training.* 28 July 1995.

Index

FM 3-05-201
30 APRIL 2003

By Order of the Secretary of the Army:

ERIC K. SHINSEKI

General, United States Army
Chief of Staff

Official:

Joel B. Hudson

JOEL B. HUDSON
Administrative Assistant to the
Secretary of the Army
0309909

DISTRIBUTION:

Active Army, Army National Guard, and US Army Reserve: To be distributed in accordance with the initial distribution number XXXXXX, requirements for FM 3-05.201.

Made in the USA
Middletown, DE
17 April 2023